Attila the Hun

Attila the Hun

Arch-enemy of Rome

Ian Hughes

Pen & Sword
MILITARY

First published in Great Britain in 2019 by
Pen & Sword Military
An imprint of
Pen & Sword Books Ltd
Yorkshire – Philadelphia

ISBN 978 1 78159 009 6

A CIP catalogue record for this book is
available from the British Library.

Printed and bound in England by TJ International Ltd,
Padstow, Cornwall

Pen & Sword Books Limited incorporates the imprints of Atlas,
Archaeology, Aviation, Discovery, Family History, Fiction, History,
Maritime, Military, Military Classics, Politics, Select, Transport,
True Crime, Air World, Frontline Publishing, Leo Cooper, Remember
When, Seaforth Publishing, The Praetorian Press, Wharncliffe
Local History, Wharncliffe Transport, Wharncliffe True Crime
and White Owl.

For a complete list of Pen & Sword titles please contact

PEN & SWORD BOOKS LIMITED
47 Church Street, Barnsley, South Yorkshire, S70 2AS, England
E-mail: enquiries@pen-and-sword.co.uk
Website: www.pen-and-sword.co.uk

Or

PEN AND SWORD BOOKS
1950 Lawrence Rd, Havertown, PA 19083, USA
E-mail: Uspen-and-sword@casematepublishers.com
Website: www.penandswordbooks.com

Contents

Acknowledgements

Yet again I must express my gratitude to Philip Sidnell for keeping faith with me. I wouldn't be surprised if, as this is my seventh book, he is now sick of hearing my voice on the telephone asking inane questions!

I would like to thank Evan Schultheis for reading the book and taking the time to discuss significant and contentious details. As usual, the comments, criticisms and corrections have been a valuable asset in the writing process. However, for any mistakes and disagreements I remain solely responsible.

For helping me to secure otherwise impossible-to-acquire books, I would once again like to thank the staff at Thurnscoe Branch Library, Barnsley, and especially Andrea World of the Inter-Library Loans Department of Barnsley Libraries. Without their help this book would have been far shorter and not as comprehensive.

I would very much like to thank the following people for kindly allowing me to use their photographs in the plates: Beast Coins (www.beastcoins. com), CNG coins (www.cngcoins.com) and Wildwinds Coins (www. wildwinds.com/coins). I would especially like to thank Pankaj Tandon of Indian Coins (http://www.coinindia.com) for allowing the use of numerous examples of the coins in his collection, as well as for information concerning the production and relevance of these coins; Helen Gooderham and Paddy Shaw for allowing the use of geographical photographs; and Peter Molnar of www.bowshop.eu for allowing the use of the photographs of the Hun bows. Their generosity is very, very much appreciated.

For their patience and for permission to use photographs from their extensive and valuable libraries I would like to thank Professor Manfred Clauss of ILS and http://www.manfredclauss.de, and Dr Andreas Faßbender and Professor Manfred G. Schmidt of CIL.

As with my earlier books, this tome would not have been the same without the contribution of the members of both www.romanarmytalk.com/rat

and www.unrv.com.forum. They have yet again been exceptionally patient, especially with regard to questions about the availability of photographs.

It goes without saying that my utmost gratitude goes to the individuals and institutions who have made available the ever-growing corpus of source material available on the internet. As with my previous books, I will refrain from mentioning individuals by name, since a look at the bibliography will show that it would need a separate book to list all of the people involved, so to single individuals out for special praise would be unfair. To all of these people, once again, my heartfelt thanks.

Yet at the top of my list remain the two people who have supported me throughout the lengthy process of writing yet another book: Joanna and Owen. Joanna remains in need of praise for her endurance and patience in reading through the book, but at least this time the book is not about 'yet another bloke from ancient Rome'. For her endless patience and understanding, I remain forever in her debt. As for Owen, he really should be given some sort of award for his stoicism in the face of my fixation with a figure from ancient history who is of no interest to him whatsoever. Well, not yet: maybe in time we will come to share the same obsession ... Then again, maybe not. Only time will tell!

Introduction

Mention the name 'Attila' (or its linguistic equivalent) to anyone over the age of 20 in the West and the chances are that they will have heard of 'Attila the Hun'. The same cannot be said of his near contemporaries whose actions were pivotal during the last years of the Western Roman Empire. The names of Gaiseric the Vandal, Euric the (Visi-) Goth, and the leaders of the other 'barbarian' nations have long since fallen from common usage; Gundobad, the king of the Burgundians, is now more famous as a mountain in Tolkien's *Lord of the Rings*.

Indeed, even the names of the so-called Germanic tribes that existed in the fifth century CE have evolved and are rarely used for the peoples of the ancient world: 'Goth' is now used as a term for a specific group of 'young people' who 'listen to depressing music and dress in black'; a 'Vandal' is anyone who destroys the property of others without consideration; and 'Frank' – apart from being an increasingly-rare personal name – is the title given to an individual who shares their views without regard to the feelings of others.

Yet, strangely, into the twentieth century 'Hun' remained in use as a title for a nomadic group who emerged from nowhere to wreak destruction on settled populations before disappearing over the horizon. It is in this context that the term 'Hun' became applied to the German army during the First World War. However, contrary to popular opinion, it was not applied to the German army by the 'Allies' due to the Germans' behaviour during this war, but rather thanks to the words of Kaiser Wilhelm II. During a speech given in Bremerhaven on 27 July 1900, when German forces were leaving to suppress the Boxer rebellion in China, Wilhelm stated:

> Should you encounter the enemy, he will be defeated! No quarter will be given! Prisoners will not be taken! Whoever falls into your hands is forfeited. Just as a thousand years ago the Huns under their King Attila

made a name for themselves, one that even today makes them seem mighty in history and legend, may the name German be affirmed by you in such a way in China that no Chinese will ever again dare to look cross-eyed at a German.

The imperialist and racist connotations of the speech resulted in the German Foreign Office omitting this paragraph from the official transcription, as diplomatically it was embarrassing and would otherwise cause political difficulties which needed to be smoothed over, especially given the nature of the rebellion.[1] However, it was only after it was used by Kipling in his 1914 poem *For All We Have and Are* that the epithet became widely applied to the German forces:

> For all we have and are,
> For all our children's fate,
> Stand up and take the war.
> The Hun is at the gate!

The question then remains as to how the image of the Huns as rapacious marauders who instilled terror in their opponents has remained in the modern mind, when the other 'barbarian' nations of the fifth century have long since had their names transmuted into less terrifying forms.

The most obvious reason is that, although they were all responsible to a greater or lesser degree for the 'Fall of the West', the other barbarian groups were Christian and, although the ancient sources were hostile, to some contemporary writers the 'Germanic' tribes were the paradigm of the 'noble barbarian' as opposed to the 'indulgent and corrupt' Romans. Furthermore, the Germanic tribes had been in contact with the Empire since the first century BCE, and long exposure to Roman customs and trade had 'civilized' them into entities which, although they were 'barbarian' (i.e. outsiders who did not speak a 'civilized' language), did not inspire terror in the citizens of Rome. In addition, after the Huns there was a cycle of eastern 'nomads' periodically appearing from the Russian steppe to terrorize western Europe: the Avars, the Magyars and especially the Mongols all appeared determined to conquer the world and repeat the 'Fall of the West' in later days.

Although in later years a minority of the Huns would convert, when they moved west in the fourth century the Huns were not Christian. In addition, their appearance on the scene in the mid-late fourth century was a new phenomenon, and the fact that they terrified the Alans and Goths with whom they came into contact resulted in Roman writers describing them in horrifying terms. For example, Ammianus Marcellinus wrote:

The people of the Huns, but little known from ancient records, dwelling beyond the Maeotic Sea near the ice-bound ocean, exceed every degree of savagery. Since there the cheeks of the children are deeply furrowed with the steel from their very birth, in order that the growth of hair, when it appears at the proper time, may be checked by the wrinkled scars, they grow old without beards and without any beauty, like eunuchs. They all have compact, strong limbs and thick necks, and are so monstrously ugly and misshapen, that one might take them for two-legged beasts or for the stumps, rough-hewn into images, that are used in putting sides to bridges. But although they have the form of men, however ugly, they are so hardy in their mode of life that they have no need of fire nor of savoury food, but eat the roots of wild plants and the half-raw flesh of any kind of animal whatever, which they put between their thighs and the backs of their horses, and thus warm it a little. They are never protected by any buildings, but they avoid these like tombs, which are set apart from everyday use. For not even a hut thatched with reed can be found among them... They dress in linen cloth or in the skins of field-mice sewn together, and they wear the same clothing indoors and out. But when they have once put their necks into a faded tunic, it is not taken off or changed until by long wear and tear it has been reduced to rags and fallen from them bit by bit. They cover their heads with round caps and protect their hairy legs with goatskins; their shoes are formed upon no lasts, and so prevent their walking with free step. For this reason they are not at all adapted to battles on foot, but they are almost glued to their horses, which are hardy, it is true, but ugly, and sometimes they sit on them woman-fashion and thus perform their ordinary tasks. From their horses by night or day every one of that nation buys and sells, eats and drinks, and bowed over the narrow neck of the animal relaxes into a sleep so deep as to be accompanied by many dreams... No one in their country ever ploughs a field or touches a plough-handle. They are all without fixed abode, without hearth, or law, or settled mode of life, and keep roaming from place to place, like fugitives, accompanied by the wagons in which they live; in wagons their wives weave for them their hideous garments, in wagons they cohabit with their husbands, bear children, and rear them to the age of puberty... In truces they are faithless and unreliable, strongly inclined to sway to the motion of every breeze of new hope that presents itself, and sacrificing every feeling to the mad impulse of the moment. Like unreasoning beasts, they are utterly ignorant of the difference between right and wrong; they are deceitful and ambiguous in speech, never bound by any reverence for religion or for superstition. They burn with an infinite thirst for gold, and they are so fickle and prone to anger, that they often quarrel with their allies without provocation, more than once on the same day, and make friends with them again without a mediator.

Ammianus Marcellinus 31.2.1–11.

The great difficulty here is that Ammianus almost certainly never encountered a Hun and was forced in part to rely on information from people who exaggerated Hunnic atrocities in their fear. In addition, Ammianus was not writing in isolation, but rather was following in the traditions of his predecessors. As a result, his description follows *topoi*: standard terminologies used throughout antiquity for characters, peoples and events which therefore do not necessarily follow the truth. In this case, the description given by Ammianus was similar to that of Herodotus' description of the Scythians in the fifth century BCE.[2] Indeed, until recently the use of *topoi* has been a neglected aspect of the study of ancient history, meaning that the words of Ammianus and his contemporaries has tended to be taken at face value. Understandably, given this invective, the Huns gained a reputation for ferocity far greater than the other invaders of the Roman Empire. However, this may not be the main reason for the continued use of Attila's name into the twenty-first century. This may be due to Christianity.

In 452 Attila invaded Italy. The emperor sent envoys, one of whom was Leo, bishop of Rome. Over time, the story of the meeting has undergone a transformation. The contemporary historian Priscus wrote that Attila was dissuaded from attacking Rome by his own men as they feared he would share the fate of Alaric, the Gothic leader who had died shortly after sacking the city in 410. On the other hand, it has been claimed that Attila withdrew due to the awe in which he held the pontiff. Later Christian writers expanded on the story concerning the pope. For example, in the eighth century Paul the Deacon claims that during the meeting Attila was threatened by a man only he could see, dressed in priestly robes and armed with a sword.[3] Alongside the inserted Christian imagery, over time Attila became the 'Scourge of God', the pagan barbarian sent by God to punish Christians for their wrongdoing. To a large degree the survival of Attila in public knowledge must be attributed to the perceived religious nature of his actions.

Reading the ancient sources without the benefit of modern analytical techniques, taking the stories concerning Pope Leo at face value, and noting the repeated invasions by marauders from the East, it was clear to the Classicists of the eighteenth and nineteenth centuries where the blame for the 'Fall of Rome' lay: it was the Huns, and their leader Attila.

For such an important historical figure it is surprising how little is actually known about Attila. A brief description of his appearance and personality survives in the fragments of the ancient writer Priscus, but few of his actions are explained in detail by the primary sources, and even where an attempt has been made, the origins of the information are obscure and the description may have more to do with the biases and goals of the ancient writer than with an intimate knowledge of Attila's modus operandi. Yet despite these limitations, Attila has remained a major figure of interest to historians, and many books and articles have been written about the man and his time.

The question then remains as to how yet another book can have any relevance to the reader who has access to so many different versions of the same story. The short answer must be very little, as most aspects of his life story have been covered in detail. However, the difference here is that an attempt has been made to relate the story of Attila from the viewpoint of Attila himself, unlike the majority of tomes that appear to focus more on how he was perceived by, and what effects his actions had upon, the Late Roman Empire, especially how his actions helped to ensure the downfall of the Western Empire. Whether the author has fulfilled this ambition is up to the reader to decide.

The Sources

The major difficulty relating to Attila's life lies in the paucity of the surviving sources. The most problematic aspect is that the 'Huns did not write a single word of their history', or at least not a word that has survived.[4] As a result, it is necessary to rely on the histories written by their opponents. Overall, the sources fall into four broad categories: Ecclesiastical Histories (which include the *Hagiographies*, Lives of the Saints), Secular Histories, Letters and Chronicles. There are also several smaller works which sometimes give relevant information, for which see the 'List of Abbreviations' following this Introduction. Unfortunately, the Ecclesiastical Histories are extremely biased against the Huns, and the other sources are of a fragmentary nature and their large number means that there are too many to analyse individually. Only brief descriptions of some of the major sources are given here. Where necessary, those not included in this list will be discussed at the appropriate point in the text.

Secular Histories

Gregory of Tours: See Renatus Profuturus Frigeridus

Jordanes (fl.550s) wrote two books: The *Romana* (*On Rome*) is a very brief epitome of events from the founding of Rome until 552. Due to the fact that it is extremely condensed, it can be useful but offers little that cannot be found elsewhere. Jordanes also wrote *De origine actibusque Getarum* (*The Origin and Deeds of the Goths*: usually shortened simply to *Getica*). This work is valuable in that it contains a lot of information that would otherwise be lost, especially those sections that demonstrate a Gothic viewpoint. Unfortunately, due to the fact that Jordanes is extremely biased towards the Goths it must be used with caution, especially when dealing with the events surrounding Attila's rule, as the Huns' actions are compared unfavourably to the Goths.[5]

Priscus of Panium (c.410/20–after 472) is the most important source for Attila. He wrote an eight-volume work, later given the title *The History of Byzantium*, which appears to have covered the period between the accession of Attila and the accession of the Eastern Emperor Zeno, so giving information dated between 433 and 475. Sadly, this only survives in fragments. In his work, he describes the court of Attila and the diplomatic exchanges that took place when he was personally involved in an embassy in 448–449. Despite the limited nature of the surviving fragments, thanks to the fact that he was an eye-witness, Priscus is far and away the most important source when attempting to describe Attila's person and personality.

Procopius (c.500–c.554) wrote the *Wars of Justinian*. In these he describes the wars fought by the general Belisarius on behalf of the Eastern Emperor Justinian. Included are many asides and brief entries concerning the history of the West, although little is written specifically concerning Attila. It is usually assumed to be reliable, but caution is needed where his work concerns events outside his own lifetime.

Renatus Profuturus Frigeridus (fl. fifth century) wrote a history that only survives in fragments. Fortunately, he was used as a source by **Gregory of Tours** for his book *Historia Francorum* (*History of the Franks*), from which many items of value can be gleaned. The accuracy of these fragments is in many cases unknown, despite many attempts by modern historians to clarify the situation.

Salvian (fl. fifth century) wrote a work known as *De gubernatione Dei* (*On the Government of God*, also known as *De praesenti judicio*) in which he describes life in fifth-century Gaul and contrasts the 'wickedness' of the Romans with the 'virtues' of the barbarians. Although written with a specific purpose, it can be used with care to furnish relevant information about conditions in Gaul and early relations with the Huns. Sadly, as it appears to have been written prior to the Hunnic invasion of 451 there is little specifically concerning Attila.

Zosimus (c.500) wrote the *Historia Nova* (*New History*) which covers the period from the mid-third century to 410. He appears to have used two main sources for his information. Eunapius was used for events to 404 and Olympiodorus was used for the years from c.407–410. Zosimus was a pagan, writing in Constantinople, who was determined to show that Christianity was the reason for the disasters suffered by the empire. He closely follows Eunapius and Olympiodorus. He is not critical of his sources, so although his work is useful concerning the arrival of the Huns, it needs a great amount of caution when it is being used. Sadly, due to the date of its ending, no specific information is given concerning Attila.

Ecclesiastical Histories and Associated Works

Hagiographies: several of the 'Lives of the Saints', for example Possidius' *Life of Saint Augustine* and Constantius' *Life of Saint Germanus of Auxerre*, contain information concerning the era during which Attila lived. However, the fact that these works are aimed almost exclusively at promoting the sanctity of the individual being described means that they are not objective and so extreme caution is needed in these cases.

Socrates Scholasticus (born c.380) wrote the *Historia Ecclesiastica* (*Church History*) which covers the years 305–439 and so only covers events up to and shortly after Attila's accession. Written solely as a history of the church, it contains much information on secular events, but mainly only where they impinge on church history. However, these items are otherwise unrecorded so they can offer unique insights.

Letters

Many letters written from this time survive. Although most are obviously of a personal nature, some include information on secular events. These can be valuable in filling in details, but their accuracy in most areas remains unknown.

Sidonius Apollinaris is the most important source for conditions in Gaul during the last years of the West. His many letters illuminate relations between the Goths and the Roman elite, as well as demonstrating the changing attitudes of the aristocracy towards their 'barbarian' overlords. However, at all times the biases of a Roman aristocrat need to be borne in mind, along with the position of the recipient of the letter: for example, a letter to a fellow aristocrat may contain disparaging remarks about the Goths, whereas a letter to a Goth would certainly not contain these.

Chronicles[6]

The chronicle was the form of history which 'so well suited the taste of the new Christian culture that it became the most popular historical genre of the Middle Ages'.[7] The positive aspect of this popularity is that several chronicles have survived. The negative aspect is that they displaced conventional history as the means of transmitting information about the past, and so no complete histories written in the West during the fifth century survive.

There is a further feature that causes difficulty when analysing the chronicles, especially the fragmentary ones. Several collections of these sources were made prior to the twentieth century. Each of these collections could give the sources different titles. For example, the works referenced as the *Anonymus Cuspiniani* in secondary sources from the early twentieth century and before are now referred to as the *Fasti Vindobonenses Priori*, following Mommsen's description in the *Chronica Minora*, Vol. 1 (see Bibliography). Therefore readers should be aware that references in this book are likely to differ from the earlier works.

The *Chronica Gallica of 452* is a continuation of the Chronicle of Jerome covering the years 379 to 452. The *Chronica Gallica of 511* also begins in 379 and continues to 511. Due to the similarity between the two, it is possible to see the Chronicle of 511 as a continuation of the Chronicle of 452. Both of these works contain useful information but need to be used with care, since the dates given may not in fact be accurate. The Gallic Chronicle of 452 only becomes accurate after 447, and here the events in Gaul are the most accurately dated. Prior to 447 the chronology is extremely confused.[8] The Gallic Chronicle of 511 has some entries undated. In these the reference is simply to the modern 'number' given to the entry. For example, the invasion of Italy by Radagaisus is undated and is therefore referenced simply as 'no. 50'.

The *Chronicon Paschale* (*Easter Chronicle*, so-called because of the author's use of Easter as the focus of his dating system) is an anonymous chronicle dating from the early seventh century, compiled in Constantinople.[9] Although it is a later document, and some of the dates and 'facts' are wrong, the *Chronicon Paschale* is useful in confirming other sources and adding detail to events. However, it must be used with caution thanks to the temporal distance between its compilation and the early-mid fifth century, due to which much of the information from earlier sources is confused and misrepresented.

Hydatius (c.400–c.469) wrote a continuation of the Chronicles of Eusebius and Jerome, beginning with the accession of Theodosius in 379 and finishing in 468, so he appears to have finished writing in 469. His work has serious errors in dating that are still confusing. These are probably caused by the fact that much of his information was late arriving in Spain, being taken there by embassies and merchants whose dating was insecure.[10] For events in Spain, especially concerning the Vandals, his work is good and relatively accurate.[11] Although potentially valuable, the errors mean that Hydatius must be used with caution, with dates especially being confirmed by other sources whenever possible.

John Malalas (fl. sixth century) wrote a chronicle intended to be used by both churchmen and laymen. Unfortunately, the work covers 'history' from the biblical period to the reign of Justinian in one book, so much is glossed over or omitted. As a result, the work is useful in places, but this is rare.

Marcellinus *comes* (fl. sixth century) wrote a chronicle that covers the period from 379 to 534 (an unknown writer continued the chronicle down to 566). It is mainly concerned with the Eastern Empire, and since in the early years of his reign Attila focused upon the East the work is potentially useful; however, it also includes some information concerning the West, drawn mainly from Orosius. Where possible this information needs to be confirmed by independent sources to ensure the accuracy of dates and the reliability of the information contained.

Orosius (fl. late-fourth–early-fifth century) wrote the *Historiarum Adversum Paganos Libri VII* (*Seven Books of History Against the Pagans*) in which he attempted to demonstrate the positive impact of Christianity. Although he does not portray the 'barbarians' in a negative manner, his work still suffers from the bias inherent in his Christianity.

Prosper Tiro (Prosper of Aquitaine: c.390–c.455) wrote a continuation of Jerome's Chronicle. Prosper's Chronicle finishes in 455, although there were two *Additamenta altera* ('additions and alterations') which commented and expanded upon the original chronicle. The early sections contain many errors, but between the years 433 and 455, when Prosper was personally involved in events, he is accepted as being the most reliable of the chroniclers, giving a 'careful and accurate' dating of events.[12] Prosper was not a clergyman, but his close association with the clergy, and especially his contacts with Pope Leo I and Saint Augustine, resulted in his viewpoint being heavily biased towards the Church. This bias needs to be taken into account when reading the chronicle.[13]

Difficulties with the Chronicles

The modern concept of a chronicle is that events are accurately dated and each single occurrence is allocated a separate entry in its relevant date. This preconception has badly affected perceptions of the chronicles, leading to accusations of inaccuracy and a poor grasp of time.

In fact, some of these observations are unfair to the chroniclers. Even in the modern era, where access to periodicals, newspapers and the internet is common, one of the most common radio competitions is 'Guess the Year'. It is clear that without modern methods of establishing specific dates such as newspaper archives, human error in reporting events is to be expected.

Furthermore, ancient chroniclers were not writing with modern expectations in mind. As long as events were in roughly the correct order, the chronicle would fulfil its purpose. Therefore it is a common occurrence for the chronicler to include later events at a convenient place earlier in his account.

Instances of the chroniclers predicting events are common. For example, in Hydatius' entry for 430 he notes the defeat of a Gothic force by Aetius before extolling Aetius' ability by noting that 'Juthungi as well as Nori were vanquished by him in the same way'. At first sight, these campaigns must therefore have taken place in 430. However, Hydatius' entry for 431 includes the sentence 'Aetius, general of both services, subdued the Nori, who were in rebellion'. On reflection, the second campaign must date to the latter entry.

A more extreme example is in the *Chronicon Paschale* in the entry dated to 437, where the chronicler describes the marriage of Valentinian III and Eudoxia: 'And he celebrated his nuptial, taking Eudoxia, the daughter of Theodosius and Aelia Eudoxia Augusti, in the month Hyperbereteaus, on day four before the Kalends of November, and by her he had two daughters, Eudocia and Placidia.' The entry highlights the fact that many chroniclers included later events at convenient places within the earlier entries, unless Eudoxia experienced two extremely fast gestation periods. The same is also true in reverse, with earlier events only being chronicled at a convenient later date.

A further problem with the chroniclers is that they use different methods for calculating dates. For example, Prosper and Hydatius use a different method of calculating Christ's passion: Prosper dates this to the fifteenth year of Tiberius, Hydatius to the start of Tiberius' fifteenth regnal year. This discrepancy helps to explain the minor differences in dates between the two chronicles.[14] The consular date used by Prosper, plus his closer proximity to events, results in his dating system being preferred on most occasions.

Panegyrics

When reading panegyrics one piece of advice is worth remembering: 'Notoriously ... the aim of the panegyrist is not to tell the truth, but to glorify his subject, exaggerating the good and suppressing or distorting the bad, the inappropriate, or the inconvenient.'[15] With this in mind, it is possible to look at the two writers of panegyrics to have survived from this period in the fifth century.

Flavius Merobaudes[16]
Merobaudes was probably of Frankish origin, having an ancestor who was either a Romanized-Frank or Frankish noble who took service with the empire, possibly the individual also named Merobaudes who lived during the reigns of Valentinian I (364–375) and Gratian (375–383).[17]

Perhaps originally from Gaul, Merobaudes appears to have moved to Hispania, where he married the daughter of Astyrius, a member of the old Hispanic aristocracy. In the early fifth century, when the majority of the aristocracy withdrew from public life, Merobaudes followed the example of his father-in-law and entered into an imperial career.[18] Famed for his talents as a rhetorician and writer, he also gained a positive reputation as a military commander. Obtaining the position of either *comes rei militaris* ('count' of the military) or *dux* (duke), his military and literary abilities resulted in entry to the senate and then a rapid rise through its ranks. On 30 July 435 he was honoured by having a statue erected to him in the Forum of Trajan in Rome.

After these successes Merobaudes appears to have focused mainly on his literary works. He may have delivered a panegyric to Aetius, as well as an ode honouring the wedding of Valentinian III and Eudoxia, daughter of Theodosius II, both in 437. The latter may have been in emulation of Claudian (d. 404), the panegyrist of Stilicho (395–408). It is possible that Aetius and Merobaudes enjoyed a similar relationship to the earlier pair, although the fragmentary nature of the evidence means that this hypothesis must remain conjecture.[19] The ode celebrating Valentinian's wedding in Constantinople may also have been at least partly responsible for Merobaudes receiving the title of *patricius* from Theodosius, the Eastern emperor. Unfortunately, both works have been lost.

In 438 Merobaudes appears to have written verses celebrating the birth of Eudocia, Valentinian and Eudoxia's first child, and probably in the winter of 441–442 he wrote a *genethliakon* ('birthday poem', 'ode composed for a person's birthday') on the first birthday of Gaudentius, Aetius' son, which work is now known as *Carmen IV*.

Also in the early 440s, although the exact date is unknown, Merobaudes wrote an *ekphrasis* (an attempt to describe physical works of art in literary form) for his friend Anicius Acilius Glabrio Faustus, which is now known as *Carmen III*. Probably in 443 he wrote two poems to celebrate the baptism of Placidia, daughter of Valentinian and Eudoxia, which may be *Carmen I* and *Carmen II*, both of which are ekphrastic poems, although it should be noted that their actual purpose and content remains the matter of debate.[20] All of these works are useful sources of information in their own right, but obviously they need to be used with care.

Shortly after writing these two poems Merobaudes was appointed *magister utriusque militiae* (Master of Both Services) and sent to Hispania, where he succeeded his father-in-law Astyrius in command. After his recall in 444 Merobaudes composed another panegyric to Aetius, which he delivered in Rome to the senate and which is now known as *Panegyric I*.[21] Shortly after this he composed yet another panegyric, now known as *Panegyric II*, which he delivered on 1 January 446.

Unfortunately, little is known of Merobaudes' later career and it is believed that he died before 460. He was obviously a man of influence and power, and of considerable literary and military ability. Like Claudian before him it would appear that Merobaudes took a full part in the regime set up by the ruling *magister utriusque militiae*, in this case Aetius. As Aetius was the leading Roman commander in the Western opposition to Attila, Merobaudes' works can give an insight into how the Huns were perceived in the West and how he interacted with Aetius.

Sidonius Apollinaris

Alongside his many letters, Sidonius also wrote a series of panegyrics, including works for the emperors Avitus, Majorian and Anthemius. Sadly, due to being written for later emperors, these only rarely mention the Huns.

Other sources

The Notitia Dignitatum

This is an extremely important document. It purports to list the bureaucratic and military organization of both the Eastern and Western empires. Hundreds of offices are listed. Dated to c.420 for the West and c.395 for the East, it is potentially a mine of statistical and legal information. Unfortunately there are many problems associated with interpreting the document. Probably originating with the Emperor Theodosius in the East, it may in theory have been intended as a complete list of offices. The Eastern section of the *Notitia* appears to date from some time around 395. As a result, it is usually believed that the surviving document is a copy preserved in the West of the Eastern *Notitia* dating from the reign of Arcadius (395–408). Unfortunately, it was not kept strictly up to date and there are many omissions and duplications. Moreover, due to the fragmentation of the Empire during and immediately after Stilicho's death in 408, it is uncertain whether many of the army units listed actually existed or existed only on paper. As a consequence, information taken from the *Notitia* should be accepted as possible rather than certain.

There appear to have been later attempts to update the Western portion of the document and evidence suggests that these were last compiled at some date in the 420s, possibly under the orders of Constantius III (*magister militum* (Master of the Troops) in the West from 411 and emperor from February to September 421).

Unfortunately, there are internal problems with the *Notitia* which suggest that it does not reflect reality. For example, although the provinces of Britain had begun to drift out of the imperial orbit in the early 410s, the leaders and troops associated with the island are still included in the *Notitia*. The same may be true of the provinces of Belgica and Germania, although the evidence is sparse and open to interpretation. The fact that these are 'unquestionably anachronistic' suggests that the document includes material reflecting what had once been available to the empire rather than the current military status.[22] Yet the document may also have been a statement of intent. If it was compiled under the orders of Constantius III in 421, it may have been his intention as emperor to restore the glory of the West and incorporate the lost provinces back into the empire.

As well as being useful in outlining what the Roman bureaucracy believed should have been the case, it is also possible to analyse the document in the hope of gleaning material concerning the condition and deployment of the army. This is covered in more depth in Chapter 6.

What is often forgotten, or at least ignored, is the fact that the *Notitia* was not updated after some time around 420. Due to the complicated nature of events from 423 onwards it is quite possible that by the time Aetius achieved sole dominance in 433, events had rendered the *Notitia* completely obsolete. As a result, it must be used with extreme caution when discussing the later army which existed during the dominance of Aetius, and the lifetime of Attila.

The *Codex Theodosianus*

The *Codex Theodosianus* is a legal codification completed during the reign of Theodosius II in the East of all the laws issued since the reign of Constantine I (306–337). Added to this body of laws were the new laws (*novella*) passed by Theodosius II (*Nov. Th.*) and Valentinian (*Nov. Val.*) after 439. These were also collected and kept with the *Codex*, and now form part of the main text.

The 'Code' and the 'Novels' are a valuable source of material for the period. It is possible to analyse the laws to establish their context and so determine the reasons for their passing. Furthermore, the laws are accompanied by the names of the emperor(s) that passed them, in most cases by the precise date on which they were passed, and by the name of the city in which the emperor passed the law. This allows us to trace some of the movements of the emperor, and also enables us to link specific laws with specific events in the lifetime of Attila. For example, the law allowing citizens to bear arms (*Nov. Val.* 9.1, dated 24 June 440) is related to the conquest of Africa by the Vandals in October 439. Therefore, close analysis of the *Codex* can open a window into aspects of imperial life and policies that would otherwise be blank.

It is also interesting to note that some of the laws dismiss laws that were destined to be 'valid for the cases of their own time only'.[23] This highlights the fact that, like modern law, some laws passed by emperors were meant to deal with specific emergencies and events. After these had passed, the laws were naturally allowed to lapse. Modern examples include the laws passed to deal with the 'emergency' that was the Second World War. Once this war was over, these laws were repealed and 'normality' resumed.

Conclusion

The information that is available in the sources should not detract us from the knowledge that they were all written with a purpose. Even when this bias is openly declared, it can easily be overlooked or forgotten. If this is the case with the major sources as listed above, it is even more the case with the multitude of minor sources not listed. The less important sources that are used are of varying accuracy and utility and where necessary an analysis of these will be dealt with in the body of the text. However, if the source only gives us one or two snippets of information then it is possible that the source will not be analysed.

One problem with all of the sources needs to be highlighted, which is where the sources inform the reader of political intrigue. The difficulty lies with the fact that the sources claim to know details of a kind which are always most suspicious: 'tales of secret intrigues and treasons which could not be known to the world at large'.[24] Whenever this kind of information is encountered, a full analysis will be attempted to decide whether or not the author was properly informed of the details of these events.

Spelling and Terminology

Wherever possible the simplest definitions and spellings have been used throughout the book. There are many examples in the ancient sources of variations in the spelling of individuals' names, such as Gaiseric being spelt 'Zinzirich'.[25] Also, in most modern works Roman spellings are usually 'modernized' by removing the common 'us' endings and substituting a modern variant; for example, 'Bonifatius' becoming 'Boniface'. Wherever possible the most widely-used variant has been employed in the hope of avoiding confusion.

When describing both the tribes along the Rhine and those who successfully invaded the Empire, at times the phrase 'barbarian' rather than 'German' has been used. Although the word 'barbarian' is now out of fashion, largely due to its negative aspects regarding comparative civilization levels with the Romans, it has been used as it is an otherwise neutral term, whereas the use of the word 'German' often implies a 'community and ethnicity on the basis of shared language', which is actually misleading.[26]

Unlike my earlier works, where in most cases the term 'Goth/s' has been used rather than 'Visigoth/s' simply because the Ostrogoths were rarely mentioned, in this work it has been necessary to use Visigoth and Ostrogoth for the two main groups simply because both feature regularly. Other 'Gothic' groups not affiliated with the main two will be given their own designations where necessary, although it should be noted that contemporary sources describe all of the 'Visigoths', 'Ostrogoths' and others simply as 'Goths'.[27]

List of Abbreviations

In order to make the references more manageable, the following abbreviations have been used for ancient sources:

Additamenta Ad Chronicon Prosperi Hauniensis	*Addit. Ad Prosp. Haun.*
Agathias	Agath.
Ammianus Marcellinus	AM
Annales Ravennae	*Ann. Rav.*
Augustine	Aug.
Aurelius Victor	Aur. Vict.
Callisthenes	Call.
Cambridge Ancient History	CAH
Cassiodorus, *Chronicle*	Cass. *Chron.*
Cassiodorus, *Variae*	Cass. Var.
Chronica Gallica of 452	*Chron. Gall. 452*
Chronica Gallica of 511	*Chron. Gall. 511*
Chronica Minora (Mommsen)	*Chron. Min.*
Chronicon Paschale	*Chron. Pasch.*
Claudian Claudianus (Claudian)	Claud.
Claudius, *In Rufinum*	Claud. In Ruf.
Codex Justinianus	*Cod. Just.*
Codex Theodosianus	*Cod. Th.*
Collectio Avellana	*Collect. Avell.*
Constantius of Lyon	Const.
Eunapius of Sardis	Eun.
Eutropius	Eut.
Evagrius	Evag.
Fasti vindobonenses posteriors	*Fast. Vind. Post.*
Fasti vindobonenses priores	*Fast. Vind. Prior*
Gaudentius	Gaud.
Gildas	Gild.
Gregory of Tours	Greg. Tur.
Hydatius	Hyd.
John of Antioch	Joh. Ant.

John Malalas	Joh. Mal.
John of Nikiu	Joh. Nik.
Jordanes, *Getica*	Jord. Get.
Libanius	Lib.
Marcellinus Comes	Marc. com.
Maurice, *Strategikon*	Maur. Strat.
Merobaudes, *Panegyric*	Merob. Pan.
Minutes of the Senate	Min. Sen.
Nestorius	Nest.
Nicephorus Callistus	Nic. Call
Notitia Dignitatum	*Not. Dig.*
Novellae Theodosianae	*Nov. Theod.*
Novellae Valentinianae	*Nov. Val.*
Olympiodorus of Thebes	Olymp.
Orosius	Oros.
Paulinus of Nola	Paul.
Paulinus of Pella	Paul. Pell.
Paulus Diaconus	Paul. Diac.
Philostorgius	Philost.
Possidius	Poss.
Priscus, *Chronica*	Prisc. *Chron.*
Priscus, *Romana*	Prisc. *Rom.*
Procopius	Proc.
Prosopography of the Later Roman Empire	PLRE
Prosper Tiro	Prosp.
Pseudo–Augustine	Pseudo–Aug.
Renatus Profuturus Frigeridus	Ren. Prof.
Saint Jerome	Jer.
Salvian	Salv.
Scriptores Historiae Augustae	*Scrip. His.*
Sidonius Apollinaris	Sid. Ap.
Sirmondian Constitutions	*Sirm.*
Socrates Scholasticus	Soc.
Sozomen	Soz.
Suidas	*Suid.*
Theoderet	Theod.
Theophanes	Theoph.
Vegetius	Veg.
Victor of Vita	Vict. Vit.
Zosimus	Zos.

Chapter One

The Origin of the Huns

I n the third quarter of the fourth century CE, the inhabitants of the Roman Empire became aware of a new threat emerging far to the east. A large group of Tervingi arrived on the banks of the River Danube and petitioned the emperor for asylum and land within the empire on which to build new homes. Shortly after, a group of Greuthungi also petitioned the emperor for asylum. Both had been driven from their homes by a people unheard of by the Romans:

> The seed and origin of all the ruin and various disasters that the wrath of Mars aroused … we have found to be this. The people of the Huns, but little known from ancient records, dwelling beyond the Maeotic Sea near the ice-bound ocean, exceed every degree of savagery.
>
> *Ammianus Marcellinus 31.2.1.*

Jordanes takes his description further even than Ammianus:

> But after a short space of time, as Orosius relates, the race of the Huns, fiercer than ferocity itself, flamed forth against the Goths. We learn from old traditions that their origin was as follows: Filimer, king of the Goths, son of Gadaric the Great, who was the fifth in succession to hold the rule of the Getae after their departure from the island of Scandza, – and who, as we have said, entered the land of Scythia with his tribe – found among his people certain witches, whom he called in his native tongue Haliurunnae. Suspecting these women, he expelled them from the midst of his race and compelled them to wander in solitary exile afar from his army. There the unclean spirits, who beheld them as they wandered through the wilderness, bestowed their embraces upon them and begat this savage race, which dwelt at first in the swamps – a stunted, foul and puny tribe, scarcely human,

and having no language save one which bore but slight resemblance
to human speech. Such was the descent of the Huns who came to the
country of the Goths.

Jordanes, Getica, *24 (121–2)*

Obviously, Jordanes' tale is simply a method used to discredit the Huns, but
when Ammianus states that the Huns were 'but little known from ancient
records' he is making a great understatement. Thanks to the lack of any
other contemporary information concerning the Huns they have remained
an enigma, even into modern times. The main question concerns their
origins. What little information we have suggests that at one point the Huns
may have been a part of the Xiongnu, an empire dating between the third
century BCE and the first century CE to the north of modern China.[1] The
hypothesis was first proposed by de Guignes in 1776, and since that time
opinion has swayed between acceptance and dismissal of his theory, which
is based largely upon linguistic and primary source analyses that are open to
different interpretations.[2]

Even more confusing is the fact that, as yet, there is no consensus
concerning the 'ethnicity' of the Xiongnu, with some early historians, for
example, even suggesting that the Huns were the 'retinue of the northern
Slavs'.[3] The primary evidence for their ethnicity is linguistic, and opinion
is divided as to whether the Huns spoke a variant of Turkic or used the Ket
language – a variant of Yeniseian – or even a different language based upon
their proposed 'Mongolian' ancestry.[4] Although only supposition, it may be
that, like the Xiongnu, the Huns, at least for the ruling classes, spoke the
original language used by the Xiongnu, which could explain their (possible)
desire to remain part of the Xiongnu legacy.

This hypothesis may be reinforced by more modern analyses, which
suggest that the 'Hunnic' language was a composite of proto-Turkic and
Old Mongolian/Ket-Yeniseian, although closer to Turkic.[5] In this model the
groups 'collected' by the Huns as they travelled west were Turkic-speakers,
while the core group was Yeniseian, hence the mix of languages with the
larger 'Turkic' population ensuring Turkic was the dominant language. The
possible presence of the Old Mongolian/Ket-Yeniseian elements in the
language can be inferred from the ruling classes speaking Ket and words
'trickling down' to be included in the common language.

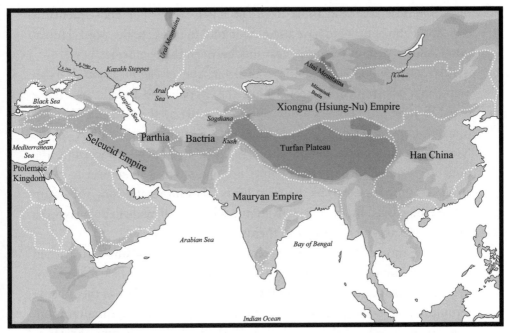

Map 1: The Xiongnu Empire at the height of its power, plus major contemporary Kingdoms.

The example just analysed clearly demonstrates that the main difficulty in assessing both origin and ethnicity is that the Xiongnu were a 'multi-ethnic, multi-cultural, polyglot and multi-tiered society with a diversified agro-pastoral economy and a highly stratified political order'.[6] Hence any theory concerning the Huns is impossible to prove, simply because the complex nature of Xiongnu society means that the Huns – if indeed they were an offshoot of the Xiongnu – could be descended from any one of a multitude of peoples with differing ethnic, social and lifestyle backgrounds, all of which are present in the 'Hunnic peoples'.

The Xiongnu Connection

The evidence linking the Huns to the Xiongnu comes primarily from two texts: one written by Zhu Fahu (Dharmaks.a) and the other by Nanaivande. Zhu Fahu was a Buddhist of Yue-zhi (Indo-Scythian) origin whose family had been settled in Dunhuang for several generations. After taking the name Zhu Fahu he translated Indian texts into Chinese and uses the name 'Hun.a' ('Huni') for a people of Xiongnu descent who are later attested in inscriptions as attacking India from the north-west.[7] The consequence is that Zhu Fahu appears to have used 'Xiongnu' to translate the word 'Hun.a' into Chinese, demonstrating a clear link between the two names.[8]

Like Zhu Fahu, Nanaivande was 'from the circle of Central Asian merchants who traded between China, the Steppe, and India'.[9] In a letter dated to June 313 he gives a description of raids by the 'Xwn', a Sogdian transcription of 'Hun.a', which thanks to Zhu Fahu are linked to the Xiongnu.[10] As a consequence, although these hypotheses concerning the transliteration of ancient tribal names are tenuous and so subject to much criticism, they appear to be the most likely basis for establishing the origin of the Huns. In addition, although attempts have been made to dismiss these theories, the arguments used can themselves be refuted.[11]

As they moved west, the Huns collected other tribes who also wished to move.[12] The decision to move would be helped by the fact that one of the commonalities of nomads on the steppes of Inner Asia was them being a multilingual society, at least to the point of efficient communication. Consequently, other tribes would have little difficulty in joining the Huns since communication would not present a barrier.[13] Since many of the tribes they ruled were likely to be multilingual, it would not be surprising if the 'complexity and fluid character of ethnogenesis' changed the Huns during their long migration, especially with regard to language.[14]

Despite the linguistic changes which are assumed to have taken place, the Huns may have kept their name 'as a political reference point', since they could use the 'prestigious name with its powerful reference to the imperial past to rule over the smaller tribes less blessed by fortune and history', or at least overawe them.[15] Although this may be considered an overstatement, it should be noted that the empire now known as 'Byzantine' called themselves 'Rhomaioi' ('Romans'), and 'the steppe has the right to have political ideas and history' as much as Europe.[16]

These are not the only problems with identifying the origins of the Huns. To make matters more complicated, the Inner and East Asian sources referring to the Xiongnu may also have 'referred to all nomadic peoples who lived beyond the Great Wall of China' generically as Xiongnu.[17] Consequently, there is doubt as to whether, if they were originally members of the Xiongnu Empire, the Huns were related to the 'Imperial family' of the Xiongnu dynasty or simply one of the constituent tribes. As noted above,

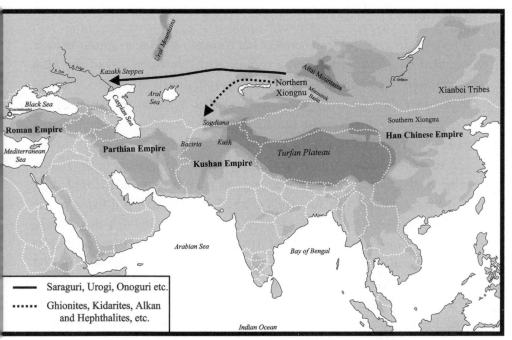

Map 2: The division of the Xiongnu (plus major contemporary Kingdoms) plus the later tribal division.

it is possible that they were indeed one of the ruling clans, forced to migrate west to retain their status.

The need to move arose in the second century CE. After a period of imperial rule beginning in the second century BCE, the Xiongnu slowly dwindled in power until eventually they were defeated by a rival nomadic force, the Xianbei – possibly in 155 CE – and split into Northern and Southern contingents. The Northern Xiongnu, who may be the ancestors of the later Huns, appear to have refused to accept Xianbei dominion. Why they were so determined to avoid this is unknown. Certainty is impossible, but there is a chance that the Xiongnu nobles had become divided over whether to resist or join the Xianbei, and those who had opposed the takeover fled west for safety, taking with them a core of their fellow tribesmen. The Southern Xiongnu were to become part of the Han Empire.

The Altai

Whatever the cause, at least some of the Xiongnu tribesmen appear to have migrated west and settled in the regions at the northern end of the Altai Mountains.[18] Assuming that the Huns migrated shortly after c.155, it would appear that they spent the next two centuries living in the Altai region, possibly conquering Kangju and Kush, and so pushing the Alanliao (the Alans) from the Aral Sea to the Don.

A surviving manuscript supports this hypothesis. A passage in the *Weishu* – the *Book of Wei*: a Chinese text written by Wei Shou in the mid-sixth century – mentions that remnants of the Xiongnu were still living in the Altai region at the beginning of the fifth century.[19] Although this passage was written long after the death of Attila, when combined with the limited archaeological and textual evidence, the concept that the Huns were indeed related to the Xiongnu becomes 'virtually certain'.[20]

Archaeologically, the Huns have left few traces with which to determine their lifestyles or their movements, but one piece of surviving evidence is the spread of 'Hunnic' cauldrons. As well as being found further west, these items have been excavated on the Orkhon River, on the northern flank of the Altai Mountains and in the Minusinsk Basin.[21] Buried near springs or rivers, these cauldrons may demonstrate continuity of ritual and culture between the Far East and the later Hunnic settlements in Europe. However, it should be noted that not all historians accept that the cauldrons are symbolic of migration: 'The very mobility of nomads means that customs, artefacts and decorative styles circulate across huge distances, and many objects that survive are the products of permanent communities acquired by trade', possibly via a number of intermediate stages.[22] It has also been noted that although the cauldrons found in the west are similar to those from the Xiongnu region, 'not one ... is decorated with the beautiful stylised animals and mythical creatures ... that are characteristic of Xiongnu design.'[23] Whatever the case, their existence can be used to suggest that the Huns, or at least some descendants of the Xiongnu, did indeed live for a time on the flanks of the Altai Mountains before migrating further west.

It is also possible that some of these Hun groups decided not to halt in the Altai region, but continued west. Writing in the second century CE, Ptolemy in his *Geographia* mentions that

And between the Peucini and the Basternae are the Carpiani, above whom are the Gevini, then the Bodini; between the Basternae and the Rhoxolani are the Chuni, and below the mountains named from these are the Amadoci and the Navari.

Ptolemy, Geographia, *3.5.10.*

Although it is tempting to interpret the inclusion of '*Chuni*' in Ptolemy's description as being evidence that a few Hunnic groups had continued to move west, this must remain a possibility rather than a fact. It may be that the names used are simply coincidental and that the Chuni are not related to the Huns at all.

The Second Migration

Why the Huns left the Altai region and moved further west is still open to debate, but two major factors probably dominated their decision. One was that the climate in the region changed: pollen and glaciation studies have shown that from the mid-fourth through the sixth century there was a sharp drop in temperatures and a rise in humidity. From c.340 CE the glaciers in the region began to advance along their valleys.[24] It would appear that the Huns found it difficult to adjust to the changes, as Chinese sources mention invasions from the Altai region from the middle of the fourth century, which may be a result of privations brought on by the temperature drop.[25]

By itself the change in temperature could explain why the Huns needed to move as they would find it more difficult to survive. Yet this wasn't the only possible reason. In the fourth century the Rouran Khanate was actively expanding and this had a domino effect on the Altai region. The Xianbei – known in the West as Sabiri – the Chinese characters of *Xianbei* were pronounced 'Sarbi' at this time – were chased out of Mongolia by the Rouran, and they may in turn have dislodged the Huns from the Altai.

For a people who had already fled once from the Xianbei to avoid assimilation, the majority of the Huns appear to have decided that foreign subjugation remained unacceptable. Although a section of the population refused to leave their homes and remained where they were – as evidenced by the remnants remaining in the Altai in the fifth century mentioned in the Chinese source above – a large proportion opted to move further west in search of homes free from external dominion. These Huns, including both those of Attila and the later Saraguri, Urogi and Onoguri of Priscus, paused after reaching the Kazakh Steppe in the mid-fourth century, before continuing their migration.[26]

At this point the scale of the migration becomes clearer. 'Tribes' such as the Saraguri, Urogi and Onoguri moved west and became well-known to the Romans. However, other groups such as the Chionites, the Kidarites, the Alkhan and possibly the Hephthalites established themselves in Sogdiana and Bactria, so posing a major threat to the Sasanid Empire and the rulers of north-western India rather than Europe.[27] Although it is usually accepted that these tribes moved to the region 'in waves', this has now been challenged and it is now proposed that the different 'tribes' attested in the sources point to changes in dynasty rather than new arrivals.[28] If true, it means that the tribes made 'one massive single migration' between c.350 and c.370.[29] The *Weishu* confirms that the 'White Huns' moved from the Altai region to Central Asia around the year 360.[30] However, the fact that together these multitudinous, disparate groups could threaten an area from Eastern Europe to India attests to the fact that a sizeable number of people must have migrated from the Altai, even accepting that other nomads would join them during their exodus. The proposed large population that migrated explains why the drop in temperatures and subsequent drop in food production has been cited as a cause for the movement of these peoples.

Whatever the case, the various groups began their move. The Chionites, Kidarites, Hephthalites and Alkhan moved off towards the south, while the Saraguri, Urogi and Onoguri, plus any attendant tribes, moved further west. Why these peoples divided is unknown. The most obvious explanation is that they believed it would be better to split up due to the problems of feeding their peoples, but there is no evidence concerning the migration of the tribes, so this must remain hypothetical.

The tribes moving west probably either crossed the Ural Mountains or, most likely, skirted the southern end of the range before following the River Volga to the south. It is almost certain that these nomadic peoples did not travel further north, entering the northern forest zones before turning south as the forests would not be suitable to the movement of large numbers of pastoralists.[31]

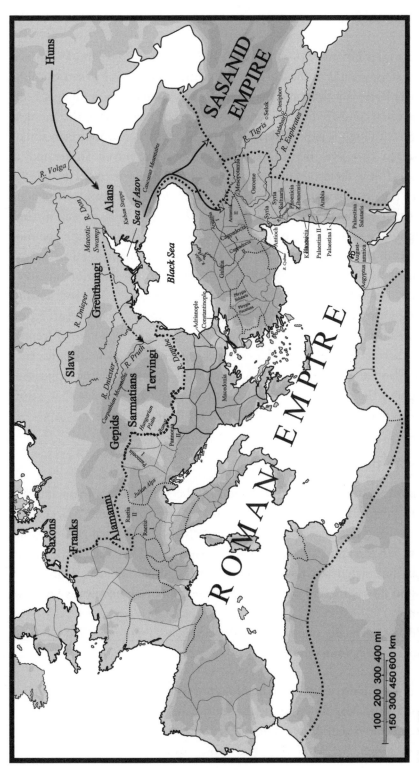

Map 3: The wars as the tribes moved west.

These migrants were to settle along the foothills of the Ural Mountains and the steppe-lands of the Caspian Sea, with some moving to settle around the Volga River. By this time they had probably undergone something of a change when compared to their ancestors who had been part of the Xiongnu Empire. Although it is possible that the ruling elite spoke Yeniseian among themselves, they and their followers probably spoke mixed Turkic and/or Ugric or Iranic dialects. Once they came into contact with the peoples of Eastern Europe, their language eventually included a Germanic component, a facet that supports the multilingual aspect of the Huns, as well as their willingness to adopt other peoples' languages, at least among the common members of the tribes. It is likely that the ruling elite maintained an antique version of Yeniseian among themselves as a sign of their superior ancestry.

Their mixed languages are mirrored by their mixed 'ethnicity'. During the long journey from their original homelands in the second century, the Huns had been joined by – or had forcibly assimilated – peoples of 'central Asian Turkic, Mongolic, and Ugric stock', plus many Iranic peoples such as the Alans and the Kushans.[32] Although they probably faced opposition throughout their migration, it is with their arrival at the Volga that we are informed that they definitely had to fight for their new lands.

War with the Alans

The move of the Huns to the region of the Volga brings them into the western historical narrative for the first time. Ammianus Marcellinus, possibly using information gleaned from refugees, notes that at some point prior to 376 the Huns attacked the Alans east of the Don: the Huns, 'aflame with an inhuman desire for plundering others' property, made their violent way amid the rapine and slaughter of the neighbouring peoples as far as the Halani.'[33]

Jordanes, allegedly quoting from Priscus, gives a more detailed but more mythologized version of events:

> This cruel tribe, as Priscus the historian relates, settled on the farther bank of the Maeotic swamp [the mouths of the River Don where it reaches the Sea of Azov]. They were fond of hunting and had no skill in any other art. After they had grown to a nation, they disturbed

the peace of neighbouring races by theft and rapine. At one time, while hunters of their tribe were as usual seeking for game on the farthest edge of Maeotis, they saw a doe unexpectedly appear to their sight and enter the swamp, acting as guide of the way; now advancing and again standing still. The hunters followed and crossed on foot the Maeotic swamp, which they had supposed was impassable as the sea. Presently the unknown land of Scythia disclosed itself and the doe disappeared. ...And the Huns, who had been wholly ignorant that there was another world beyond Maeotis, were now filled with admiration for the Scythian land. As they were quick of mind, they believed that this path, utterly unknown to any age of the past, had been divinely revealed to them. They returned to their tribe, told them what had happened, praised Scythia and persuaded the people to hasten thither along the way they had found by the guidance of the doe. As many as they captured, when they thus entered Scythia for the first time, they sacrificed to Victory. The remainder they conquered and made subject to themselves. Like a whirlwind of nations they swept across the great swamp and at once fell upon the Alpidzuri, Alcildzuri, Itimari, Tuncarsi and Boisci, who bordered on that part of Scythia. The Alani also, who were their equals in battle, but unlike them in civilization, manners and appearance, they exhausted by their incessant attacks and subdued.

Jordanes, Getica, *24 [123–6] = Priscus, fragment 10.*

As already stated, the story of the doe is a mythologized version of events: the concept that the Huns did not know that there was land beyond the Maeotis is hardly believable. However, the story may be an accurate account of a Hunnic claim to 'divine revelation' and hence their 'right' to rule the lands they found beyond the Maeotis and the Don.[34]

Ammianus confirms that the Huns were met with resistance from the Alans, but they proved to be irresistible:

The Huns, then, having overrun the territories of those Halani ... to whom usage has given the surname Tanaïtes, killed and plundered many of them, and joined the survivors to themselves in a treaty of alliance.

Ammianus Marcellinus, 31.3.1.

This seems at first glance to be a straightforward description of events and for many years was accepted as such. However, recently a more detailed analysis of both the sources and the events recorded suggests otherwise. Ammianus makes no mention of battles, nor does he give a specific indication of the length of the war. Yet the Alans had a 'warlike reputation', and in fact were to remain a feature of the political landscape in the region until their defeat by the Mongols in the thirteenth century. It is clear that the Alans were no easy victims and it would have taken a long time for the Huns to overcome them, a fact reinforced by the phrase used by Priscus/Jordanes that the Alans were 'exhausted by their incessant attacks'.[35]

A further complication is that the political situation among the Alans is unclear. Although it is known that later the Tervingi divided along political lines under Hun pressure, the same information is not given for other tribes. It is possible that divisions among the Alans helped the Huns, with some Alan leaders becoming allies of the Huns in the hope of usurping the positions of their opponents with Hun assistance, with others resisting and later being forced to flee west as they were overcome.

Chronologically, the problem then is that as the political situation among the Alans and the duration of the war is unknown, it is uncertain when the Huns moved to the region. It is therefore necessary to 'work forward' until a date is known and then attempt to work backwards from that date in the hope of constructing a viable chronology.

However, the Alans were not the only group of tribes encountered by the Huns. Also living west of the Volga were tribes such as the Apilzuri/ Alcidzuri, Itimari, Tuncassi and Boisci – all of which are assumed to be of Turkic origin – who 'bordered on the shore of Scythia'. These tribes also were overwhelmed by the Huns.[36] Either now or later the Apilzuri and Alcidzuri joined together and were later known as the Amilzouri.[37] In the fifth century they were all to be found bordering the Roman Empire along the Danube, though whether they had fled to the region or had been forced to live there by the Huns is unknown.[38] It is possible that these tribes were actually ethnically the same and spoke the same language as the Huns. In fact, they may have been the 'Huns' fighting for the Romans and Goths in Ammianus and other accounts before 400 AD.[39]

War with the Goths: the Greuthungi and Tervingi

Having been defeated, some of the Alan tribes fled west while others joined with the Huns. At this point the Hunno-Alanic alliance 'made the more boldly a sudden inroad into the extensive and rich cantons of Ermenrichus [Ermanarich], a most warlike monarch, dreaded by the neighbouring nations because of his many and varied deeds of valour'.[40]

It is usually accepted that these attacks were the first attempt by the Huns to expand their territories further west into the lands of the Greuthungi, but this is only an assumption. It is far more likely that the first attacks were simply raids aimed at discouraging Gothic attacks on the newly-founded Hunnic settlements and attempting to establish Hunnic supremacy in the region, as well as simply gathering booty. This is more likely to be the case if the Alans actually had put up a firm resistance to their conquest. After a long, hard war, both the Huns and their new Alan allies would need time to rest and regroup prior to further major campaigns. In this context, large raids may have been the first indication to Ermanarich that a new enemy had entered the picture to the east.

In the quote in the previous paragraph it is noted that Ermanarich was 'a most warlike monarch' and later Ammianus notes that:

> He was struck with consternation at the violence of this sudden storm; for a long time he did his best to maintain a firm and continued stand, but since rumour gave wide currency to and exaggerated the horror of the impending dangers, he put an end to his fear of these great perils by a voluntary death.[41]

It is clear from Ammianus that Ermanarich had a reputation for bravery and military ability. That he committed suicide in despair implies that the war against the Huns and Alans was of longer duration and brutality than is usually accepted. Again, though, there is no indication of exactly how long the war lasted.

In addition:

> After his [Ermanarich's] demise Vithimiris [Vithimer] was made king and resisted the Halani for a time, relying on other Huns, whom he had

paid to take his side. But after many defeats which he sustained, he was overcome by force of arms and died in battle.

Ammianus Marcellinus 31.3.3.

It is interesting to note here that Ammianus has Vithimer hiring Huns to fight the Alans.[42] Although uncertain, it is possible that displaced Alans had invaded Greuthungi territory when fleeing from the Huns. Knowing that the Huns had defeated the Alans, it would be an obvious move to hire Hunnic mercenaries to fight against them: these may have been the Alpidzuri and other tribes mentioned earlier as being 'Hunnic' without being affiliated directly with the Huns later ruled by Attila.[43] Alongside other fragmentary evidence, the episode suggests that after the conquest of the Alans the Huns had not advanced as a large, single 'people', but rather as 'multiple, small-scale warbands operating on a more or less individual basis', but with a centralized core around which the tribes could focus at need.[44] In effect, the Goths were being overwhelmed not by a massive force repeatedly engaging the main Gothic army, but rather that Ermanarich had been demoralized by the sheer number of smaller-scale attacks which he had no way of countering. It is possible that the Huns had conquered the Alans in the same manner, but given the nature of the proposed migration of the Huns it is more likely that the Alans were simply inundated by large numbers of Huns and their associated peoples.

Vithimer, son of Ermanarich, is not placed into the same military category as his father by Ammianus, yet he is attested as having suffered 'many defeats', which suggests several years of fighting. Consequently, it is possible to suggest that from the start of their raids on Ermanarich's territory to the defeat and death of Vithimer, the Huns and Alans were at war for between four and ten years, if not more. With the death of Vithimer, rule passed to his son Viderichus. However, as Viderichus was a minor, two experienced generals named Alatheus and Saphrax took command of the defence. They decided to retreat behind the River Danastius (Dniester), 'which flows through the wide extent of plain between the Hister [Danube] and the Borysthenes [Dnieper]'.[45]

At this point they received help from the Tervingi. Athanaric, king of the Tervingi, heard of the war and he established his camp near the banks of the Danastius, conveniently at some distance from the stockade of the Greuthungi, and sent Munderichus … with Lagarimanus and some other men of high rank, to a distance of twenty miles … to observe the advance of the enemy, while he himself in the meantime, disturbed by no one, was preparing his army for battle.[46]

Although not usually analysed, it is interesting to note that the Tervingi advanced to the vicinity of the Greuthungi. There can be little doubt that during the Hunnic attacks the Greuthungi had sent envoys and arranged a treaty with the Tervingi. The alliance was swiftly defeated:

For the Huns, who are shrewd in arriving at conclusions, suspecting that there was some large force farther off, disregarded the troops which they had seen, and who had disposed themselves to rest, as if there was nothing to disturb them; then, when the moon broke into the darkness of night, they chose what seemed to be the best course, crossed the river by a ford, and fearing lest some informer should get ahead of them and frighten off the enemy who were at a distance, they made a swift attack on Athanaricus himself. As he was stunned by their first onset, they forced him to take speedy refuge in the steep mountains, after losing a few of their own men.

Ammianus Marcellinus, 31.3.6–7.

If Athanaric was forced to retire, there can be little doubt that the Greuthungi who were encamped not far from the battle also retreated in the face of the Huns. Tellingly, Ammianus now recounts Athanaric's next move:

Athanaricus, troubled by this unexpected attack and still more through fear of what might come, had walls built high, skirting the lands of the Taifali from the banks of the River Gerasus [Pruth] as far as the Danube, thinking that by this hastily but diligently constructed barrier his security and safety would be assured [and this work] was being pushed on.

Ammianus Marcellinus, 31.3.7–8.

To plan, organize and begin construction of a barrier of any length would take more than a few weeks.[47] Although Ammianus implies that the Huns quickly pursued the Tervingi, it is more likely that the defeat at the River Dniester was the last battle in the campaigning season and that the Huns renewed their attack in the following year, during which respite Athanaric ordered the construction of the walls. Yet it should be noted that rather than being built from scratch, Athanaric may have simply ordered the repair of the old Roman fortifications along the Dacian limes.[48] Whatever the case, his plans were not implemented within the time allotted:

> While this well-planned work was being pushed on, the Huns swiftly fell upon him, and would have crushed him at once on their arrival had they not been so loaded down with booty that they gave up the attempt.
>
> *Ammianus Marcellinus, 31.3.8.*

Athanaric's defeat was the last recorded act in the war between the 'Hunno-Alanic alliance' and the two main Gothic confederations.[49] This is largely due to the fact that Gothic unity collapsed and the various cantons decided individually or in small groups on their next course of action. The Greuthungi split into at least two factions. Ammianus describes the choices of one group:

> Yet when the report spread widely among the other Gothic peoples, that a race of men hitherto unknown had now arisen from a hidden nook of the earth, like a tempest of snows from the high mountains, and was seizing or destroying everything in its way, the greater part of the people, who, worn out by lack of the necessities of life, had deserted Athanaricus, looked for a home removed from all knowledge of the savages; and after long deliberation what abode to choose they thought that Thrace offered them a convenient refuge, for two reasons: both because it has a very fertile soil, and because it is separated by the mighty flood of the Hister [Danube] from the fields that were already exposed to the thunderbolts of a foreign war; and the rest of the nation as if with one mind agreed to this plan.
>
> *Ammianus Marcellinus 31.3.8.*

Athanaric led the other assemblage, which withdrew across the Carpathian Mountains into the 'Banat region' ('Caucalanda'), where he drove out the Sarmatian inhabitants – who fled to Roman territory – before holding out for a further four years, after which he too sought sanctuary in the Empire.[50]

All of the above suggests that the wars between the Huns, the Alans, the Greuthungi and the Tervingi lasted for a long time, possibly a decade or more, with some historians suggesting as long as twenty years.[51] In fact, the ferocity of the resistance helps to explain why the majority of the Huns were to then spend around a generation living between the Rivers Volga and Don.[52]

'Independent Huns'

As already noted, the Huns may have conquered the Alans by simply overwhelming them in a series of battles, before settling between the Volga and the Don. On the other hand, the attacks on the Greuthungi and the Tervingi may have been on a smaller scale, with roaming warbands delivering morale-sapping defeats upon an enemy unable to cope with the Huns' superior horsemanship, archery and hit-and-run tactics.[53] There is little evidence that the Huns quickly conquered the two Gothic peoples and moved their centre of operations across the Carpathians and into the Hungarian Plain. That movement only happened much later.

The main centre of Hunnic control was in the region of the Kuban Steppe until around the year 400. The evidence for Huns further west before this date indicates that only small numbers of Huns were involved. The implication is that the main body of the Huns remained in the east and that only an 'advance guard' of tribes was active on the Danube from the 370s onwards, probably settling on lands vacated by the Greuthungi and Tervingi.[54] However, these groups took an active part in affairs along the frontier, sometimes acting alongside the Romans, at other times invading Roman territory.

As is well-known, large numbers of the two Gothic confederations sought refuge within the Roman Empire. After they were treated badly by the Romans, the Tervingi under Fritigern rebelled and were joined by the Greuthungi under Alatheus and Saphrax.[55] What has sometimes been overlooked is that the united Goths 'gained an alliance with some of the Huns and Halani by holding out the hope of immense booty'.[56] After their victory at the Battle of Adrianople in 378 the allies then marched on Constantinople but, finding the walls to be too vast to assault, instead moved away from the city, plundering as they went.[57] Sadly, the history of Ammianus stops here, so it is impossible to be certain what happened to these Huns. The Goths, however, won another victory in 380 over the new Eastern Emperor Theodosius before being contained and eventually signing a treaty with the East in 382.

The Huns, however, have a slightly different history. In late 378 or early 379 the alliance is recorded by Ammianus as ravaging the Balkans as far as the Julian Alps, and they may have inflicted a defeat on the *comes rei militaris* ('count' of the military) Vitalianus.[58] However, Marcellinus *comes*, in an entry dated to 427, claims that some Huns had settled in Pannonia many years before.[59] There are two different possible dates given in transcriptions of the source. One reads '*quinquaginta*' (fifty), which, when deducted from 427 gives a date of 377. The second reads '*sexaginta*' (sixty), but this date is unlikely since it would be before the Battle of Adrianople in 378. Although the first date is also before 378, it is probable that Marcellinus was giving a vague date of 'around fifty years' rather than attempting to be specific.

All that can be suggested from this brief and uncorroborated entry is that it may be that early in Theodosius' reign a group of Huns were allowed to settle in Pannonia. It is sometimes claimed that they were settled by Theodosius himself, but as in 379 Pannonia was still part of the Western Empire, this is unlikely.[60] It is more feasible that these were the Huns who had fought at Adrianople, settled on advantageous terms by the Western Emperor Gratian after separating from the main Gothic horde. Gratian is recorded as fighting Alans at Castra Martis, west of the Carpathians, in 378.[61] Gratian was to recruit Alans into his army, although whether it was these same Alans is unknown.[62] It is likely that these Alans were working alongside the Hunnic tribe that had fought at Adrianople. These Huns may have been the Alpidzuri, who appear to have had a distinct history to the main body of the Huns.[63] If this is true, there is little indication of where exactly they were settled, but it is most likely that it was somewhere in Pannonia II, at which time there may even have been an attempt to convert them to Christianity, although the attempt failed.[64]

In 381–2, prior to the treaty between the Goths and Romans in 382, one group of Huns took part in an attack on those parts of the Balkans held by the East. Zosimus records that 'Theodosius ... defeated the Sciri and the Carpodaces, among whom were some Huns, and forced them to cross the Danube and return home.'[65] Whether it was a tribe still ravaging Thrace or a newly-arrived tribe is unknown. This may have been the group of Huns Theodosius then settled in Pannonia, but them being new arrivals is the more likely, as the phrasing used by Zosimus suggests that in this attack the Huns were not the instigators, but instead simply joined the Sciri and the Carpodaces in their raid.[66]

The fact that the Huns were 'untrustworthy nomads' was doubtless imprinted on Roman minds by events in 384. In that year the Western Empire was embroiled in tumult. The child–emperor Valentinian II (born 371) was in conflict with Magnus Maximus, the commander of the British armies, who had revolted and declared himself emperor in 383. Taking advantage of the confusion, in 384 the Juthungi invaded Raetia, and Bauto, one of the Western *magistri militum* ('masters of the soldiers'), appears to have requested that an unknown group of Huns and Alans – most probably those settled in Pannonia – attack the invaders. This they did, but sadly, they then proceeded to ravage Roman territory until halted by the intervention of imperial forces.[67] Interestingly, they then appear to have helped the West again, this time against an invasion by the Sarmatians. However, in this case it is likely that their homes were at risk, so their participation in the campaign is understandable.[68]

Alongside the other evidence, this all implies that the Huns settled in the Danube region were not necessarily the major polity as sometimes believed by modern sources. Although there was indeed a core of 'Hunnic' tribes, the majority were probably a series of related tribal groups who were not united under one or two leaders, but instead followed their individual policies with regard to both the Romans and to the tribes among whom they now lived. This hypothesis is reinforced to some extent by Ammianus when he writes that the Huns 'are not subject to any king, but broke through any obstacle in the path under the improvised command of their chief men'.[69]

The Final Migration

It is worth reiterating that sources for the activities of the Huns are sparse, especially when it comes to events away from the Roman borders. As a result, when talking about the main Hunnic forces, it is necessary to resort to speculation using the few sources that exist as guides but, as usual, it is possible to use the sources to reach different conclusions to those reached here.

The recorded activities of the Huns in the early 380s suggest that these were the actions of (a) smaller, disparate group(s) intent upon establishing themselves in the region and of extorting from their new neighbours – especially Rome – as much as they could get. Interestingly, the other 'barbarian' groups in the region had a similar reaction to events, so it would appear that between 376 and c.385 affairs on the frontiers quietened down and some form of stability ensued.

However, in 386 there was a new invasion of Roman territory by a large number of people, under their leader Odotheus. The invasion was defeated by Promotus, *magister militum per Thracias* (Master of the Troops in Thrace), and Odotheus was killed.[70] The survivors were either recruited by Theodosius for his campaign against Magnus Maximus or settled in the East, especially Phrygia.[71]

Odotheus is alleged to have been a king of the Greuthungi, and the fact that another large tribal group attempted to leave the regions to the north of the Danube has major implications. Although disputed, it is possible that the exodus was caused by the Huns beginning to expand their control towards the west. At the least it is probably indicative of the Huns launching major attacks, though whether they followed these up by moving their centre of power from the Don to the Hungarian Plain at this time is unknown.[72]

That the latter must remain only a possibility may be implied by events at the end of the fourth century. In 388 some Huns served under Theodosius I, the Eastern Emperor, during his attack on the usurper Maximus in the West. Although these may have been the first generation of Huns living on the Hungarian Steppes, their most likely origin is that they were the Huns who had originally fought alongside the Goths in 377–8 and had been settled in Pannonia after the Gothic Treaty of 382.[73] Certainty is impossible, but it may be that these same Huns then 'deserted' the Roman army alongside a larger Gothic force and terrorized Macedonia for the next four years.[74] In 391 the situation became so bad that Theodosius granted affected citizens the right to bear arms, but shortly after he was himself defeated in the field and almost killed.[75]

Affairs were finally brought under control, but in 394 war broke out between the Eastern Emperor Theodosius and the Western usurper Eugenius. Events in this war were to have a major impact upon the Balkans. Shortly after his victory, Theodosius died in January 395. It has been suggested that after his passing there was a massive invasion of the Balkans in the campaign season of 395. In this hypothesis this was a 'pincer movement' launched by a new Hunnic 'Khanate' centred on the Hungarian Steppe, as it appeared at the same time as an invasion was launched by the Huns through the Caucasus into Asia Minor, in which the 'eastern pincer' attacked both the Sasanids and the Eastern Romans. That there were two simultaneous attacks has been interpreted as having great implications for the nature of Hunnic society.

Adherents of this hypothesis suggest that the Huns had resurrected the political institutions of their (alleged) Xiongnu ancestors. In this model, the 'Eastern' Huns and the 'Western' Huns were simply part of the same Empire, with the two halves being ruled by the kings of the 'Left' and of the 'Right', under the supreme control of a single emperor. These two kings were usually either the sons or brothers of the emperor.[76] In the proposition, this would explain the simultaneous nature of the two attacks, as a large single Hunnic Empire would probably be capable of organizing the manpower and logistics of such a dual campaign.[77]

Unfortunately, this whole theoretical edifice appears to be based upon entries in Philostorgius, Orosius and Claudian. Philostorgius wrote:

> The Huns, who had seized upon that part of Scythia which lies across the Ister [Danube] and laid it waste, afterwards crossed the river when it was frozen over, and made an irruption into the Roman territory: then spreading themselves over the entire surface of Thrace, they laid waste all Europe.
>
> *Philostorgius 11.8.*

It should be noted that 'Europe' ('Europa') does not imply the whole of modern continental Europe: 'Europa' was the province in the Diocese of Thrace which included Constantinople.[78]

In his *In Rufinum* (*Attack on Rufinus*), Claudian claims that:

Some pour across the frozen surface of quick-flowing Danube and break with the chariot wheel what erstwhile knew but the oar; others invade the wealthy East, led through the Caspian Gates and over the Armenian snows by a newly-discovered pass ... [and have devastated] ... all that tract of land lying between the stormy Euxine [Black Sea] and the Adriatic.

Claudian, In Rufinus, 2. 2736–8.

At first glance it would appear that Claudian is speaking of the Huns, as it is obvious that the attack by 'others ... through the Caspian Gates' was undertaken by the Huns in the east. However, the context and other references in Claudian make it clear that while the East was being overrun by Huns, the threat in Thrace was the 'rebellion' of the Gothic leader Alaric, who was taking advantage of the recent death of the Emperor Theodosius I (379–395) who would later go on to sack Rome. In addition, the events described by Socrates and Sozomen (see below) and interpreted as supporting a Hunnic invasion of Thrace in 395 actually refer to events in 404–405.[79]

On the contrary, although some Huns joined Alaric in his 'rebellion', there is no indication in the sources that large numbers of Huns either joined the Goths or invaded on their own. Although Stilicho, the Western *magister militum*, is recorded as campaigning against Alaric and the Goths, there is no mention in these sources of any major Hunnic threat in the same region.[80] In fact, Alaric's rebellion was most likely caused by the treatment of his men by the Roman commanders, since it was the Goths who bore the brunt of the fighting in the victory against Eugenius at the Battle of the River Frigidus in 394. Interestingly, John of Antioch records that for this campaign Theodosius had employed some Huns as well as the Gothic *foederati*.[81] The most likely scenario is that when the Goths 'rebelled', the Eastern Huns in the Roman army simply joined in the rebellion.

That there was no major Hunnic invasion aimed at taking advantage of both Theodosius' death and the rebellion of Alaric by actually invading Thrace in large numbers implies that they had no strong presence on the Danube at this time. Similar problems later in the fifth century would cause the Huns to invade both East and West.[82] Rather than suggesting that the Huns were of a strength capable of attacking both halves of the major Empire in the region – as suggested by the hypothesis analysed above – the fact that the only major invasion from the Huns came over the Caucasus suggests that the Huns remained centred to the East at this time, although they do appear to have unified by this time.

In support of the above hypothesis, it is notable that in 395 Rufinus, the Eastern Praetorian Prefect, was forced to negotiate a separate peace with the Goths and the Huns. The fact that the Goths and the Huns were treated separately and as equals reinforces the concept that Hunnic attacks were most likely raids by ex-Roman army forces rather than a full-scale invasion comparable to that in the East.[83] Consequently, the hypothesis concerning the invasion and its implications is here dismissed. On the other hand, the suggestion that the Huns employed the same political practices as their Xiongnu ancestors may be true and will be discussed later.

The Persian Assault

In contrast to the tone of the sources concerning the 'revolt' in the Balkans, the attacks across the Caucasus terrified the courts of East Rome and the Sasanids. For example, Ephraim the Syrian wrote: 'The Huns ate children, drank the blood of women, and were the reincarnation of the devil, Gog, and Magog.'[84] The terror inspired by the Huns in both East and West would reverberate down the centuries, passing in turn to their successors, the Avars and the Mongols.

The attack on the East was initially a success. Splitting into two, one group moved to attack the Sasanids, while the other attacked the Roman Empire. The names of the leaders of the two groups are given as Basich and Kursich:

> Basich and Kursich, who later came to Rome to make an alliance, men of the Royal Scythians and rulers of a vast horde, advanced into the lands of the Medes ... A Persian host came on them as they were plundering and overrunning the land and, being on higher ground than they, filled the air with missiles, so that, encompassed by danger, the Huns had to retreat and retire across the mountains with little loot, for the greatest part was seized by the Medes.
>
> *Priscus, fragment 8.*

Basich and Kursich are the first Huns named definitively in the sources. The fact that they are both classed as kings has led to conjecture that even at this early stage the Huns were practising the 'dual-monarchy' used by their predecessors the Xiongnu. This theory may be supported by the fact that Priscus notes that the two men together later made an alliance with Rome, possibly in either 404 or 407.[85] However, it is possible that they were simply the leaders of two separate tribes or groups of tribes which joined to make a simultaneous attack on the Eastern Roman and Sasanid empires before making a simultaneous agreement with Rome.

It has also been posited that the two men were leaders of a political entity that was based in Europe. Although the paucity of the evidence is such that proof is impossible, the little we have can be used to support this theory:

> Romulus answered that the land of the Medes was separated by no great distance from Scythia and that the Huns were not ignorant of this route. Long ago they had come upon it when a famine was in their country … Those who went across say that they traversed a desert country, crossed a swamp which Romulus thought was the Maeotis, spent fifteen days crossing mountains and so descended into Media.
>
> *Priscus, fragment 11.2.595f.*

This small passage is often used as conclusive proof that the Huns had indeed crossed from the Hungarian Steppes via the mouths of the Don to the passes over the Caucasus Mountains. However, this evidence is of dubious accuracy. Priscus' statement that he was relating information which had been related to Romulus suggests that perhaps the information was inaccurate or exaggerated in order to impress Romulus. On the contrary, it may be that the Huns at the time of the invasion were still in 'Scythia', as evidenced by the phrase 'no great distance from Scythia'. If so, they were settled to the north of the Black Sea and the Sea of Azov, their crossing of the Don being the marshes in the quote.

The attack caused havoc in the Roman East:

> In the year just gone by the wolves (no longer of Arabia but of the whole North) were let loose upon us from the remotest fastnesses of Caucasus and in a short time overran these great provinces. What a

number of monasteries they captured! What many rivers they caused to run red with blood! They laid siege to Antioch and invested other cities on the Halys, the Cydnus, the Orontes, and the Euphrates. They carried off troops of captives. Arabia, Phoenicia, Palestine and Egypt in their terror fancied themselves already enslaved.

Jerome, Epistle, *60.16.*

In support of Jerome, the *Chronicle of Edessa* states that: 'In the year 706, the month of Tammuz [July 395], the Huns reached Osroene in northern Mesopotamia.'[86]

The 'troops of captives' is confirmed to some degree by a statement in the *Chronicon miscellaneum ad annum Domini 724*:

And in this year, the accursed people of the Huns came into the lands of the Romans and passed over Sophene, Armenia, Mesopotamia, Syria, Cappadocia, as far as Galatia; they took a great number of captives and turned back so that they might return to their (own) country. But they went down to the banks of the Euphrates and Tigris, in the province of the Persians, and reached the Persians' royal city; they did no damage there, but laid waste many villages by the Euphrates and Tigris, and killed (many) and took a great number of captives. But when the Huns heard that the Persians were marching against them, they prepared to flee, and (the Persians) pursued them and killed one of their detachments, and took back from them all the spoils they had seized; and they freed male captives from them 18,000 in number, and led them to their cities Selok and Kaukaba, which are called Ardashir and Ctesiphon, where they were for many years. The Persian king assigned rations for them – bread, wine, date wine and oil. From these 18,000 there remained but a few ... the first thousand; and the Persians let them go so that they might return to their (own) land.

Chronicon miscellaneum ad annum Domini
724, 3.136–137 = 4.106–7

Unlike the Sasanids, at the start of the campaign the East was unable to respond as the focus of the court at Constantinople was upon the activities of Stilicho – the Western *magister militum* and guardian of the young

Western Emperor Honorius – and the increasing tension between Stilicho and Rufinus, the Eastern Praetorian Prefect.

The Huns retreated back across the Caucasus, yet the claims of the Eastern Empire of a 'victory' over the retreating Hunnic raiders suggests that at least one – possibly successful – attack on the retiring Huns took place, perhaps under the command of Eutropius, a eunuch who became the young Eastern Emperor Arcadius' leading advisor after the death of Rufinus late in 395.[87] If so, the Roman victory was probably won against a small raid that occurred in 397 rather than 395: the account of Pseudo-Dionysus claims that this victory was in 395, but this is disputed.[88] Sadly, the sources give no decisive dates concerning the duration of the war.

The Huns in the East

Placing the attacks and other events into context can lead to a hypothesis concerning the movement of the Huns between the mid-360s and the early 400s. Having analysed the course and outcome of the various attacks on the empire, it is possible to suggest that prior to the 370s – and maybe as early as the late third century – the Huns migrated from the Altai Mountains to the River Don, either displacing or absorbing the various tribes in the region. Once settled, they launched raids that virtually destroyed the Greuthungi and terrified the Tervingi to the point where a large proportion of both peoples asked for asylum within the empire. At this point the only Huns who were present in the West were small groups who offered their services to whoever could offer them reward, such as those that joined the Tervingi for the Battle of Adrianople in 378 and the subsequent attempt on Constantinople.[89]

Although it is sometimes assumed that the Huns had emigrated to the Hungarian Steppes by CE 400, the evidence shows that this claim is debatable. It is better to assume that there were 'two main phases of population movement' among the barbarians living to the north of the Roman Empire. The first of these was c.376–86, with the second coming much later, in 405–408, but both were 'directly caused by the intrusion of Hunnic power into the fringes of Europe'.[90] It is here assumed that only with the later attacks can the Huns be assumed to have been on the move again.

As a consequence, it is best to assume that the majority of the united Hunnic tribes remained around the Don and the Volga, where they were to remain for nearly a generation, terrorizing the surrounding peoples and regaining their strength. During this period they launched a large attack on the Greuthungi and/or Tervingi who had remained in their homes north of the Danube, with the result that Odotheus attempted to invade the empire rather than submit to Hunnic domination.

Part of the evidence for Hunnic 'disunity' in this period is the emergence between 395 and 400 of a new Hunnic political entity to the north of the Danube, led by the first Hun on the Danubian frontier named in the sources. Yet the nature of Hunnic society, both during their migrations and their final settlements, remains a mystery – largely due to the lack of written evidence – so for any analysis it is necessary to resort to analysis of the few viable sources and speculation.

Chapter Two

The Huns: Nomadic Society

Perceptions

The little surviving evidence suggests that at least the core of the new settlers was nomadic. The greatest difficulty in assessing the nature of nomadism in its various forms, and especially when it comes to ancient sources, is that from time immemorial nomads have been seen by the agriculturalists with whom they came into contact as 'the Other', and it is agriculturalists who have left written records. Furthermore, over time the original description has transformed into the view that nomads were 'excessively savage and wild', an observation that passed into Western lore – largely thanks to the arrival of the Huns – when it was coupled with the biblical representation of the nomad as violent and 'a means through which God can chastise different peoples'.[1]

From the time that Ammianus described the nomadic Huns as uncivilized men who 'dress in linen cloth or in the skins of field-mice sewn together', the view of the unrefined nomad who has little in common with more 'civilized' city-dwellers has lingered. Only in recent decades has study of the nomad lifestyle shown that the old perceptions were wrong and do not do justice to the complex social and political reality of nomadic society. Far from being uncultured and having only rudimentary political and social institutions, recent research has demonstrated that nomads are a 'political entity with their own internal and external mechanisms, not ... an isolated entity with no external ties'.[2]

In fact, it is now clear that nomadism is far more complicated than first thought. For example, on the Eurasian steppes semi-nomadism – the mixture of mobile nomadism and more settled agriculturalism – was widespread. It was even possible to cross from pure nomadism to pure agriculturalism, and vice versa, over time.[3] Such flexibility was necessary as although 'Inner Asia' is commonly perceived as miles of unbroken grassland, in reality the steppes are contiguous with mountains, deserts, arctic tundra and forests, all of which respond differently to small changes in climate. As a consequence, the region is home to a wide variety of 'pastoralists, agriculturalists, hunter-gatherers and urban dwellers'.[4] Given that wide-ranging nomads would interact with a variety of different lifestyles as well as different cultures, they would have knowledge of alternative lifestyles to nomadism. This ability to change needs to be remembered when discussing the nature of Hunnic society.

Pure nomadism was (and is) based on 'a fundamental activity ... [of] ... livestock production which was carried out through the purposeful seasonal movement of livestock and their human masters (living in portable dwellings) over a series of already delineated pasturages in the course of a year.'[5] Yet even here there was some agriculture being used to supply the basics needed for survival, so the concept that change was possible is reinforced.

Those nomads that retained a distinctly nomadic lifestyle still had complex interactions to make. Each group may have been composed of eight to twelve family units, which by themselves were too small to have major political influence.[6] Consequently, there was a constant need for the 'mounted warrior elites ... [to direct] ... affairs through elaborate networks of authority and dependence', and although the various nomadic groups 'shared certain traits of herding, trading and fighting', they all lived 'in complex synergy with local agricultural and commercial communities'. In this way, they could make good on commodities that they did not produce, as well as take advantage of long-distance trade.[7]

Obviously, the small scale of these basic groups meant that grievances between families outside of the group could result in internal conflict, yet this was rarely allowed to influence the nomads' interaction with the outside world, to which they tended to display a 'common front'.[8] However, this may not always have been the case: as the Hunnic polity grew, political affiliations and feuds may have become more strained, accounting for the existence in the late fourth and early fifth centuries of roving bands of Huns who appear to have had little or no affiliation with the main polity.

To add to the confusion, the Huns had now moved to a region where political and social complexity was even more evident than normal: the western steppes in Asia. Here there are four interlocking zones: the Eurasian Steppe (the Hungarian Plain to the Gobi Desert); Sasanian Persia (the

Iranian Plateau across the Caucasus Mountains to the fringes of the Eurasian Steppe); trans-Danubian Europe; and Roman Europe.[9] Followers of the Huns who were non- or semi-nomadic would find land on which to settle and grow crops. The nomadic sections of the migrants would obviously live in tandem with their fellow agricultural settlers, but would also be able to interact with the Sasanians and Romans, who were largely agricultural and who had important settlements where the nomads would be able to trade their own goods – livestock, excess grain and other resources available on the steppes – for those items that were otherwise inaccessible, especially rare goods from distant lands that would be more readily available at the large towns in Rome and Persia. In addition, they would be able to trade with the inhabitants of the European forests who had access to commodities unavailable on the steppes, allowing access to additional goods wanted by the Roman and Sasanid empires and so boosting the Huns' ability to trade.

The majority of the goods supplied by nomads for markets were probably based on hunting and herding. Hunting would produce, among other things, furs and slaves. With regard to herding, it should be noted that the nomads in the period under question placed reliance on sheep, goats, camels and horses, not cattle.[10] As a result, they could have supplied meat, skins and wool, as well as the animals themselves, so that agriculturalists could use the sheep to rear small herds of their own. The tribes could also facilitate trade links between the two large empires to the south and their northern neighbours, which would be of benefit as they could impose a 'tax' on traders attempting to cross their lands.

The converse of this is that the refusal of the Romans or Sasanids to trade, or an inequality in the prices at trade centres, or even an unexpected rise in the price of goods – for example, prices being raised as a result of Roman tax reforms – could have serious consequences. Rather than accepting an unequal trade deal, the nomads could revert to raiding to either obtain the goods they wanted or attempt to force the other side to lower the price of their goods, or both.[11] It is probably fair to say that the greatest cause of 'nomadic irruptions' was the need to interact economically with sedentary societies.[12]

Yet there is an even more fundamental issue when analysing the Huns. Although they are attested as being 'nomads', questions are still being asked as to which particular form of 'nomadism' they used. The problem lies in the fact that over time they moved from regions suitable to 'pure' nomadism to territories where the local topography was less suitable. The question then is did any of the nomad groups who formed the Huns retain their nomadism, or did they convert to semi-nomadism, or even to agriculturalism?

Obviously, in the past it has been accepted that they retained their nomadic state:

> There is no need to labour the point that the Huns all but lived on horseback, and in sheer horsemanship they far surpassed the best Roman and Gothic cavalry.
>
> *E.A. Thompson*, A History of Attila and the Huns
> (*Oxford, 1948*), *p.51*.

> In the seventy years between the first clash of the marauders with Roman frontier troops and the battle at the locus Mauriacus, the warfare of the Huns remained essentially the same. Attila's horsemen were still the same mounted archers who in the 380s had ridden down the Vardar valley and followed the standards of Theodosius.
>
> *O. Maenchen-Helfen*, The World of the Huns
> (*Berkeley, 1973*), *p.201*.

This may not do justice to the complexity of Hunnic society, especially when it is accepted that in their travels the Huns almost certainly collected in their wake tribes who were not nomadic or only partially nomadic. In addition, the nature of their movement also impacted upon the nature of their own society:

> In times of turbulence the tribal and ethnic composition of these steppes became a richly hued mosaic, the colours and textures of which are only partially reflected in our sources. The latter largely stem from and were written in the languages of the surrounding sedentary societies. They are frequently incomplete, on occasion ill-informed and universally tend to view the nomad through the prisms of their own cultures. The movement of the Huns toward Europe undoubtedly introduced new ethnic elements into the Ponto-Caspian steppes. These included Turkic speakers who later became the dominant ethno-linguistic grouping in

this region. We have, however, scraps of evidence that appear to indicate that Turkic nomads were present here even before the Huns crossed the Volga.

Golden, The Peoples of the South Russian Steppes, *1990*

In fact, even some of the ancient sources may have been able to differentiate to some degree between the different 'nomadic' 'Hunnic' tribes:

The Ephthalitae are of the stock of the Huns in fact as well as in name; however they do not mingle with any of the Huns known to us, for they occupy a land neither adjoining nor even very near to them; but their territory lies immediately to the north of Persia; indeed their city, called Gorgo, is located over against the Persian frontier, and is consequently the centre of frequent contests concerning boundary lines between the two peoples. For they are not nomads like the other Hunnic peoples, but for a long period have been established in a goodly land. As a result of this they have never made any incursion into the Roman territory except in company with the Median army. They are the only ones among the Huns who have white bodies and countenances which are not ugly. It is also true that their manner of living is unlike that of their kinsmen, nor do they live a savage life as they do; but they are ruled by one king, and since they possess a lawful constitution, they observe right and justice in their dealings both with one another and with their neighbours, in no degree less than the Romans and the Persians.

Procopius, Wars, *1.3.2–8.*

On a final note, it should be acknowledged that nomadic empires may have followed a cyclic pattern, in that the mobile nomads could effect the conquest of a sedentary people, but this usually resulted in the sedentarization of the ruling clan and the nomadic elite, since they needed a 'capital' from which to govern their new empire.[13] This in effect left them vulnerable in at least two respects, in that they now had a capital city that was open to attack, plus the loss of their nomadic lifestyle may have resulted in them losing those martial abilities which had gained them their empire in the first place.

On the other hand, the 'core' of the Huns may have remained nomadic after their migration. It is possible they retained their nomadic fighting techniques due to their pride in their ancient heritage, but the chances are that many tribes named in the sources as 'Huns' either were or became semi-nomadic or agriculturalist. This factor needs to be remembered when the later history of the Huns is explored.

Warfare

There remains the question of how the Huns were able to traverse such vast distances while retaining their cohesion – or at least the cohesion of the tribal core – without being assimilated by the peoples they encountered. One factor in this was almost certainly the 'arrogance' of the Huns. Proud of their ancestors, the Huns were able to retain their identity against all challengers, none of whom were able to display a more grandiose ancestry than the imperial Xiongnu.

A second may have been their expertise in warfare. The core of the Huns was certainly composed of nomads imbued with the skills required to fight and win from the backs of their horses. Their main 'weapons' are attested as being their superb horsemanship, their asymmetrical composite bows and their lassos, along with the usual sword and possibly a javelin or lance, although the claim that they were the world's best at the time may be overstating the case.[14]

The Hun Army

As far as their horsemanship goes, there can be little doubt that they were highly-skilled cavalrymen. The fact that they had ridden since their early childhood and so had a close connection to their horses contrasts with the long and intense training necessary for Roman cavalry units in order for them to work efficiently. Their superior skills gave the Huns advantages when using large numbers of cavalry. Among these was great tactical and strategic flexibility: there can be little doubt that Hunnic cavalry were capable of independent action, whether this was harassing the flanks of an enemy in battle, scouting enemy positions or foraging for food far away from the main body.

An often overlooked aspect was the ability to mount a devastating pursuit of an enemy routed in battle: it was when the enemy battle-lines began to fragment that the vast majority of casualties were usually caused. Equally, the large numbers of fast-moving Hunnic horsemen would deter any enemy from pursuing defeated Huns by covering the retreat, meaning that Hunnic losses would usually be minimal.

When it comes to archery, questions have been raised both as to the effectiveness of the Huns' bows, as well as to whether the Hunnic army – and especially that employed by Attila, which contained large numbers of 'allied' troops from conquered tribes and had long exposure to Roman and Sasanid military methods – really was composed mainly of Hunnic horse-archers.[15]

In this context, it is interesting to note that the slightly later Roman military manual called the *Strategikon*, attributed to the emperor Mauricius, suggests that Roman cavalrymen carried bows individually suited to the strength of each soldier. In addition, unskilled men were instructed to use lighter bows as these would be easier to draw. Mauricius also suggests that it was essential for even the most unskilled to learn how to shoot a bow. In fact, he dedicates a section in the *Strategikon* specifically to archery training. Soldiers were trained to shoot rapidly, 'either in a Roman or Persian manner'.[16] Although it has been noted that in this context Mauricius may be describing a 'Roman' method that followed Hunnic exemplars of drawing the bowstring with thumb and forefinger – whereas the 'Persian' method employed the lower three fingers – it is also likely that the two styles employed different tactical approaches to archery.

It is possible that it was the method in which archery was employed by the Huns that was the main difference between the Huns and both the earlier and contemporary enemies of Rome who made use of horse-archers. In this hypothesis, the Sasanids – and possibly the Sarmatians and Alans – used mounted archery in an 'old-fashioned' manner, relying upon massed archery fired quickly without specific aim at a large target. This may have been a tactic enforced upon them by both the rigidity of their formations and the fact that training may have begun later in life, especially for the Sasanids. A side-effect of the method was that it required vast numbers of arrows.

On the other hand, and aided by their training from childhood, the Huns appear to have used heavier bows and arrows and to have focused upon smaller volumes of arrows being aimed at specific targets. In this they would be helped by the mobility and agility of their steppe-bred horses which, in conjunction with a lack of 'formal' formations, allowed the Huns to get in close to the enemy to help their aim. Obviously, this meant that the Huns did not use nearly as many arrows as did the Sasanids. In addition, the lower number of arrows being fired would mean that the Huns would not tire as fast as the archers of other armies. It is the combination of strong bows and heavy arrows employed by archers who did not tire that accounts for Ammianus' claim that the Huns fought with superior bows.[17]

The factors outlined above were the foundation of the Huns' reputation, so much so that their success was a factor in the reorganization of the later East-Roman army, which by the time of Belisarius had adopted the horse-archer tactics of the Huns. Interestingly, despite the fact that they had been exposed to massed horse-archers from at least the first century BCE when fighting against the Parthians and Sasanids, it is only after exposure to Hunnic methods that the empire decided to convert to an army based around horse-archers.

It has been claimed that the expertise necessary in both woodworking and metalworking to manufacture the bows and the swords with which many of the Huns were equipped proves that these were acquired from 'settled communities' via trade and raid.[18] However, there are problems with this hypothesis. One is the question of why the communities who manufactured these weapons sold them to a nomadic people who could then use the weapons against their makers. A second question must be why there is no record of settled peoples on the steppes using these same weapons to defend themselves: surely, if they manufactured and so had access to these weapons, the superiority of the Huns would not have been so pronounced. The third, and possibly most important question, is that for this to be true there must have been settlements all along the journey from the Altai Mountains to the west that had the skills to keep the Huns supplied with the same equipment – especially bows – as those that had been damaged during either the journey or the fighting that inevitably took place when the Huns faced obdurate opponents.

Although there is a lack of archaeological evidence to either support or disprove the theory – for example, the discovery of smelting or smithing sites within those areas ruled by the Huns and dated to their occupation – it is surely far more logical that the Huns had experts within their ranks who knew how to manufacture swords and bows, both of which operations could easily be carried out by the Huns themselves without recourse to trade. In fact, one theory has it that the word 'Turk' comes from the word for helmet: the Ashina peoples of the Altai were famed as ironsmiths.

On the other hand, the acquisition of the basic metals needed for the production of weapons, cauldrons and other items may have been at the focus of trade agreements on the steppes, and the need to obtain metals difficult to obtain elsewhere may be a reason for some of the raids carried out by nomads throughout history. There is no need to think of the Huns – or nomads in general – as being simply 'parasites', relying on settled communities for all of their needs except for some types of food, clothes and drink.

Priscus: Hunnic Society

In any analysis of Hunnic society there is one major difficulty: the use of *topoi* (singular *topos*: 'a method of treating new material by referring to traditional descriptions') by ancient writers. The technique can mask any differences that may have been seen by more observant eyewitnesses. For example, the description of the ancient Scythians by Herodotus in the fifth century BCE remained the model for depicting nomadism among the Greeks, and as Roman education focused upon the reading of the 'Classics', Herodotus' account continued to be the model for later Roman writers.

However, there is one first-hand account of the Hunnic court and society that has intrigued historians for centuries. This is by the historian Priscus and, although it concerns his later embassy to Attila, it is here assumed that in the area of Hunnic society Attila made no major changes when he became sole ruler. The following extracts are taken from the translation by J.B. Bury (Priscus, fragment 8, in *Fragmenta Historicorum Graecorum*):

> We set out ... and arrived at Sardica. Halting there we considered it advisable to invite Edecon and the barbarians with him to dinner. The inhabitants of the place sold us sheep and oxen, which we slaughtered, and we prepared a meal. In the course of the feast, as the barbarians lauded Attila and we lauded the Emperor, Bigilas remarked that it was not fair to compare a man and a god, meaning Attila by the man and Theodosius by the god. The Huns grew excited and hot at this remark.

But we turned the conversation in another direction, and soothed their wounded feelings; and after dinner, when we separated, Maximin presented Edecon and Orestes with silk garments and Indian gems.

This extract can be taken as evidence that the Huns were extremely sensitive to any perceived slights to Attila, so giving proof that Attila was highly-regarded by his followers. What is more interesting is that the envoys sent by the empire to the Huns appear to have been incompetent in that they did not understand that such remarks would cause offence, this despite modern historians claiming that contacts with the Hunnic Empire 'were characterised by extreme sensitivity to the niceties of procedure'.[19] Although the 'niceties of procedure' may have been followed when in close contact with the Hunnic ruler, when dealing with his underlings it would seem that Roman arrogance remained the norm:

Having crossed the Danube, and proceeded with the barbarians about seventy stadia [sing. *stadion*: a unit of distance that varied from place to place but averages c.160 metres], we were compelled to wait in a certain plain, that Edecon and his party might go on in front and inform Attila of our arrival .... and two Scythians arrived with directions that we were to set out to Attila ...On the next day, under their guidance, we arrived at the tents of Attila, which were numerous, at about three o'clock, and when we wished to pitch our tent on a hill the barbarians who met us prevented us, because the tent of Attila was on low ground, so we halted where the Scythians desired.

Obviously there was a strict hierarchy within Hunnic society, as part of which a subordinate would not be allowed to occupy a position – in this example higher on a hill – which could suggest dominance over the Hunnic ruler:

[Having been told by Attila to leave] ...When it was day we expected a gentle and courteous message from the barbarian, but he again bade us depart if we had no further mandates beyond what he already knew. We made no reply, and prepared to set out, though Bigilas insisted that we should feign to have some other communication to make. When

I saw that Maximin was very dejected, I went to Scottas (one of the Hun nobles, brother of Onegesius), taking with me Rusticius, who understood the Hun language. ...I informed Scottas, Rusticius acting as interpreter, that Maximin would give him many presents if he would procure him an interview with Attila; and, moreover, that the embassy would not only conduce to the public interests of the two powers, but to the private interest of Onegesius, for the Emperor desired that he should be sent as an ambassador to Byzantium, to arrange the disputes of the Huns and Romans, and that there he would receive splendid gifts. As Onegesius was not present it was for Scottas, I said, to help us, or rather help his brother, and at the same time prove that the report was true which ascribed to him an influence with Attila equal to that possessed by his brother. Scottas mounted his horse and rode to Attila's tent ... Scottas came to fetch us, and we entered Attila's tent, which was surrounded by a multitude of barbarians. We found Attila sitting on a wooden chair. We stood at a little distance and Maximin advanced and saluted the barbarian, to whom he gave the Emperor's letter, saying that the Emperor prayed for the safety of him and his. The king replied, 'It shall be unto the Romans as they wish it to be unto me', and immediately addressed Bigilas, calling him a shameless beast, and asking him why he ventured to come when all the deserters had not been given up ... [a reference to earlier negotiations].

This passage can be interpreted in at least two different ways. In the first, important persons within Hunnic society could be petitioned in order to use their influence with the king: on this occasion, Scottas intervening and gaining the envoys access to Attila in order to gain an advantage for himself and his brother. On the other hand, it may be that a politically-astute king would place his subordinates in positions from where they could reap the rewards, assuming that Attila knew all along that he would 'change his mind', simply waiting until one of his entourage should gain from the ensuing discussions. Following this interview:

After the departure of Bigilas, who returned to the Empire (nominally to find the deserters whose restoration Attila demanded, but really to get the money for his fellow-conspirator Edecon[20]), we remained one day in that place, and then set out with Attila for the northern parts of the country. We accompanied the barbarian for a time, but when we reached a certain point took another route by the command of the Scythians who conducted us, as Attila was proceeding to a village where he intended to marry the daughter of Eskam, though he had many other wives, for the Scythians practise polygamy.

It is interesting to note that the Huns practised polygamy. Although to Christian Romans polygamy was unacceptable, to the more mobile Huns this was a natural form of marriage that had great political and personal benefits. One of these may be dimly viewed in this extract. Although Eskam is otherwise unknown, it is most likely that the marriage was political, being a means of tying Eskam to the royal house and so ensuring his loyalty. With polygamy, this method could be used several times, whereas in the Greek and Roman world a marriage for diplomatic reasons would necessarily enforce the divorce of any previous spouse, meaning that the divorcee's relatives would possibly become hostile to the ex-husband.

> [Proceeding by a different route to Attila] ... met with navigable rivers – of which the greatest, next to the Danube, are the Drecon, Tigas, and Tiphesas [Theiss] – which we crossed in the Monoxyles, boats made of one piece, used by the dwellers on the banks: the smaller rivers we traversed on rafts which the barbarians carry about with them on carts, for the purpose of crossing morasses.

It would appear that when the Huns (or their subordinates) were expecting to cross rivers and swamps they had ready-made rafts carried on wagons with which to cross. This seems a little odd, as having crossed on a raft they would then be unable to use the wagons left behind on the far bank. This would suggest that the Huns had relays of raft-loaded wagons ready to cross rivers and marshes on routes that were often used. This may point to a level of organization that is usually interpreted as being beyond the abilities of 'nomadic horsemen':

> In the villages we were supplied with food – millet instead of corn, and mead, as the natives call it, instead of wine. The attendants who followed

us received millet, and a drink made of barley, which the barbarians call kam. Late in the evening, having travelled a long distance, we pitched our tents on the banks of a fresh-water lake, used for water by the inhabitants of the neighbouring village. But a wind and storm, accompanied by thunder and lightning and heavy rain, arose … all our utensils were rolled into the waters of the lake. Terrified by the mishap and the atmospheric disturbance, we left the place and lost one another in the dark and the rain, each following the road that seemed most easy. But we all reached the village by different ways, and raised an alarm to obtain what we lacked. The Scythians of the village sprang out of their huts at the noise, and, lighting the reeds which they use for kindling fires, asked what we wanted. Our conductors replied that the storm had alarmed us; so they invited us to their huts and provided warmth for us by lighting large fires of reeds.

Although possibly only a divergent story to add flavour to the account, it is interesting to note that, although the envoys had lost a lot of equipment and been scattered, the villagers gave the envoys a welcome and sheltered them during the remainder of the storm. In fact, things went further:

The lady who governed the village – she had been one of Bleda's wives – sent us provisions and good-looking girls to console us (this is a Scythian compliment). We treated the young women to a share in the eatables, but declined to take any further advantage of their presence.

There are several points of interest in this small extract. One is that, although the settlement is only classed as a 'village', it is governed by Attila's sister-in-law. The polygamy practised among the Huns resulted in a large number of 'imperial princesses', all of whom would require positions of importance: although it was Attila who had killed her husband, the lady still needed a position that would earn her respect as a member of the imperial family. On the other hand, it should also be noted that she was only 'one' of Bleda's wives, so it is intriguing to consider how many 'imperial princesses' there were in Hunnic territory governing small settlements.

There is also the question of sexual morality. No doubt in part the offer of 'good-looking girls' was seen as repellent by Priscus due to the difference in sexual practices between the Huns and the Romans, especially when taken in conjunction with their practice of polygamy. Overall, it offers the impression that when it came to sex the Huns had a more permissive attitude when compared to their neighbours. After a night's sleep:

> Having looked after our horses and cattle, we directed our steps to the princess, to whom we paid our respects and presented gifts in return for her courtesy. The gifts consisted of things which are esteemed by the barbarians as not produced in the country – three silver phials, red skins, Indian pepper, palm fruit, and other delicacies.

As with the Romans and the Germanic tribes, the act of giving gifts as a thank-you for services appears to have been an established practice, and here Priscus gives us a small insight into those types of items not available in general to at least the majority of the Huns and their subsidiaries:

> Having advanced a distance of seven days farther, we halted at a village; for as the rest of the route was the same for us and Attila, it behoved us to wait, so that he might go in front.

Although much has been inferred from this sentence, it should be noted that except for individuals expressly permitted to advance in front of a ruler by tradition, in the majority of cases a monarch would expect to go first in any ceremonial procession, so the fact that Attila (and presumably his predecessors) would demand priority is not in itself informative:

> Having waited for some time until Attila advanced in front of us, we proceeded, and having crossed some rivers we arrived at a large village, where Attila's house was said to be more splendid than his residences in other places. It was made of polished boards, and surrounded with a wooden enclosure, designed, not for protection, but for appearance.

The description of Attila's house immediately brings to mind the 'round houses' and 'rectangular huts' predominant among mid-late twentieth century historical recreations of the buildings of 'barbarians'. It also stands in stark contrast to the massive stone buildings with which the Roman Empire's cities were decorated. Yet this should not be used to imply that

Hunnic society was less sophisticated and politically adept as that of the Romans. Recent research has done much to dispel the myth of the 'crude barbarian', emphasizing the grandeur and workmanship of the wooden halls built for barbarian kings. In fact, the description of the sheer size of Attila's 'house' is remarkable:

> The house of Onegesius was second to the king's in splendour, and was also encircled with a wooden enclosure, but it was not adorned with towers like that of the king. Not far from the enclosure was a large bath which Onegesius – who was the second in power among the Scythians – built, having transported the stones from Pannonia; for the barbarians in this district had no stones or trees, but used imported material.

That the enclosure around Attila's main residence had towers built into it implies a far grander structure than that envisioned by historians in the recent past, who have been misled by the 'noble barbarian' tradition inherent in the ancient sources.

This small passage also gives a little further information. Onegesius has apparently attempted to emulate Roman practices by having a bath-house built – guided by a captured Roman specialist – outside his enclosure. The fact that the bath-house was built outside the enclosure implies that in some ways Onegesius was in effect enriching the lives of the local community by building a communal baths, which would both elevate his standing among his compatriots as well as please his overlord. The construction would have cost a great deal, since the stones had had to be transported from Pannonia for the building. The fact that the Huns had no skilled workers capable of producing stone of their own is also notable.

> The builder of the bath was a captive from Sirmium, who expected to win his freedom as payment for making the bath. But he was disappointed, and greater trouble befell him than mere captivity among the Scythians, for Onegesius appointed him bathman, and he used to minister to him and his family when they bathed.

Although this passage can be used to suggest that Onegesius had promised the captive his freedom, this can be seen as being unlikely: Onegesius would have needed somebody who knew how to operate, maintain and repair the structure.

> When Attila entered the village he was met by girls advancing in rows, under thin white canopies of linen, which were held up by the outside women who stood under them, and were so large that seven or more girls walked beneath each. There were many lines of damsels thus canopied, and they sang Scythian songs.

Although less flamboyant than the processions of either the Roman or the Sasanid rulers, it is clear that the Huns employed specific ceremonies to acknowledge the arrival of their ruler. It is unlikely that every village or town under Hunnic rule would have the necessary equipment – especially in respect of large volumes of linen – needed to undertake this ceremony every time Attila entered a settlement, so this may only have happened in places where Attila had permanent residences.

> When he came near the house of Onegesius, which lay on his way, the wife of Onegesius issued from the door, with a number of servants, bearing meat and wine, and saluted him and begged him to partake of her hospitality. This is the highest honour that can be shown among the Scythians. To gratify the wife of his friend, he ate, just as he sat on his horse, his attendants raising the tray to his saddlebow; and having tasted the wine, he went on to the palace, which was higher than the other houses and built on an elevated site.

Again, this episode simply shows the many customs by which the ruler both demonstrated that he was the first among the people, while at the same time using his position to bolster the standing of one of his most powerful followers. Although specific customs doubtless varied – especially the partaking of food and drink from horseback – it is likely that these traditions were in some ways echoed by other 'barbarian' societies lying beyond the Roman frontier.

> But we remained in the house of Onegesius, at his invitation, for he had returned from his expedition with Attila's son. His wife and kinsfolk

entertained us to dinner, for he had no leisure himself, as he had to relate to Attila the result of his expedition, and explain the accident which had happened to the young prince, who had slipped and broken his right arm.

It would appear from this excerpt that Onegesius was in command of the 'expedition', not, as would sometimes be expected, Attila's son. Sadly, as the son is not named there is no indication of his age, so it is unknown whether Onegesius was in command due to his political standing, putting him above Attila's son, or whether the latter was simply too young to command and was included in the affair to give him military experience.

After dinner we left the house of Onegesius, and took up our quarters nearer the palace, so that Maximin might be at a convenient distance for visiting Attila or holding intercourse with his court. The next morning, at dawn of day, Maximin sent me to Onegesius, with presents offered by himself as well as those which the Emperor had sent, and I was to find out whether he would have an interview with Maximin and at what time. When I arrived at the house, along with the attendants who carried the gifts, I found the doors closed, and had to wait until some one should come out and announce our arrival.

The Huns are depicted as having a hierarchy and a framework which visiting dignitaries had to utilize, as evidenced by the repetitive 'giving of gifts' in Priscus' narrative, yet it is certain that they did not have as much ceremonial impediment as the Romans. Whether this is to the credit of the Huns or the Romans is a matter for debate.

As I waited and walked up and down in front of the enclosure which surrounded the house, a man, whom from his Scythian dress I took for a barbarian, came up and addressed me in Greek, with the word *Xaire*, 'Hail!' I was surprised at a Scythian speaking Greek. For the subjects of the Huns, swept together from various lands, speak, besides their own barbarous tongues, either Hunnic or Gothic, or – as many have commercial dealings with the western Romans – Latin; but none of them easily speak Greek, except captives from the Thracian or Illyrian sea-coast; and these last are easily known to any stranger by their torn garments and the squalor of their heads, as men who have met with a reverse.

The multilingual nature of Hunnic society is here presented in clear and certain manner. Strangely, it is also highlighted that among the Huns Greek was not a language in common use, implying that in trade dealings even those traders from the East spoke Latin.

> This man, on the contrary, resembled a well-to-do Scythian, being well dressed, and having his hair cut in a circle after Scythian fashion.

Although the majority of analysis of Priscus' meeting with this man has focused on the next section, there is a useful piece of information here concerning the Huns. Contrary to Ammianus' description of the Huns wearing 'mice-skins', the better-off Huns were well-dressed and had fashions concerning hair and probably clothes.

> Having returned his salutation, I asked him who he was and whence he had come into a foreign land and adopted Scythian life. When he asked me why I wanted to know, I told him that his Hellenic speech had prompted my curiosity. Then he smiled and said that he was born a Greek and had gone as a merchant to Viminacium, on the Danube, where he had stayed a long time, and married a very rich wife. But the city fell a prey to the barbarians, and he was stripped of his prosperity, and on account of his riches was allotted to Onegesius in the division of the spoil, as it was the custom among the Scythians for the chiefs to reserve for themselves the rich prisoners.

As may have been expected, Hunnic nobles reserved the right to take the rich prisoners for themselves. In this manner they would expect to have slaves with better manners who knew what service would be best appreciated by their new masters. However, it would also mean that should any of the new slaves later be ransomed by Rome, the nobles would be the ones who received the greatest share of the ransom money.

Having fought bravely against the Romans and the Acatiri, he had paid the spoils he won to his master, and so obtained freedom. He then married a barbarian wife and had children, and had the privilege of eating at the table of Onegesius.

There are three things of note in this small extract. One is that the captive appears to have had neither scruples nor embarrassment at having fought alongside the Huns against 'his own people', the Romans. Another would be that Hunnic slaves could, in the right circumstances, buy their freedom from their new masters, although whether this was open to members of the lower castes is open to doubt. Finally, having been released, the man had not only married a 'barbarian wife', but had been allowed to eat at Onegesius' table. This suggests that in Hunnic society ability and loyalty could overcome origin or slave-status:

He considered his new life among the Scythians better than his old life among the Romans, and the reasons he gave were as follows: 'After war the Scythians live in inactivity, enjoying what they have got, and not at all, or very little, harassed. The Romans, on the other hand, are in the first place very liable to perish in war, as they have to rest their hopes of safety on others, and are not allowed, on account of their tyrants to use arms.'

The man goes on to complain about the fact that Roman citizens were barred by Roman law from carrying weapons and so defending themselves, unlike the Huns: although the law against Romans carrying arms had been repealed in 440 by Valentinian – due to the threat of Vandal attack following their capture of Carthage – this only applied in the West. Furthermore, the man then criticizes the Roman generals as being cowards who are unable to conduct wars, again a contrast to the perceived abilities of the Hunnic commanders.

It is with his complaints concerning Roman taxation and the treatment of poorer people in law courts that most historians have exerted their utmost in analysis. However, all that needs to be said here is that this gives the impression that among the Huns legal battles were fought on a 'fairer' basis, but it would be odd if the highest nobles were unable to arrange matters so that they could not be held accountable for breaking the law, especially when treating members of the lowest classes badly. Sadly, he does not mention specifically how Hunnic taxation – should it have been imposed on Hunnic citizens – was raised.

Priscus goes on to a lengthy defence of the empire, using the paradigms of earlier centuries as evidence that Roman law was better than that of the Huns. In this he gives one small piece of evidence concerning Hunnic legal affairs:

> '[The Romans] are not allowed, like the Scythians, to inflict death on them [slaves]. They [the Romans] have numerous ways of conferring freedom; they can manumit not only during life, but also by their wills, and the testamentary wishes of a Roman in regard to his property are law.' My interlocutor shed tears, and confessed that the laws and constitution of the Romans were fair, but deplored that the governors, not possessing the spirit of former generations, were ruining the State.

Despite the high volume of interest in this section, it should be noted that it may not reflect reality. It is possible that Priscus has either invented or exaggerated the conversation simply as a means of comparing Roman and Hunnic society.[21]

It would appear that one of the few ways of manumission among the Huns was for slaves to buy their freedom, but doubtless this was difficult for slaves ordered to complete menial tasks, rather than those from richer families allowed to fight alongside the Huns and so gain large amounts of booty. In addition, Priscus decries the apparently common usage among the Huns of the death penalty. Although no context is given, it is probable that the kings and nobles were allowed to use the death penalty on a more regular basis than those in Rome (except possibly for the emperor) and that at times these could be classed as unfair. Although the unnamed man accepted that this was true, he then derided the Roman 'judges' for their bias and response to bribery and corruption. It was allegedly at this point that Priscus returned to the task at hand: arranging peace between Rome and the Huns:

> I ... addressed him [Onegesius], saying, 'The Roman ambassador salutes you, and I have come with gifts from him, and with the gold

which the Emperor sent you. The ambassador is anxious to meet you, and begs you to appoint a time and place.' Onegesius bade his servants receive the gold and the gifts, and told me to announce to Maximin that he would go to him immediately. I delivered the message, and Onegesius appeared in the tent without delay. He expressed his thanks to Maximin and the Emperor for the presents, and asked why he sent for him. Maximin said that the time had come for Onegesius to have greater renown among men, if he would go to the Emperor, and by his wisdom arrange the objects of dispute between the Romans and Huns, and establish concord between them; thereby he will procure many advantages for his own family, as all his children will always be friends of the Emperor and the Imperial family. Onegesius inquired what measures would gratify the Emperor and how he could arrange the disputes. Maximin replied: 'If you cross into the lands of the Roman Empire you will lay the Emperor under an obligation, and you will arrange the matters at issue by investigating their causes and deciding them on the basis of the peace.' Onegesius said he would inform the Emperor and his ministers of Attila's wishes, but the Romans need not think they could ever prevail with him to betray his master or neglect his Scythian training and his wives and children, or to prefer wealth among the Romans to bondage with Attila. He added that he would be of more service to the Romans by remaining in his own land and softening the anger of his master, if he were indignant for aught with the Romans, than by visiting them and subjecting himself to blame if he made arrangements that Attila did not approve of. He then retired, having consented that I should act as an intermediary in conveying messages from Maximin to himself, for it would not have been consistent with Maximin's dignity as ambassador to visit him constantly.

The impression given is that there were strict protocols to be followed in Hunnic society, especially when treating with ambassadors from major powers. Both Onegesius and Maximin are acutely aware of their personal standings and as such have little option but to work within their respective frameworks:

The next day I entered the enclosure of Attila's palace, bearing gifts to his wife, whose name was Kreka. She had three sons, of whom the eldest governed the Acatiri and the other nations who dwell in Pontic Scythia.

It is known from later information that at least the Goths and the Gepids were ruled by their own kings, so the fact that one of Attila's sons was made ruler of the Acatiri suggests that these subordinate tribes were allowed to retain their own rulers and institutions as long as they followed Hunnic instructions. Should they fail in this duty, the ruler would be deposed and replaced by either one of Attila's many sons or a trustworthy subordinate. However, whether this was a regular rule followed throughout the period of Hunnic rule or only during Attila's reign is uncertain.

Within the enclosure were numerous buildings, some of carved boards beautifully fitted together, others of straight, fastened on round wooden blocks which rose to a moderate height from the ground. Attila's wife lived here, and, having been admitted by the barbarians at the door, I found her reclining on a soft couch. The floor of the room was covered with woollen mats for walking on.

Although these buildings are obviously seen as inferior to those built of stone by the Romans, the fact that Priscus took the time to comment on the quality of the beautifully-fitted carved boards on some of the buildings adds weight to the concept that the Huns and their followers were capable of switching between nomadic, semi-nomadic and agricultural lifestyles depending upon the topography of the region in which they were dwelling and the need of 'permanent' structures to act as centres of rule, both for internal politics as well as for the reception of visiting foreign dignitaries.

A number of servants stood round her, and maids sitting on the floor in front of her embroidered with colours linen cloths intended to be placed over the Scythian dress for ornament.

Alongside the mention of the ex-slave man above, who was well-dressed, this extract also gives a different view to that of Ammianus in that the servants' embroidered cloth suggests that the stereotype of nomads as poorly-clad barbarians is deceptive and belongs alongside the standard *topoi* used of steppe nomads, rather than being accurate.

> Having approached, saluted, and presented the gifts, I went out, and walked to another house, where Attila was, and waited for Onegesius, who, as I knew, was with Attila. I stood in the middle of a great crowd – the guards of Attila and his attendants knew me, and so no one hindered me. I saw a number of people advancing, and a great commotion and noise, Attila's egress being expected. And he came forth from the house with a dignified gait, looking round on this side and on that. He was accompanied by Onegesius, and stood in front of the house; and many persons who had lawsuits with one another came up and received his judgment. Then he returned into the house, and received ambassadors of barbarous peoples.

As is to be expected, this segment simply shows that Attila – and doubtless his predecessors and successors – spent at least some of their time as judges in disputes within their realm, as well as dealing with foreign envoys:

> When the hour arrived we went to the palace, along with the embassy from the western Romans, and stood on the threshold of the hall in the presence of Attila. The cup-bearers gave us a cup, according to the national custom, that we might pray before we sat down. Having tasted the cup, we proceeded to take our seats; all the chairs were ranged along the walls of the room on either side. Attila sat in the middle on a couch; a second couch was set behind him, and from it steps led up to his bed, which was covered with linen sheets and wrought coverlets for ornament, such as Greeks and Romans use to deck bridal beds.

This section reinforces the impression that Hunnic society relied to a large extent upon the tradition of saluting the king with a ceremonial drink. However, it also shows that Ammianus' description of the Huns is definitely awry, in that the bed is described using Roman comparisons. The only unfavourable aspect may be that Priscus is derisive concerning the fact that Attila's bed was dressed as for a new bride – hinting that Attila may have been less than manly in some respects – although it is possible that the bed was attired in this way because Attila had only recently introduced his latest bride to his main residence.

> The places on the right of Attila were held chief in honour, those on the left, where we sat, were only second. Berichus, a noble among the Scythians, sat on our side, but had the precedence of us. Onegesius sat on a chair on the right of Attila's couch, and over against Onegesius on a chair sat two of Attila's sons; his eldest son sat on his couch, not near him, but at the extreme end, with his eyes fixed on the ground, in shy respect for his father.

As with the majority of recorded societies, the place of honour was on the right hand of the ruler. Interestingly, Priscus accepts that the place of envoys – even those sent by the ruler of the Roman Empire – was below that of the nobles of Attila's court. This suggests that precedence and power were strictly regulated by the Hunnic kings to ensure the smooth operation of the court and of external politics.

> When all were arranged, a cup-bearer came and handed Attila a wooden cup of wine. He took it, and saluted the first in precedence, who, honoured by the salutation, stood up, and might not sit down until the king, having tasted or drained the wine, returned the cup to the attendant. All the guests then honoured Attila in the same way, saluting him, and then tasting the cups; but he did not stand up. Each of us had a special cup-bearer, who would come forward in order to present the wine, when the cup-bearer of Attila retired. When the second in precedence and those next to him had been honoured in like manner, Attila toasted us in the same way according to the order of the seats.

Again, as earlier, much is made of the ceremonial drinking of wine as a means of reinforcing bonds and of displaying and enhancing respect for Attila.

> When this ceremony was over the cup-bearers retired, and tables, large enough for three or four, or even more, to sit at, were placed next the table of Attila, so that each could take of the food on the dishes without

leaving his seat. The attendant of Attila first entered with a dish full of meat, and behind him came the other attendants with bread and viands, which they laid on the tables. A luxurious meal, served on silver plate, had been made ready for us and the barbarian guests, but Attila ate nothing but meat on a wooden trencher. In everything else, too, he showed himself temperate; his cup was of wood, while to the guests were given goblets of gold and silver. His dress, too, was quite simple, affecting only to be clean. The sword he carried at his side, the latchets of his Scythian shoes, the bridle of his horse were not adorned, like those of the other Scythians, with gold or gems or anything costly. When the viands of the first course had been consumed we all stood up, and did not resume our seats until each one, in the order before observed, drank to the health of Attila in the goblet of wine presented to him. We then sat down, and a second dish was placed on each table with eatables of another kind. After this course the same ceremony was observed as after the first.

As is by now expected, the guests ate and drank seated in a specified order due to custom and politics and Attila was lauded and entertained during the meal:

When evening fell torches were lit, and two barbarians coming forward in front of Attila sang songs they had composed, celebrating his victories and deeds of valour in war. And of the guests, as they looked at the singers, some were pleased with the verses, others reminded of wars were excited in their souls, while yet others, whose bodies were feeble with age and their spirits compelled to rest, shed tears. After the songs a Scythian, whose mind was deranged, appeared, and by uttering outlandish and senseless words forced the company to laugh. After him Zerkon, the Moorish dwarf, entered. He had been sent by Attila as a gift to Aetius, and Edecon had persuaded him to come to Attila in order to recover his wife, whom he had left behind him in Scythia; the lady was a Scythian whom he had obtained in marriage through the influence of his patron Bleda. He did not succeed in recovering her, for Attila was angry with him for returning. On the occasion of the banquet he made his appearance, and threw all except Attila into fits of unquenchable laughter by his appearance, his dress, his voice, and his words, which were a confused jumble of Latin, Hunnic, and Gothic. Attila, however, remained immovable and of unchanging countenance nor by word or act did he betray anything approaching to a smile of merriment except at the entry of Ernas, his youngest son, whom he pulled by the cheek, and gazed on with a calm look of satisfaction. I was surprised that he made so much of this son, and neglected his other children but a barbarian who sat beside me and knew Latin, bidding me not reveal what he told, gave me to understand that prophets had forewarned Attila that his race would fall, but would be restored by this boy. When the night had advanced we retired from the banquet, not wishing to assist further at the potations.

Although the lengthiest of the extracts used here, this actually tells little that could not be found from the *topoi* used by ancient writers. The Huns were fond of songs and entertainment at their banquets and as was to be expected, everything was on a large scale due to Attila's presence.

The only real thing of note comes at the end, where it is revealed that Attila was influenced by 'prophets'. Although the precise nature of the method used is unknown, it is possible that Attila was responding to divination by scapulimancy, a means of foretelling the future using the heated shoulder-blades of sacrificial cattle or sheep.[22]

Although the Romans made at least one attempt to convert the Huns to Christianity, they may have failed. Armenian sources record that some members of the Hunnic 'tribe' called Xailandur were being drawn towards Christianity, but that the majority of the Huns remained staunchly Pagan and it is believed that they practised a form of shamanism, an animistic belief system in which all things have spirits.[23] As evidence of this factor, it has been suggested that the suffix 'Kam' in, for example, the name of Eskam (the father of one of Attila's wives[24]) derives from 'qam', the common Turkish word for shaman, and it is further interesting to note that the majority of named examples in the sources belong to high-ranking Huns, the implication being that the spiritual (shamanistic) leaders among the Huns were part of the nobility in Hunnic society.[25]

Overall, the long fragment of Priscus from which the above is taken shows little that could not be surmised from other sources: the Huns had a strict hierarchical society where proximity to the ruler was a mark of power and influence; the king had to deal with everyday matters regarding the running of his kingdom; foreign envoys were required to follow a strict protocol when dealing with a Hunnic king; and during banquets there were several courses during which the guests repeatedly paid their respects to the king.

The only things of note are the manner in which Priscus gently contradicts the expectations of his readers by not using the stereotypes common among his predecessors – for example, in the context of clothing and housing – and with the depiction of Attila himself, who is depicted as a stern ruler who disdains the trappings of luxury and remains true to his nomadic roots. The latter could indeed be a realistic portrayal, but could also simply be a propaganda exercise by Attila put on whenever foreign dignitaries were present to impress them with the picture of a stern and calculating king.

Yet there is evidence from other fragments of Priscus that Hunnic society was even more complicated than depicted above, although this can only be applied definitively to the reign of Attila and may not be applicable to either his predecessors or successors. Some evidence exists for the manner in which Attila was to organize his army and realm as they grew. For example, Attila himself – and possibly also Bleda – had a personal bodyguard known as *intimates* (*epitedeios*), though how these were chosen or organized is not stated.

Apart from the king, the most important people in the court were the *logades* ('picked men'), who according to Priscus both commanded military units – almost certainly along either numerical or tribal lines – and had administrative functions.[26] Examples of *logades* include Edeco, attested as the 'ruler' of the Sciri; Orestes, who later served the Roman Empire; and Berik, the 'ruler of many villages in Scythia', allegedly due to his noble birth.[27] The administrative duties of the *logades* appear to have been the collection of taxes and tribute, although in most cases this may have been collected by lower-ranking officials, and later such demands would 'become so ruthless that the Goths rebelled in the late 460s'.[28]

There was also a hierarchy among the *logades*. The seating arrangements attested by Priscus above demonstrate that the seats to the right of Attila were given to the *logades* of higher status. Although it has been claimed that this was 'characteristic' of Inner Asian tribes, the seating or placement of people and even army units to the right as a sign of honour is a common feature throughout history.[29] As a result of these observations, it is possible to discern a hierarchy and administration that is usually ignored by historians intent upon retaining the 'barbaric' image of the Huns. Interestingly, the supply by Rome of 'secretaries' to Attila may have influenced the growth of a bureaucracy increasingly based upon Roman practice, which may have been reinforced by the employment of Roman defectors and captured Roman administrators, adapted to Hunnic requirements. Whether these men were required to learn the Hunnic language or whether Latin was used is not known, but it should be noted that later an Eastern bishop who entered the lands of the Caucasian Huns returned bringing books written in the Hunnic language.[30] It may only be the lack of sources that allows the traditional attitude to persist.

Nomadism and Horses

Attila himself is depicted on horseback, but this has not stopped modern historians from questioning the nature of the Huns during their time as a major threat to the Roman and Sasanid empires. On the vast Asian steppes there would be little problem for the Huns regarding the rearing of the large numbers of horses they needed to preserve their lifestyle. On the other hand, the Hungarian Steppe is nowhere near as large and it has been suggested that once they crossed the Carpathian Mountains the Huns would have been unable to maintain the large number of horses they needed. As a result, many would have become either semi-nomadic or agriculturalists.[31]

Furthermore, it has been suggested that later sources support the thesis that the Huns on the whole adopted a more sedentary way of life and that horses became less important in Hunnic society. Much of the evidence is anecdotal and has been interpreted solely to support this viewpoint. For example, it is noted that the Huns took part in long sieges, such as that of Aquileia in 452, and that it would be difficult to feed horses during a long siege.[32] This may be true, although it should be noted that one man can lead a large string of horses away from a siege in search of fodder, leaving their riders behind to continue the siege. In addition, the Huns had many allies and conquered peoples who would be obliged to supply troops that were primarily infantry. It is equally possible that a siege was undertaken by these foot troops while the Hunnic cavalry was away foraging for food both for the horses and the men holding the siege. The latter becomes more of a possibility when it is noted that during the siege of Asimus the men of the fort 'ambushed and forced the men away'.[33] Although this has been used as evidence that the Huns had stopped using large numbers of cavalry, the episode can also be interpreted as the defenders attacking the besiegers when the Hunnic cavalry was away foraging, or even that the men laying siege were infantry and that the cavalry had gone to continue the campaign elsewhere, leaving the infantry to continue the siege alone. Whatever the reality of the case, these examples cannot be used to prove that the majority of the Huns had lost their horses and settled down as agriculturalists.

On a final note, it has also been suggested that the fact that Priscus, in his description of his embassy to Attila, does not mention horses, and that the tactics used at the Battle of the Catalaunian Plains in 451 are those of an infantry army, not a nomadic horde.[34] Although at first glance conclusive, in reality both of these can be explained. Although it is true that Priscus does not mention horses during his description, the episodes described take place in 'permanent' Hunnic settlements so the omission is understandable. As for the battle, the tactics used by nomadic tribesmen would be unsuitable since a large part of the 'Hunnic' army was in fact composed of Franks, Goths, Gepids and many other smaller tribes, the majority of which relied for a large part upon masses of infantry. So although the hypothesis remains a possibility, it should not be taken as proven.

There is one further factor to assess concerning the impact that the Huns (and their successors) had upon Europe as a whole. Starting with Herodotus and his description of the Scythians, the nomad has always been seen as a major threat to 'western' sedentary societies. In part this is obviously due to the historical tradition of portraying the nomad as 'other', 'savage' and 'backward'. Yet in reality there is one aspect where the stereotype comes close to reality: warfare. Although the Sasanid and especially the Roman empires should in reality have been able to deal with the Huns simply due to their vast population advantage, the 'military potential of nomads was far superior to that of peasants and villagers'.[35] By gathering their military resources into one vast army and invading Hunnic territory, the Romans or the Sasanids may have been able to destroy the Huns as a political force.

This was never going to be possible due to the threats posed on the two empires' other frontiers. That the vast majority of their populations were simple agriculturalists who had no response to Hunnic attacks explains how the Huns were able to strike at will with little chance of reprisal in their own homeland.

Having reached conclusions regarding the political and military nature of the Huns, it is now possible to analyse the story of the first Hun who was based on the borders of the Roman Empire and named in the sources. This man's name was Uldin.

Chapter Three

Contact

Uldin

In the context of Hunnic history, Uldin is an important but baffling character who may have ruled in the region of modern Muntenia, although the precise location is far from secure.[1] The first problem surrounds his name. One modern expert in Philology and Onomastics has suggested that his name has a Mongolian core and the original form was *öl-di-n*, meaning 'auspicious', 'happy', 'lucky', 'fortunate'.[2] However, another has suggested that 'Uldin' is derived from 'Uld' ('Six'). In the latter hypothesis, the author has suggested that the Huns followed the Xiongnu political structure and that 'Uldin' is the sixth-ranking noble in the hierarchy: in other words, Uldin is simply a western sub-king of the Huns who at this time had recently moved to the Hungarian Steppes.[3] This small example clearly demonstrates the difficulty of using philology in order to clarify the origins of the Huns: many different options are available for experts and these tend to be mutually exclusive.

However, if the philological aspects are removed, there remains a further possibility. As noted in Chapter 1, at an earlier but unknown date Theodosius I may have settled a group of Huns in Pannonia.[4] It is feasible that Uldin was either the leader of this group, or maybe the successor to that individual, who after the settlement had extended his authority across the Danube, either by conquest or by settlement.

Certainty is impossible, but later events as recorded by Roman historians suggest that Uldin was probably a minor Hunnic king, and in reality may have later accepted a position as a subordinate of the main Hunnic rulers, but only if these had recently moved to the Hungarian Steppes they would be busy settling their people into new homes and establishing their dominance over neighbouring tribes, not interfering in Roman politics. However, below it will be suggested that they had not yet moved and so it is more

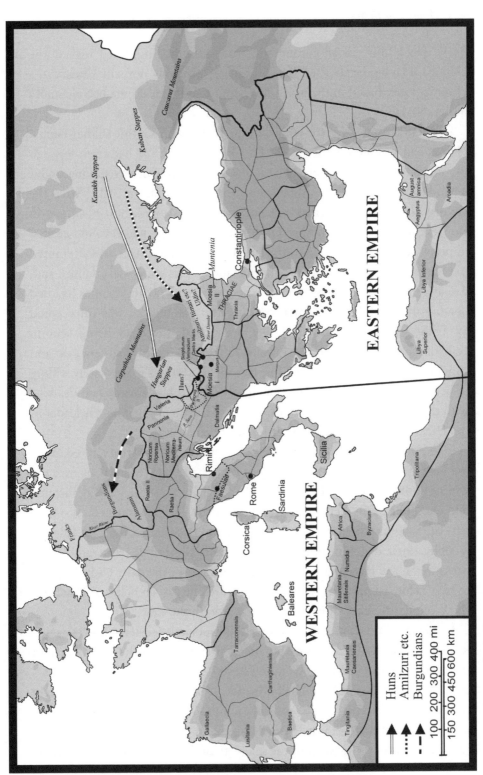

Map 4: The Huns arrive in Europe.

likely that Uldin was an autonomous ruler who had migrated west to the Danube. Having established that Uldin was probably not subordinate to a Hunnic polity based in the north, his actions and later events become more understandable.

Uldin first appears in the record in the year 400. A Gothic soldier named Gainas had accepted service in the East Roman army and had risen through the ranks to the point where he was one of the commanders serving under Theodosius I against the Western usurper Eugenius in 394.[5] After the victory Gainas had returned east and rapidly became *magister militum* in Constantinople. When another Goth named Tribigild had revolted against imperial rule, Gainas had used the situation to his advantage and attempted to secure complete control of Constantinople.[6] His coup was a failure and, defeated by Roman troops under the new *magister* Fravitta, Gainas had fled north with his followers. After crossing the Danube he was intercepted by Uldin and, after several battles, was killed, his head being sent to Constantinople.[7] In return, the Eastern Emperor Arcadius had sent gifts and concluded a treaty with Uldin.[8] The fact that Uldin was immediately willing to help the East against Gainas may imply that he had already had dealings with the empire, and possibly adds weight to the theory that he was leader of the Huns who previously been settled by Theodosius.

The peace was not to last. For an unknown reason the treaty agreed with the East after the death of Gainas appears to have broken down, as over the winter of 404–405 'The Huns crossed the Hister [Danube] and devastated Thrace.'[9] The most likely cause is that either the East had reneged on at least part of its commitments and Uldin wanted to ensure that the East fulfilled its obligations, or Uldin simply wanted a more favourable treaty and so put pressure on the East to give concessions. Whatever the case, Uldin appears to have achieved his aim, as shortly afterwards he is seen helping Stilicho in the West, hardly likely if he was still at war with the East.

In 405 the Goth Radagaisus and his followers invaded Italy. Radagaisus is usually seen as leading Goths who, under pressure from the Huns north of the Danube – and possibly beginning to settle on the Hungarian Steppes – attacked Italy to escape Hunnic dominance. If this is true, then it adds weight to the hypothesis that Uldin was only a minor Hunnic leader, that he was probably not affiliated to the main Hunnic polity, and that he attacked the East on his own: if the focus of the majority of the Huns had been attacking the East in 404 and 405, then it is unlikely that the Huns were also moving to the Hungarian Steppes, forcing Radagaisus to flee.

In 406 Uldin joined the West Romans and, in alliance with Stilicho, the Western *magister militum*, took part in the defeat of Radagaisus at the Battle of Faesulae.[10] That he would turn from assaults upon the East to supporting the West by attacking Radagaisus may seem a little unlikely. The whole episode adds weight to the assumption that Uldin was only a minor player in events and, rebuffed by the East, was willing to join the West in return for financial and political gain.

There is then the question of why the Huns who were allegedly settled in Pannonia – possibly Valeria – had not opposed the attack by Radagaisus as it crossed their territory.[11] There are most likely two reasons for this. One is that if Radagaisus had crossed their lands they were too few in number to risk facing him in battle on their own. The second is that although the route taken by Radagaisus is unknown, it is probable that he travelled through Noricum and Pannonia Superior. If so, the Huns would have not needed to resist the invasion.

It has been suggested that at an unknown date Stilicho settled some other Huns in Italy and in Pannonia Inferior. Although this remains a possibility – especially as many unaffiliated groups of Huns may have joined the various forces invading Italy prior to Stilicho's death in 408 – the accuracy of the hypothesis has been questioned, and so this must remain a possibility rather than a fact.[12]

It may be that throughout this period Uldin was acting under the direction of the main Hunnic body on the Kuban Steppes, although the distances involved implies that such quick reversals of decisions – for example changing from attacking the East to helping the West – would be unlikely. Whether he was acting on orders from a central Hunnic power or on his own initiative is in one respect immaterial: it was clear to everyone that the separation of the empire into two halves offered all of its opponents the opportunity to play the game of divide and conquer.

Accordingly, and despite the arrangement with the West, tension remained high with the East and in the summer of 408 Uldin led his forces in a large invasion of Thrace.[13] In this Uldin may have been setting a further precedent for later Hunnic rulers by taking advantage of imperial difficulties. In May 408 Arcadius, the Eastern Emperor, died and his successor – his son

Theodosius II – was only 7 years old. At the same time Alaric the Goth, who had been serving the Western Empire in Illyricum, chose this moment to invade Italy. Apparently the Huns settled in Pannonia Inferior did not join the invasion in any great numbers.[14] With the removal of the Gothic threat in the Balkans, the East took the opportunity to move troops that had been stationed nearby to keep the Goths under control to the far eastern frontier to face the Sasanid Persians.[15] Uldin simply took advantage of the death of Arcadius and the weakening of the Roman defences by launching a massive invasion of the Balkans.

A strange tale is now recorded by Sozomen:

Uldis [Uldin], the leader of the barbarous tribes who dwell near the Ister [Danube], crossed that river at the head of a large army, and encamped on the frontiers of Thrace. He took possession by treachery of a city of Moesia, called Castra Martis, and thence made incursions into the rest of Thrace, and insolently refused to enter into terms of alliance with the Romans. The prefect of the Thracian soldiers made propositions of peace to him, but he replied by pointing to the sun, and declaring that it would be easy to him, if he desired to do so, to subjugate every region of the earth that is enlightened by that luminary. But while Uldis was uttering menaces of this description, and was ordering as large a tribute as he pleased, and that on this condition peace could be established with the Romans or the war would continue – when affairs were so helpless, God gave manifest proofs of special favour towards the present reign; for, shortly afterwards, the immediate attendants and the leaders of the tribes of Uldis were discussing the Roman form of government, the philanthropy of the emperor, and his promptitude and liberality in rewarding the best and good men. It was not without God that they turned to the love of the points so discussed and seceded to the Romans, to whose camp they joined themselves, together with the troops ranged under themselves. Finding himself thus abandoned, Uldis escaped with difficulty to the opposite bank of the river. Many of his troops were slain; and among others the whole of the barbarous tribe called the Sciri. This tribe had been very strong in point of numbers before falling into this misfortune. Some of them were killed; and others were taken prisoners, and conveyed in chains to Constantinople.

Sozomen 9.5.[16]

The fact that Jerome, at the time living in Jerusalem, described the attack demonstrates the ferocity of the initial assault.[17] Yet after the first fury, the invasion quickly diminished in severity and it was over by 23 March 409, when Theodosius issued a decree concerning the aftermath of the attack.[18]

The main point to note in this account is that Uldin was abandoned by many of his troops. If he had been the major power in Hunnic politics this would have been a disaster and it would be expected that this defeat would have major repercussions recorded in Roman sources. No such record exists, so again it is better to assume that he was a relatively minor power, possibly on the southern fringe of the newly-established Hunnic polity. In addition, it is clear from events that Uldin's rhetoric was a considerable 'bluff, not the calculated arrogance of a true precursor of Attila'.[19] Sadly, unless new evidence comes to light, whether Uldin was an independent ruler or whether he was merely a subordinate of the rulers of the main Hunnic body will remain elusive.[20]

At this point, although war still loomed between Uldin and the Eastern Emperor Theodosius, there were Huns serving in the Roman West. Despite the claim that these Huns were not serving under Uldin being proof of the collapse of Uldin's power after his defeat of 408, this is not certain: it is also possible that these were independent tribesmen who had never acknowledged Uldin as their leader.[21] For example, before his death in 408 Stilicho had a bodyguard formed of Hun mercenaries.[22] In addition, it may be that these later decided to join Alaric and the Goths against Rome after Stilicho's execution, and so had no connection to Uldin.

After Uldin

According to Zosimus, in 409 Honorius attempted to hire 10,000 Huns to face Alaric in Italy.[23] However, the number claimed is open to doubt, with one historian suggesting that the Huns numbered only 'a few hundred' rather than 10,000.[24] If the claim of 10,000 is anywhere near accurate, it should be noted that it is unlikely that such a large force would be recruited from Uldin. The easy way in which the Romans had bribed his men in 408 implies that he could only field a much smaller force.

Although it is questioned whether these Huns actually arrived in Italy, an entry in Zosimus suggests that some Huns did enter the peninsula –

possibly in late 409 – to help the Western government against Alaric.[25] Even more suggestive is the fact that although the Goths under Alaric had sacked Rome in 410, in the following year the new *magister militum* Constantius was 'able to cast off the military paralysis which had gripped Ravenna' and take the initiative against the West's enemies.[26] It may have been only in 411 that the new Hunnic *foederati*/mercenaries could be supplied in numbers and the confusion in Italy in 410 after the Gothic sack of Rome would have limited imperial responses.[27] Yet the Western government was not totally reliant upon treaties to ensure continuing peace. In 409 the Roman troops in Upper Pannonia, Noricum and Raetia were placed under the command of a man named Generidus, possibly with a mandate to oppose the Huns should the treaty be broken.[28]

To add to Hunnic woes, it would appear that at around this time the alliance between the Huns and at least some of the Alans collapsed, although it should be remembered that some Alans had joined in the barbarian invasion of Gaul in 406, so not all Alans were allied to the Huns. It is notable that after the early fifth century no source speaks of the alliance. One, Orosius, even notes that the Goths, Alans and Huns serving in the Roman army came to blows: 'I say nothing of the many internecine conflicts between the barbarians themselves, when two *cunei* [Roman military units] of the Goths, and then the Alans and Huns, destroyed one another in mutual slaughter.'[29] Although many of the other tribes served alongside the Huns, especially under the later rule of Attila, it should be remembered that many of these peoples were unhappy at Hunnic dominance. Nevertheless, some would willingly continue to fight alongside the Huns in the hope of plunder or in bonds of alliance.

Italy and Aetius[30]

The East had suffered the most from Hunnic attacks, yet it may be that Uldin's attacks had also made inroads into those territories still ruled by the Western Empire. The West desperately needed peace on its eastern frontiers in order to deal with its other problems: Honorius was facing usurpers in Gaul and the Gothic king Alaric in Italy; indeed, in 408 and 409 Alaric took the decision to besiege Rome, greatly increasing the pressure on Honorius.

The Treaty of 409

As noted above, probably in 409 a treaty was agreed between the West and the Huns. It may be that, following Uldin's abortive attack on Thrace and the loss of many of his troops, he needed the political benefits of a treaty to recover from his losses. In that case, the treaty was beneficial to both parties.

On the other hand, although it is possible that Uldin was the Hunnic signatory, it is possibly more likely that by this point the main Hunnic body had finally settled on the Hungarian Steppes and that, following Uldin's defeat, either the remainder of his people had thrown off their allegiance to Uldin and pledged to the new, more powerful Hunnic political entity to the north or Uldin had been forced to accept the authority of the Huns on the Hungarian Steppes.

As part of the treaty the Western Empire sent a man named Aetius – he had already been a hostage with the Goths in Italy – to be a hostage with the Huns.[31] He may have begun at Uldin's court, but whether he did or not he soon ended at the court of a different Hunnic leader.

Charaton

While Roman sources are focused upon internal events plus the attacks of the Huns of Uldin and the Goths of Radagaisus and Alaric, away from the Danube it would appear that major changes had been taking place. The successful attempt by Radagaisus in 405 and the Asding Vandals, Siling Vandals, Sueves and (some) Alans in 406 to enter the empire, plus the fact that by 411 the Burgundians had moved from east of the Alamanni to the banks of the Rhine, all imply that the main body of the Huns were expanding their power and that other tribes were determined to avoid subjugation by the new Hunnic 'Empire'. Therefore it is most likely in the early-mid 400s that the Huns moved their centre of power to the 'Carpathian (Hungarian) Steppe'.[32] This would help explain the claim that Honorius had arranged for 10,000 Huns to support him in Italy against Alaric. As already noted, it is unlikely that Uldin would have the resources available for such a claim to be made, so it is more likely that Honorius was dealing with the new Hunnic power in Hungary.

Although no reason is given in the sources, one of the most likely factors in the decision of the Huns to migrate was the need to avoid friction with their cousins to the east. The decision was to their great benefit. Within a short time they became the predominant political force on the Hungarian Steppes. At around this time (c.409–10) a man named Charaton/Karaton/ Qaraton (the spelling of his name varies in the sources) was the 'King of the Huns'.[33] It is feasible that he was the man who had led the Huns to their new home. It is also remotely possible that he was simply the successor to Uldin, although the above analysis makes this unlikely.

The appearance of the Huns on the Hungarian Steppes had a major impact on the policy of East Rome, who in January 412 strengthened the Danubian fleet and began work on new land walls around Constantinople.[34] Although it may be that these improvements were the result of Uldin's attacks in 408–409, the fact that the East would have then waited for three years before taking these measures suggests a different cause.

At the same time, in late 412 or early 413, either the Western Emperor Honorius or the Eastern Emperor Theodosius II sent the writer Olympiodorus:

> on a mission to them [the Huns] and Donatus, and [he] gives a tragic account of his wanderings and perils by the sea. How Donatus, being deceived by an oath, was unlawfully put to death. How Charaton, the first of the kings, being incensed by the murder, was appeased by presents from the emperor.
>
> *Olympiodorus, fragment 18.*

Although sometimes seen as being from the Eastern Empire to the Huns on the Danube, it is possible from other evidence that Olympiodorus was sent by the West.[35] Who Donatus was remains unknown, since this is the only mention of him in the sources and he died before the end of the passage. He may have been a Hun, or a renegade Roman, or possibly even one of the hostages sent alongside Aetius in 409 or 410.[36] Given the esteem in which Aetius appears to have been held by the Huns, and the similar esteem Donatus was held by Charaton, the most likely answer may be that Donatus was either a fellow of Aetius as a hostage among the Huns, or a diplomat in charge of or accompanying the embassy sent alongside Aetius.[37]

There is no other mention of Charaton, and no reliable source gives a genealogy for the Hunnic rulers. The only clue as to Charaton's authority comes in Olympiodorus' final line, 'Charaton, the first of the kings'. It would appear that, for the first time, the Romans are dealing with the most powerful Hunnic king, ruling on the Hungarian Steppes, rather than a subordinate or the 'king' of a smaller Hunnic entity.[38] Prior to this, 'the piecemeal activity of numerous Hunnic bands destabilized the general situation, provoking several prolonged crises for the Goths and other inhabitants of the Pontic regions.'[39] This would explain both the fragmentary notices of Hunnic activity in the sources prior to 412, and the fact that a 'central monarchy' and the concept of succession is nowhere clearly identified until after 420. In effect, before 412 there were numerous Hun tribes exploring new territories and either taking employment or attacking the West.

After 412 things were to change. Although Charaton appears to have been the true 'King of the Huns', there remains the slight possibility that he may have been simply the local successor to Uldin. This concept is based on later evidence, where it is notable that the main Hunnic body based on the Hungarian Steppes had a short tradition of dual rule.[40] On the other hand, the close connections between Aetius and the later Hunnic rulers suggests that Charaton was a major player in Hunnic politics and that Aetius was a hostage at the main Hunnic court, not simply that of a minor Hunnic noble on the frontiers.

The 420s

After the embassy of 412/413 there is no mention of Hunnic rulers until the 420s. The most likely reason for the silence is that the Huns were adhering to a treaty with Rome, instead concentrating on expanding their authority over the tribes surrounding their new base in the Hungarian Steppes. This appears to have become established by the early 420s, as there is a report by Marcellinus *comes* that a Hunnic army raided Thrace in 422.[41] This is made more likely when events in the east are analysed.

In 421 the East was at war with Persia and the *Chronicon Paschale* records a Roman victory on 6 September, although this may only have been a small-scale battle.[42] It is possible that the East withdrew troops from the Danube to help in the war effort and the Huns took advantage of the weakening of the defences to launch an invasion, although the scale of any assault is nowhere given.[43]

Yet there may be another reason behind the proposed Hunnic assault and one that also answers the question of why the East believed that they were free from attack by the Huns. There is the possibility that in 421 the East was using politics against the Huns. Theophanes notes that the Emperor Theodosius II had at some time in the 420s settled Goths in Thrace.[44] Although convoluted, and irrelevant in most respects to the story of Attila, the hypothesis is that Theodosius managed to detach a group of Goths from their allegiance to the Huns and settled them in Thrace – probably in 421, although not all historians accept this date – in the belief that they would protect the region from Hunnic attack.[45] In this context, the Huns' anger and the East's removal of troops to face the Sasanids are both explained.

Probably due to the Hunnic attack, in 422 the Romans made peace with the Sasanids and troops were recalled from the eastern frontier and billeted within the walls of Constantinople, with the implication that the Hunnic attack was more than simply a small-scale raid.[46] Although Theodoret claims that during this attack the Hunnic leader Rua died, it would appear that in this he is mistaken, as Rua did not die in Thrace but on Hunnic soil.[47] However, as Theodoret completed his work decades after the events portrayed, it is possible that he has conflated events, joining the Hunnic invasion of 422 with the death of Rua, usually dated to 434 or 435.[48] Yet from his source Theodoret may have taken one piece of valuable information: by 422 a man named 'Rhoïlas' – usually called Rua – was leader of the Huns.

It is probable that in 422/3 a treaty was signed between Rua and the Eastern Empire. Priscus, writing of the treaty signed in 435 between Attila and the East, notes that

> The treaty should be maintained and last as long as the Romans paid seven hundred pounds of gold each year to the Scythian kings (previously the payments had been three hundred and fifty pounds of gold).
>
> *Priscus, fragment 2, trans. Blockley.*

It may be that Priscus is giving details of an earlier treaty signed between Rua and the East in order to halt the attacks.[49]

Rua and Octar

As noted above, the tradition of dual rule on the Hungarian Steppes may first have been recorded during the attack across the Caucasus by the Huns in 395. In contrast, during Aetius' mission to the Huns in 424 (see below), the dual kings are definitively named as Rua and Octar.[50] In theory it may have been a 'triple' or even 'quadruple' rule, as they had other brothers named Mundiuch and Oebarsius. However, although the latter is a possibility, it is not mentioned anywhere in the sources and so must remain hypothetical.[51]

The premise is that the expansion of Hunnic power in some ways had led to a political entity that had come to resemble that of the earlier Xiongnu Empire, at least in the eyes of contemporaries, and as a result the Huns had resurrected the tradition of a dual monarchy reminiscent of their proposed Xiongnu ancestors far to the east. If this is the case, it would appear that Rua became the king of the western territories, with Octar leader in the East. Yet on the contrary, the limited evidence suggests that Octar was ruler in the West, as it was he that is later attested as campaigning in the West. Sadly, however, no indication is given in any of the sources for the boundaries of the Hunnic Empire and therefore any attempt to define either their individual areas of rule or even the limits of the whole empire is speculation. The only information given is that Rua and Octar 'are said to have held the kingship before Attila, though by no means over all the peoples whom he ruled.'[52]

The next concrete mention of the Huns is thanks to the confused political position in the West after the death of Emperor Honorius in 423. An individual named John was made emperor by the Western *magister militum*, and when the Eastern Emperor Theodosius II declared this invalid and prepared for war, John sent Aetius, who had earlier been a hostage among them, to the Huns requesting aid.[53] John may also have sent 'regular' units of Huns serving in the Roman army to Africa in an attempt to conquer the province from Bonifacius, who had remained loyal to the imperial dynasty, but this is uncertain.[54] Aetius travelled to the Hunnic capital in 424. It may be that by this time Charaton was dead and his place – if indeed he was the main Hunnic leader – had been taken by the two brothers, but this is unclear.

Rua and Octar immediately promised to aid Aetius in his hour of need.[55] The fact that Rua (and Octar) were willing to help Aetius can, in part at least, be due to the growing 'barbarian' tradition of helping to cause chaos within the empire using the principle of 'divide and conquer'. Obviously there also remains the hypothesis that they wanted to retain their predecessors' high profile, maintaining their political position by working within the Roman political system, a standing that would be massively reinforced by having the emperor of the Western Empire beholden for their help in keeping his throne. All of the above likely played a part in their decision to help John.

Yet possibly one of the main factors is the status of Aetius. He had been a hostage among the Huns for a long time, possibly up to the late 410s or early 420s.[56] There is little doubt that during this time he had established strong personal relationships with many among the Huns, including Rua and Octar, who were most likely near him in age. Brought up with the future kings, it is hardly surprising that, if their opinion of Aetius was high, they would agree to help him.

Returning to Italy with a Hunnic army, Aetius found that he was too late: John had been defeated and executed.[57] However, with the help of the Huns, Aetius was able to negotiate a treaty with Rome that brought a peaceful end to their 'invasion': the Huns were paid a sum of gold, hostages were returned and oaths exchanged.[58]

Pannonia

It has been suggested that, as part of this agreement, in 425 Valentinian and Aetius ceded part of Pannonia to the Huns.[59] Although tempting, there is no definitive notice in the sources, which suggest on the contrary a more 'traditional' agreement:

> [The Huns were] persuaded to lay aside their anger and their arms with the assistance of gold, and having given hostages and accepted pledges, they retired to their own lands.
>
> *Philostorgius 12.14.*

Xiongnu gold stag with eagle's head. From a Xiongnu tomb on the frontier, fourth to third century BC.

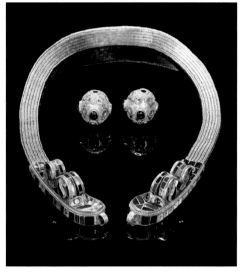

Xiongnu gold torque. The fine workmanship demonstrates that these 'nomads' had access to fine goldsmiths.

Alkhon coin, showing the distinctive skull shape associated with some nomadic societies.

Xiongnu gold wolf. The artisans were capable of exquisite work.

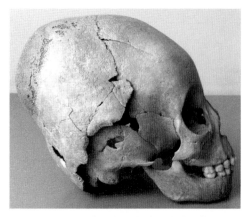

A 'bound' skull, showing the level of deformity of the bones.

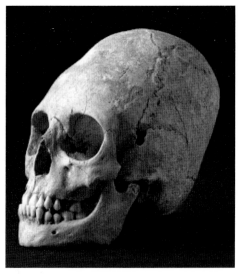

A 'bound' skull from France, clearly showing the extent of the distribution of the 'Hunnic skulls'.

A Hun cauldron, one of the artefacts usually accepted as demonstrating the spread of Hunnic society in the West.

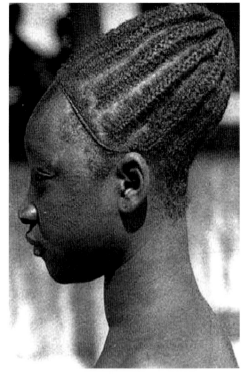

An African woman with a deformed skull. The effect is other-worldly.

The Altai Range. Climate change would easily have resulted in the loss of land as glaciers expanded.

The Kazakh Steppes, far more amenable to the breeding of large numbers of horses than the valleys of the Altai.

The Hungarian Steppes. Away from the Carpathian Mountains the land is capable of supporting a large nomadic force. (© *Paddy Shaw*)

The Theodosian Walls. The sheer scale of the defences clearly demonstrates why Attila was determined to assault them after they had been damaged by an earthquake.

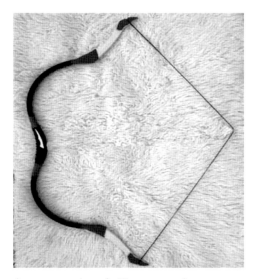

A reconstruction of a Hun recurve bow, © www.bowshop.eu. Whether a Hun warrior used this or the asymmetrical bow was probably a matter of personal preference.

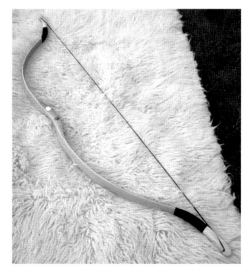

A reconstruction of a Hun asymmetrical bow, © www.bowshop.eu. Despite the apparent clumsiness of the asymmetrical shape, in reality the bow has some superior features that become apparent when used on horseback.

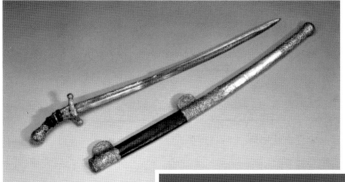

A Hun sword. The shape of the handgrip is a forerunner of the later British 'pistol-grip' swords used by cavalry during the Napoleonic Wars.

Roman ruins in Aquileia. The city was captured by Attila after a long siege during the invasion of Italy.

Roman ruins at Naissus. The city was devastated by the Huns after a siege and reportedly left ruined and depopulated.

The Roman amphitheatre at Aquincum. The amphitheatre may have been used by Attila as the location to gather his troops before the invasion of Italy.

A coin of Honoria. Her decision to ask Attila for help was to have tremendous consequences for the Western Empire.

A coin of Marcian. When he became Roman emperor and confident in his own military abilities, he stopped payments to Attila.

Bust of Valentinian III, the Roman emperor who was Attila's opponent in the West.

The meeting between Attila and Pope Leo I, a work by Giuseppe Maria Mitelli dating to the seventeenth century.

A bust of Theodosius II. He rarely attempted to face Attila in battle, instead reverting to paying 'subsidies' to halt Attila's attacks.

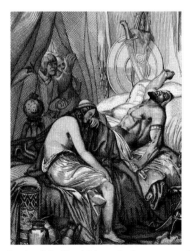

The death of Attila. Although there are variations of the story, the most commonly accepted is that he died of internal haemorrhaging after drinking too much on his wedding night.

The classical view of Attila. Up to the twentieth century Attila was seen as the 'Scourge of God' and a demoniacal appearance was usually exaggerated, as seen by the horns in this drawing.

Attila on horseback. The painting by Eugene Ferdinand Victor Delacroix is less 'demonic' than that depicted in the image on the left; however, the wearing of a wolfskin highlights his 'barbarian' identity.

A statue of Attila in Budapest. In parts of Eastern Europe Attila is not seen as a 'demon' but as a founding father of East European culture, hence his 'noble' appearance in this statue.

A bust of Attila. In Eastern Europe any possible traces of 'Mongoloid' features tend to be minimized, in accordance with the political desires of the regimes that erect the statues and busts.

That there was no agreement to cede part of Pannonia in this treaty is reinforced by the Chronicle of Marcellinus *comes*. He notes in the entry for 427 that the Huns were 'evicted' from Pannonia, an account reinforced by Jordanes, who states that they were driven out by the Romans and Goths.[60]

These entries are confusing, yet the information carries great ramifications for the study of the Huns. For example, it is unlikely that the Romans would evict the Huns if they had only recently ceded the territory to them: the strength of the main Hunnic army, as evidenced by its ability to ensure Aetius' acceptance in the West, would be a cause for concern should Rome instigate a war with the Huns. Another possibility is that, although it was the West that had signed the treaty, it may have been the East that evicted the Huns to stop them interfering in Roman politics.[61] This remains a possibility, but again there is the threat of the main Hunnic force and there is no evidence of a Hunnic invasion of either East or West in response to the Roman action. Of greater import, it may be that the Hunnic removal from Pannonia was agreed as part of the negotiations of 425, but this is not supported by the sources, which state that it was a Romano-Gothic army that forced them out, rather than the affair being a voluntary migration.[62]

There are a variety of options available to explain the brief notices in the sources, but their brevity causes confusion.[63] It is impossible to establish whether the action was taken by the East or the West, as the claim by Jordanes that a Gothic force was involved does not help to clarify matters: the ancient sources refer to both the 'Visigoths' in Gaul and the 'Ostrogoths' – at this time in Thrace – simply as Goths, and both halves of the Roman Empire had access to 'Gothic' troops.

Therefore it is probably best to assume that at this point there were two Hunnic 'realms': the main body centred on the Hungarian Steppes with which the West had now reached an agreement, and a smaller, independent entity that had earlier been allowed to settle in Pannonia and that had no allegiance to the main body.

The hypothesis has two far-reaching implications. One is that even at this late date the Huns were not yet totally unified, despite possible modern claims to the contrary. The second is that it may reinforce the theory that Uldin was the ruler of a small, independent group of Hunnic tribes that had invaded the empire in the late fourth century and settled on the banks of the Danube.

If true, then this can lead to a further possibility. It may be that Rua and/or Octar had suggested the eviction of the Huns in Pannonia, as this independent Hunnic entity could then be absorbed by the main body.[64] The latter may be reinforced by events later in the century.

Octar and Aetius

Reinforcing the concept that the eviction of the Huns from Pannonia did not hamper Romano-Hunnic relations, there are no recorded Hunnic attacks on the empire. In fact, they may have been attempting to extend their control further into *Germania*, as in 430 the Huns attacked the Burgundians:

> The Huns, by making continual irruptions on this people, devastated their country, and often destroyed great numbers of them ... the Burgundians resolved to commit themselves to the protection of ... God ....Accordingly becoming confident thenceforth, they marched against their invaders; nor were they disappointed in their hope. For the king of the Huns, Uptar [Octar] by name, having died in the night from the effects of a surfeit, the Burgundians attacked that people then without a commander-in-chief; and although they were few in numbers and their opponents very many, they obtained a complete victory; for the Burgundians were altogether but three thousand men, and destroyed no less than ten thousand of the enemy.
>
> *Socrates*, Historia Ecclesiastica, *7. 30.*

Obviously, the numbers quoted are unlikely to be accurate as Socrates was not an eyewitness to the event, but doubtless relied on sources likely to exaggerate the defeat of the Huns. However, there is a good chance that the underlying events are accurate: a victory over the Huns by the Burgundians would help to account for how a small people managed to rise to prominence over the course of the next century.[65] The Huns would be allowed to get their revenge due to events in the Roman West.

Aetius again

In 432 there was a civil war between Aetius, based in Gaul and Italy, and Bonifacius, whose base was in Africa. At the Battle of Rimini Aetius was defeated and shortly after fled to the Huns.[66] Interestingly, he travelled *per Pannonias*, possible evidence that the Huns were no longer in these provinces.[67] It is possible that his destination was the region near Margus, where Hunnic royal tombs have been found and dated to, at the latest, the 440s.[68]

Again the Hunnic king – almost certainly now just Rua following the death of Octar – agreed to help Aetius and in the following year a large Hunnic army led by Aetius appeared on the borders of the empire.[69] Opposition collapsed and Aetius returned in triumph as the sole *magister utriusque militiae* in the West.[70] He was to hold this post for the next twenty-one years.

Doubtless Aetius had to make some promises to ensure that the Huns would help him, but what these were is nowhere delineated and so it is necessary to resort to deduction to arrive at a feasible conclusion. The most logical assumption is that Aetius had agreed to give the territory in Pannonia from which the 'independent' Huns had been evicted in 427 to the main body of Huns led by Rua. It has been suggested that the treaty that granted parts of Pannonia to the Huns was on condition that the Huns settled in the region became *foederati*.[71] This is possible, but the exact terms were probably slightly different: the phrase *foederati* usually placed the non-Roman in a subordinate position to Rome. It is highly unlikely that Rua and his Huns would accept a subordinate position to the Roman Empire. On the other hand, it may have been agreed that only the Huns settled in Pannonia were to act as *foederati*. Sadly, the exact truth will never be known.

Obviously this agreement could not be concluded without the consent of the Western Emperor Valentinian III, so until his victory Aetius was acting solely on his own word. However, the assumption makes sense when it is noted that in 434 or 435 an embassy was sent from the West, led by Carpilio, Aetius' son, and Cassiodorus, to the Huns.[72] It may be assumed that this embassy simply confirmed and concluded the details of the agreement Aetius had agreed with Rua.[73]

There remains the question of which parts of Pannonia were granted to the Huns, an issue which has resulted in furious debate.[74] Priscus mentions 'a region of Pannonia close to the river Sava', but this is the only information available.[75] The phrase 'a region' means that a single area, not a whole province or a fragmented group of territories, near to the Sava was allotted to the Huns, a concept reinforced by a second fragment of Priscus when he notes that a man named Constantiolus was 'from the part of Pannonia subject to Attila'.[76] The agreement probably excluded large towns, which were needed for Roman administrative purposes.[77]

Obviously certainty is impossible, yet the territory conceded to Rua would appear to be vastly overstated. A look at the map indicates that according to some authorities the West gave lands as large as the Hungarian Steppes to the Huns, and it is not usually indicated how the newly-donated 'territories' would link with each other. Instead it is possibly better to assume that, while extensive, the lands granted were a cohesive whole that was linked directly to territories controlled by the Huns on the northern banks of the Danube.

In that case, it is probable that only a distinct region encompassing the south of Pannonia II, a large part of Valeria, and extensive tracts of Savia near to the River Save were allocated to the Huns. The extreme south of Pannonia I may also have been included. The main roads throughout the region were, wherever possible, excluded from the agreement, since the Romans would not want their main arteries of communication and trade jeopardized.[78] Obviously the region surrounding the city of Sirmium was not included in the treaty, as otherwise it would not have been attacked in the later war of 441–2.

Rua

The Hunnic rulers had learned that the best way of dealing with the empire from a position of strength was to use the practice of 'divide and conquer'. Possibly with this in mind, and with his frontier with the west settled, in 434 Rua turned to affairs in the east. He was helped by the fact that both halves of the empire were facing a crisis. In 429 the Vandals had crossed to continental Africa and were threatening Africa Proconsularis, the West's most vital province. In response, the East had sent Aspar, the

Eastern *magister militum*, to Africa in 431 in an attempt to help the West control the Vandals.

Yet the Romans were not the only ones facing political problems. It would appear that some of the tribes who had been conquered when the Huns migrated to the Don and the Volga were attempting to throw off the Hunnic yoke and join their forces to the Romans.[79] Taking advantage of Roman difficulties, Rua decided to go on the political offensive:

> When Rua was king of the Huns, the Amilzuri, Itimari, Tounsoures, Boisci and other tribes who were living near the Danube were fleeing to fight on the side of the Romans. Rua decided to go to war with these tribes and sent Eslas, a man who usually handled negotiations over differences between himself and the Romans, threatening to break the present peace if they did not hand over all who had fled to them. The Romans wished to send an embassy to the Huns, and both Plinthas and Dionysius wished to go. Plinthas was a Scythian, Dionysius a Thracian: both were generals and had held the Roman consulship. Since it seemed that Eslas would reach Rua before the embassy was dispatched, Plinthas sent along with him Sengilach, one of his own retainers, to persuade Rua to negotiate with none of the Romans but himself.
>
> *Priscus, fragment 2, trans. Blockley*

It is nowhere stated whether these tribes had first migrated to the region of the Danube in an attempt to flee from the Huns or whether they had been forced to settle in the area by their Hunnic overlords. Whatever the case, it is clear that Rua was facing a problem as the tribes haemorrhaged across the Danube into the Roman East.

Unhappy with the lack of a Roman response, it would appear that Rua led an army into Thrace and brushed aside the Roman forces facing him.[80] Yet despite the convoluted arrangements made by Plinthas to organize an embassy, no peace treaty was to be signed with Rua:

> So when Rhoïlas [Rua], Prince of the Scythian Nomads, had crossed the Danube with a vast host and was ravaging and plundering Thrace, and was threatening to besiege the imperial city, and summarily seize it and deliver it to destruction, God smote him from on high with

thunderbolt and storm, burning up the invader and destroying all his host.

Theodoret, 5.36.4.

Theodoret has confused his sources and combined the earlier invasion of Thrace by the Huns with the death of Rua, so it is uncertain whether the Huns actually invaded Roman territory in 434. However, there does seem to be some truth in the manner of Rua's death, as this information is also given by Socrates Scholasticus.[81] Given the complicated and possibly protracted nature of the negotiations, it is unknown whether Rua died in 434 or 435. He was succeeded by his two nephews, one of whom would become one of the most famous military commanders of all time.

Chapter Four

Attila

Attila was probably born at some point between c.390 and 410 CE. Although claims to specific dates have been made, there is no evidence to confirm any such date and any claim made on such a date is based on personal preference, not the sources. There are only two pieces of evidence that may help. One is the description given by Jordanes, probably referencing Priscus, which claims 'his beard thin and sprinkled with grey'.[1] The other is that he became king in 434 and died in 453. To succeed in 434, he must have been a fully-grown man, and the fact that his beard was 'sprinkled with grey' suggests a man in his late thirties or early forties. However, the nature of his death in 453 gives no clear indication of his age. As a result, his age is entirely unknown.

Attila's father was Mundiuch, the brother of the Hunnic kings Rua and Octar. Mundiuch had another brother, Oebarsius, who is not named as a king.[2] Attila's co-ruler, Bleda, is named as his brother – although given the nature of Hunnic marriages mentioned in Chapter 2 he may have been a half-brother – and was probably the older of the two.[3] The meaning of Attila's name is uncertain, but it may have been a title meaning 'great father', in which case he would have also had an unknown, proper Hun name as well.[4] As just noted, the only description of Attila is from Jordanes, although it is generally believed that the extract has been taken from an otherwise lost fragment of Priscus:[5]

> He was a man born into the world to shake the nations, the scourge of all lands, who in some way terrified all mankind by the dreadful rumours noised abroad concerning him. He was haughty in his walk, rolling his eyes hither and thither, so that the power of his proud spirit appeared in the movement of his body. He was indeed a lover of war, yet restrained in action, mighty in counsel, gracious to suppliants and lenient to those who were once received into his protection. He was

short of stature, with a broad chest and a large head; his eyes were small, his beard thin and sprinkled with grey; and he had a flat nose and a swarthy complexion, showing the evidences of his origin.

Jordanes, *Getica*, 35 (182)

Although the origins of the Huns are disputed, superficially it would seem that Priscus/Jordanes is not describing someone who is of Turkic origin: although the colour of the skin may indeed denote anyone from the Inner Asian Steppe, when coupled with the description of the nose it is tempting to suggest that Attila was of 'Mongol' origin; however, this is supposition based upon fragile evidence. On the contrary, Priscus, and possibly also John Malalas, suggest that Attila was 'of the Gepid Huns'. Although the meaning of this phrase is unclear, it may simply mean that Attila was one of the 'western' Huns, rather than one of those residing further east.[6]

Of more interest, however, is the description of Attila's personality. That he was a 'lover of war' is understandable: the majority of 'barbarian' leaders relied on success in war to extend their personal power and reward their followers, who otherwise could abandon them for a more successful warlord. On the other hand, the portrayal of Attila as 'restrained in action' and 'mighty in counsel' suggests that he relied to a great degree on his personality to command respect: not reverting to violence at every opportunity and giving good advice to his followers and subordinate leaders was a way to win loyalty beyond the mere pragmatism of the usual warlord. This is reinforced by the fact that he was known as being 'gracious to suppliants and lenient to those who were once received into his protection'. The latter gives a compelling reason for the rapid spread of his empire: those tribes who accepted Hunnic leadership without recourse to fighting would be allowed to keep their leaders and a large measure of autonomy, whereas those who fought and lost would still be accepted into the Hunnic hierarchy, as long as there was no doubt over their new loyalty. This would explain why, at the Battle of the Catalaunian Fields in 451, Attila's main commanders were not Huns but the 'kings' of other tribes. Although Attila was to be sole decision-maker, the leaders of defeated tribes could expect roles of real power under the new regime. Sadly for the Huns, Attila's sons do not seem to have been endowed with their father's political abilities.

Attila's upbringing and training are completely unknown. It has been suggested that he would have been taught to ride and care for four horses simultaneously, and had training in archery, swordplay and the use of the lasso. Apart from Hunnic, he probably also spoke Gothic, as this was the language of one of his largest 'allied' groups, and he would have spoken at least a little Latin. Priscus in his writings does not clarify whether Attila himself needed a translator or not: he does state that negotiations were conducted in Latin, but not Greek as the latter was not widely spoken at Attila's court.[7]

Such linguistic ability would have been useful, as doubtless Attila was present during the political negotiations undertaken by his uncles, both with Rome and the conquered indigenous peoples of Europe, and doubtless took part in many raids and wars in order to build up his experience of warfare to the point where he was capable of commanding troops, as befitted the role of an 'imperial prince'.[8]

Little is known of Attila's personal life. Following traditional Hunnic marriage patterns he definitely had several wives, and these gave birth to numerous sons. The eldest son was named Ellac, and others named include Dengizich and Ernach.[9] Sadly, the names of his wives are unknown and of his sons only Ellac appears to have been mentioned by the sources as being active during his father's reign. The others come to prominence only after Attila's death.

Sadly, there is little information concerning Attila's brother and co-ruler Bleda. No description survives of either his physical appearance or his personality, which has allowed historians in the past to make differing suggestions for the style of his rule and for Attila's later actions concerning Bleda. These proposals will be assessed at the relevant place later.

The brothers assumed control of the Hunnic kingdom, but there is no statement in the sources as to either the size or the extent of the Hunnic realm upon their succession, so it is impossible to determine with accuracy either their division of their new kingdom or give a definitive account of their campaigns over the next few years. As a result, it is necessary to revert to hypothesis for all but the most basic of statements. For example, since it is recorded that both East and West were sending embassies to Attila, it has been seen as reasonable to assume that Attila was the king of the Huns in the West.[10] If the brothers simply divided their realm equally on a geographic basis, this must remain the most likely division. However, there is another option. This is the hypothesis that the brothers ruled equally but that Bleda, as the senior sibling, assumed control of part of the army and led the subjugation of the tribes to the north, east and west of the Hunnic homeland, in this way keeping the glory of conquest for himself. In this model, Attila took personal control of the Hunnic heartland with the remaining forces and assumed the lead when dealing with the two halves of the Roman Empire to the south. Sadly, it is impossible to state with certainty which of these propositions is the more accurate, but for the purposes of this book the latter has been assumed as more likely for reasons which will become clear.

The Treaty of 435

In 434 Rua had invaded Thrace with the aim of making the East come to terms; an invasion that had resulted in the Eastern Empire's military commander Aspar being recalled from Africa, where he had been restricting the Vandals to minimal gains following their invasion in 429.

It is probable that by this time at the latest the Huns had based their centre of power to the north of the Danube, possibly opposite the Roman town of Margus, as evidenced by the recorded existence of Hunnic royal tombs in the region. However, Attila's main base appears to have been centred on the Hungarian Plain.[11] Although this was not ideally located for their dealings with the tribes with whom they were in contact to the north, east and west, it was a good location for negotiations with the Roman Empire. This observation reinforces the possibility that Attila was to deal with the empire, while Bleda had the sole task of conquering or negotiating with the tribes outside the empire.

Following Rua's invasion, but before negotiations could be concluded, Rua had died and Bleda and Attila had become the new rulers of the Huns and so received the imperial delegation. The Roman envoys were probably Plinta, who had been one of Theodosius' most senior generals and a consul in 419, and Epigenes, probably at this time the *magister epistularum* (Master of the Letters/Correspondence).[12] The importance to Rome of gaining a treaty can be confirmed by the appointment of two such senior figures to act as ambassadors, for the empire had problems. Partly due to the protracted negotiations with the Huns, both Eastern and Western Rome had been

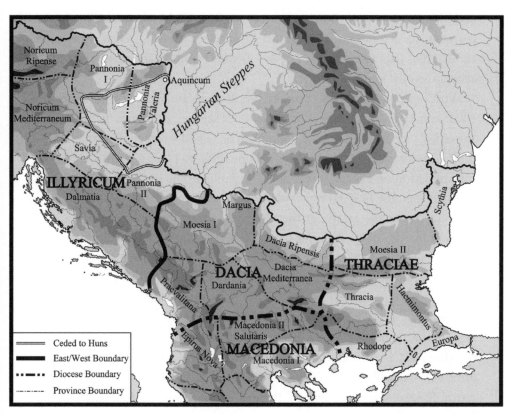

Map 5: The Hunnic Steppes, including the territory suggested as being ceded in Pannonia.

forced to accept the unpalatable inevitable. Earlier in 435 they had signed a treaty with the Vandals wherein the Vandals received a part of Africa in which to settle. Although this took pressure off the important province of Africa Proconsularis, it was a major blow, especially to the Western Empire.

On the other hand, the signing of the treaty with the Vandals meant that the Eastern army under Aspar, which had been in Africa facing the Vandals since 431, had been freed to return home and shore up the defences of the Balkans. Doubtless this was a factor that put pressure on Bleda and Attila to agree terms: the new Hunnic kings were facing a much larger Roman army than that which Rua had threatened before his death.

More importantly, the demands on Attila and Bleda were already mounting. Their assumption of power may not have gone unchallenged. Other members of the 'royal dynasty' may have attempted to secure the throne for themselves, as at least two members were later to be found seeking sanctuary in the Roman Empire (see below). In addition, they almost certainly needed to campaign against subservient tribes who had either seen the death of Rua as a chance to throw off the Hunnic yoke or who refused to accept the new kings.

With both sides desiring a treaty, the Roman ambassadors were met by Bleda and Attila on horseback. This has been seen as an attempt to 'humiliate' the envoys, as the Roman tradition was to be seated when conducting talks.[13] This may have been true, but it is also possible to place a slightly different interpretation on events: it was not to 'humiliate' the Romans, but to signal to them that the new Hunnic rulers were not prepared to adopt 'Roman' customs to put the envoys at their ease. In effect, they were attempting to discomfort the envoys in order to gain even the slightest possible advantage during the talks. In fact, it is probably only the preliminary talks that took place on horseback. After ensuring their 'supremacy', Bleda and Attila almost certainly resorted to talks in the more comfortable seated positions necessary to record agreements in writing. Finally, in 435 a treaty was signed. It is commonly known as the Treaty of *Horreum Margi*, or the Treaty of Margus.[14] It is sometimes suggested that the treaty should be dated after February 438 and no later than 440.[15] This is due to the fact that the envoy Epigenes is described by Priscus as *quaestor sacri palatii* (Quaestor of the Sacred Palace), a post he did not hold until after 438. However, the attribution of posts to individuals at an earlier date than they were actually held is not uncommon in the ancient sources. It was probably intended to identify individuals to a reader by using their contemporary post when describing their actions in the past.

Terms

In one of the previous treaties – probably that signed with Rua in 422 – the Romans had promised to pay 350lb of gold as a 'tribute', though doubtless the Romans had called it a subsidy for internal political consumption. This amount was now doubled to 700lb of gold.[16] In addition, the new kings demanded that the payment be made directly to themselves. They were not yet in a strong position politically and did not want the money to be given to an envoy: envoys were usually powerful individuals within the Hunnic polity and the new kings would not have wanted a large amount of gold to fall into the hands of a potential challenger.[17]

Priscus records more of the terms.[18] No further refugees from Hunnic areas were to be allowed to enter the empire, and all of those who had already sought sanctuary were to be returned to the Huns. Priscus gives the names and fate of two of the returned fugitives. Mamas and Atakam, who were members of the 'royal family', were to be handed over to Bleda and Attila, after which they were impaled near to Carsum in Thrace. The episode lends credence to the proposal that the accession of Bleda and Attila was not fully accepted, and that there were members of the royal dynasty who were unhappy with their assumption of power.

An unexpected – at least to modern eyes – clause required that all Romans who had been captured by the Huns during the war and had since escaped were to be returned to their Hunnic masters unless a ransom of 8 *solidi* was paid. Obviously this was a major demand. Although sometimes overlooked, the question then is how the Huns and Romans came to an agreement concerning the number of Romans who had escaped captivity. Doubtless the Huns exaggerated the number in order to extract the maximum amount of money from the empire, with Rome claiming a far lower figure. There is no answer to this question.

The final terms of the treaty were of a more standard type that are acceptable to modern readers. Rome was not to make an alliance with any tribes against the Huns, including when the Huns were the aggressors. Finally, there were to be safe markets where the Huns could trade their goods and where Hunnic and Roman traders were to be given equal rights. It may be that this was in response to Roman taxation. It is likely that prior to this the tax on goods traded by Hunnic merchants was higher than that imposed on Roman merchants. This was now to be discontinued and both sets of traders were to pay the same in tax.

There is one further possible clause in the treaty, although this is far from certain. In a later entry, Priscus states that a man named Orestes, who was then working as a *notarius* ('secretary') for Attila, was from the part of Pannonia ceded to Attila.[19] Sadly Priscus gives no date for the cession of Pannonia. It has been suggested that the loss of parts of Pannonia was due to this treaty. This must remain a possibility, but it is more likely that Pannonia was lost due to a different agreement, since at this date Pannonia was officially attached to the Western Empire and so would not have been included by the Eastern envoys. As noted earlier, it is probable that the

Western *magister militum* Aetius had either agreed to give the Huns part of Pannonia when he solicited their aid in 432–3 (after having fled following his defeat by Bonifacius at the Battle of Rimini) or, just as likely, that part of Pannonia was now demanded by Bleda and Attila after the death of Rua in order to maintain their support of Aetius.

War

With the embassies concluded and peace on their southern and western flanks, the new Hunnic kings took action to cement their place as rulers. Bleda now led his forces against the (otherwise unknown) Sorosgi in 'Scythia'.[20] At the same time, Attila appears to have taken the opportunity of secure southern and south-western borders to secure the brothers' power throughout the already-conquered regions of *barbaricum*. The limited information available suggests that for several years after their succession the brothers were campaigning against the Goths and the Gepids – and probably other tribes later attested as serving under Attila – forcing some into subservience and others into alliance.[21]

Except for those living in forests or mountainous regions, these peoples would have had little chance of resisting the Huns, and although they could probably escape from Hunnic attacks it would make sense for them simply to come to terms. The peoples living between the Atlantic and the Crimea who were not part of the Roman Empire were primarily 'sedentary agriculturalists' surviving on 'subsistence agriculture', ruled by 'warlords who lived beyond their village'. They had little defence and so repeated large-scale raids would quickly force them into starvation.[22] The only alternative for these peoples was to flee – usually to the Roman Empire – or accept Hunnic control. Those leaders who stayed and accepted Hunnic rule without a fight appear to have been richly rewarded by the Huns. For example, the 'Pietrosa treasure' was probably owned by a Gothic leader serving alongside his Hunnic masters.[23] Yet for the average 'peasant', the change in masters probably had little effect.

After several years of fighting, by the early 440s the Hunnic Empire probably directly encompassed three major Gothic groups, plus the Gepids, Sarmatians, Heruli, Alans, Rugi, Suevi and Sciri, as well as exerting influence over the Alamanni, the Burgundians and possibly the Thuringii and Lombards. In addition, they may also have begun interfering in politics further west, as by the 450s they are attested as interfering in the dynastic succession of the Franks.[24]

One further factor of note is the movement of tribes who may have been subservient to the Huns. Prior to 450 only the Gepids, the Sarmatians and the Suevi are attested as being west of the Carpathians. After this, the three groups of Goths, plus the Alans, Sciri, Heruli and Rugi are all attested as having moved to the middle Danube. Sadly, it is unknown whether their movement was the result of Hunnic 'resettlement' or whether it was on their own initiative and an attempt to solicit aid from the Roman Empire once they were settled directly on the borders.[25] All of these changes took place away from the Roman orbit, so no details are given in the sources concerning these events. Instead, Roman writers concentrated upon events taking place in the 430s and 440s that had direct relevance to the empire.

Chapter Five

Joint Rule

Although the Huns' main concentration was upon expanding their power to the west, north and east – and possibly along the Danube – at times their actions were either in alliance with Rome, or directly influenced events taking place on the empire's borders. Possibly to be included in these events is an attack on the town of Noviodunum.

435

According to an undated fragment of Priscus, a man named Valips, who 'ruled' at least some of the Rugi, not only attacked but seized the city of Noviodunum.[1] This event has been dated by historians to either 435 or 441. Those who date the event to 435 see it as Valips and his men attempting to escape from the expanding Huns, whereas those preferring 441 interpret the event as being part of the Huns' invasion of the East in that year, largely because the Rugi are later attested by Jordanes as being included in the Hunnic Empire.

As a further complication, the Rugi are noted as forming a large proportion of the Roman army in Italy in the mid-late fifth century, so it has recently been proposed that Valips was commanding Rugian *foederati* in the province of Scythia and simply rebelled against the local Roman commanders in the hope of either securing a better deal for his men or, especially if the attack took place at a later date, of taking control of the region for himself as Roman power waned. The latter remains a possibility, as at least some Rugi were later attested as being in the region of Noricum in the Life of St. Severinus (d. AD 482), so at least one group remained at large after the fall of Rome.[2] As a consequence, it should be noted that in reality the attack could easily date to any year from the mid-430s to at least the early-mid 440s.

The little evidence imparted by Priscus suggests an early date for the event. Priscus states that after the Rugi had seized Noviodunum the Roman

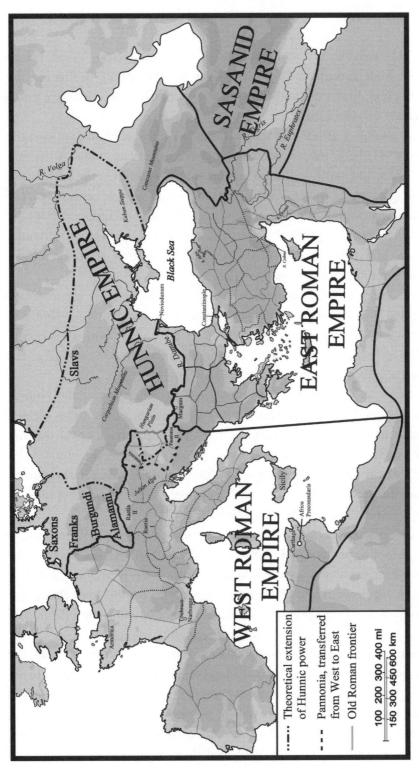

Map 6: The Hunnic Empire. Where in *'barbaricum'* Hunnic influence ended is unknown.

army besieged the city and, faced with imminent defeat, Valips placed children from the city on the walls to deter Roman attacks. In this way the siege became protracted and the situation was only concluded by a peace treaty rather than a battle.

It is certainly feasible that Valips was attacking in conjunction with the Huns in 441; later, tribal leaders are attested as serving under Attila in a semi-independent role, so this must remain a possibility. On the other hand, the fact that a treaty was agreed suggests that Valips was not acting as part of the Hunnic attack, since being a Hunnic vassal should exclude him from the possibility of an independent agreement with Rome. In addition, although Valips extended the duration of the siege using children, at no point did a Hunnic force attempt to raise the siege.

Sadly, later information does not help: the fact is that the constant protracted and complicated demands placed by the Huns on Rome to 'repatriate traitors' in treaty negotiations could refer to both a successful attempt by Valips to escape from Hunnic dominion in 435, as well as the 'secession' of Valips from the Huns to Rome in 441.

However, as Valips is nowhere mentioned as being part of the Hunnic polity, and the Rugi are not specifically named as one of the tribes seeking sanctuary in the empire, it is assumed here that Valips' attack was an attempt to escape Hunnic dominion and so took place in 435/6 as the Huns under Attila took advantage of the Roman peace to extend their sway in *barbaricum*. If true, the episode clearly demonstrates that Attila was starting to exert Hunnic power along the Danubian frontier.

These actions were mirrored by the activities of Bleda in the West. Possibly also in 435, but perhaps in 436, Bleda, in alliance with Aetius, attacked the Burgundians, who by this point had settled just to the west of the Rhine. It has been suggested that it was during negotiations for this joint attack that Aetius gave the Huns permission to expand their dominions into Pannonia.[3] This must remain a possibility, but sadly certainty is impossible.

The main reasons behind Aetius' desire to attack are easy to establish. For Rome, not only was the existence of a large tribe on the border a threat to the empire, but they had earlier probably raided one of the Belgic provinces in tandem with a Gothic revolt, as well as crossing the frontier and settling in deserted agricultural areas under the nominal control of Rome.[4] In addition, the Burgundians had recently enhanced their reputation by defeating an invasion, so probably causing other tribes to join them in the hope of retaining some measure of autonomy. The newly-enlarged tribal confederation would be a threat to the security of the Rhine frontier, especially if they now failed to abide by the terms of any treaty with Rome signed earlier.

The Huns' motives may also be straightforward. The 'recently defeated invasion' was that of the Huns under Octar in 430. Octar had died during the attack – allegedly of natural causes – and his demoralized army had consequently been defeated by the Burgundians.[5] As well as enhancing the reputation of the Burgundians, the reverse would have been a blow to Hunnic prestige, and one that would need to be redressed: the Huns had 'unfinished business' with the Burgundians. There are, however, two additional factors. One is that, as the elder of the two brothers, it is possible that Bleda had served for a long time under his uncles Rua and Octar. In this context, not only would he hold a personal grudge against the Burgundians, it is possible that, like them, he had established a strong relationship with Aetius and so was more amenable to an alliance with the Western Empire. A second is that such an attack would be more likely to succeed with imperial support, and Bleda was desirous of both avenging his uncle's defeat and boosting his own reputation.

Whatever the cause, in either 435 or 436 – and more likely the latter to allow for joint plans to be made for the attack and after consideration of ensuing events – the Huns and Romans launched their attack. Sadly for the Romans, the campaign appears to have been short-lived. Learning of the upcoming war, the Goths in Toulouse took advantage of the removal of Roman troops from Gaul by gathering their forces and laying siege to the city of Narbo (Narbonne). The Roman army was forced to limit the Burgundian campaign, with many troops returning to Gaul to face the Goths. In addition, more troops were needed in Armorica, where a man named Tibatto was leading a band of *bacaudae* – groups of rebelling Roman citizens – against Roman rule.[6] Aetius sent a *comes* (count) named Litorius with a small army to deal with Tibatto. Although the campaign against the Burgundians may have continued on a smaller scale, the diversion of troops may have caused its postponement. It would be resumed in the following year.

437

There was one major political change that took place in 437 which was to have a major effect on relations between Attila and the Roman Empire: as part of the marriage celebrations between the Western Emperor Valentinian III and Licinia Eudoxia, daughter of the Eastern Emperor Theodosius II, it would appear that at least part of Pannonia would pass from Western to Eastern control (see Map 6).[7] No doubt this was an attempt to help deal politically with the Huns. Hunnic control of Pannonia was both an embarrassment and a liability to the West, as they were forced to deal with the Huns from a position of weakness. With the stronger East in control of the territory, the result was that the Huns were now forced to deal with the East concerning Pannonia, and could not now use the territory as part of a 'divide and conquer' policy. For the foreseeable future the majority of direct contact between the Huns and Rome would be with Constantinople but, of equal import, it was now the East that had to deal with the Huns settled in Pannonia.

Also in 437 the aborted campaign against the Burgundians was resumed. This time there was to be no distraction: the allied forces decimated the Burgundians, killing the Burgundian king Gundahar and 20,000 of his men.[8] The limited evidence implies that there was a single major battle followed by a savage attack on Burgundian settlements, so it must have been a fast campaign. This was important for the West, as there were still affairs in Gaul to be dealt with. Finally, the *comes* Litorius managed to defeat the *bacaudae* under Tibatto before turning south and forcing the Goths to lift the siege of Narbo.[9]

The battles fought by Litorius would not be of great interest to a study of Attila and the Huns were it not for the fact that Litorius was commanding a body of Huns during his operations. Although it is possible that these were simply a contingent of independent Huns rather than the continuation of the allied operation, the fact that the Huns are specifically mentioned fighting against both Tibatto and the Goths implies that the alliance was holding firm and that these were troops supplied by Bleda.

The Goths

Despite the destruction of the Burgundians and *bacaudae*, plus their defeat at Narbo, the Goths continued their war against Rome. Aetius took personal control of the main Roman army and defeated the Goths at the battle of Mons Colubrarius.[10] However, Litorius – now probably *magister militum per Gallias* (Master of the Troops in Gaul) – became over-confident and in 439 he pushed the Goths back to their capital of Toulouse. Here, according to Jordanes, he consulted soothsayers that were Huns.[11] These men used scapulimancy – the art of using the shoulder blades of sacrificial animals – to foretell events.[12] Having secured proof of his victory, Litorius then gave battle to the Goths, but the efficacy of the seers using scapulimancy appears to have been poor: after a long, hard-fought battle the Hunnic forces were defeated. Litorius himself was captured and later executed.[13] The episode suggests that the Huns formed a large proportion of the Roman army at the battle, so it is possible that they were at least equal to the Roman forces present, reinforcing the concept that they were allies rather than Litorius' personal bodyguard (*bucellarii*).[14]

If the Huns at the battle were allies, they were only a fraction of the forces now available to the Huns. Simultaneous with these developments both Bleda and Attila were expanding their central power base. In the west, it is possibly around this time that the Hunnic Empire reached the Baltic Sea, although concrete evidence for this is yet to be found.[15] In the east, and according to Priscus, Attila's realm 'spread from the Volga to central Gaul'.[16] Although obviously an exaggeration – unless he is including the territories crossed by Attila in his invasion of Gaul in 451 – and of a later date, the statement suggests that the Huns will certainly have been making great inroads into *barbaricum* during this time, although as it does not affect the Roman Empire there is no record of when or how far they expanded.

It is probably from the late-430s onwards that the influence of the Huns was such that Hunnic practices began to be adopted by the tribes in the west, especially with regard to military and elite culture. Apart from the possible adoption of the Hunnic cauldrons mentioned in Chapter 1, there is also archaeological evidence that some members of the elite adopted 'skull-binding'. In this process, the heads of newly-born infants were wrapped in bandages in order to force the skull to grow in an elongated fashion. Unfortunately, those specimens found in the west are yet to be analysed in order to establish whether they were indeed 'Germanic', or whether they were actually Huns who had either joined the western tribes or been imposed upon them by the Huns as leaders.[17]

The Vandals

With the Huns expanding Hunnic control to the north and with a treaty in place with Rome, the situation along the Roman border appeared stable. This was to change in dramatic circumstances. In October 439 the Vandals, settled in Africa since 435, broke their treaty with Rome and captured Carthage.

Although the Huns theoretically remained in alliance with the West and bound by treaty with the East, the disastrous loss of Africa meant that the focus of Rome would shift to the Mediterranean. Although pure speculation, it is possible that it was in late 439 or, more likely, early 440 that a division first appeared between Bleda and Attila. There is no evidence that Bleda was involved in any attempt to use the African disaster to either gain plunder or obtain more advantageous terms from the Roman Empire, and interestingly the West – the region most affected by the loss of its African territories – was to be left alone by the Huns.

With the East, however, things were to be different. Although the East was only indirectly affected by the loss of Africa, Attila appears determined to have used the event to wrest more concessions from Constantinople. It may be that the refusal of Bleda to agree with this strategy was the first sign of a growing schism with Attila. If the course of events as analysed below is accurate, it may be that in 440–441 Bleda would be forced into an unwanted war with Rome, further exacerbating the discord between the brothers.

This hypothesis gives a further reason for Attila wishing to break with the East, despite Bleda's unwillingness: although as the elder brother Bleda had been able to range far afield in the north and west, gaining glory and plunder, as the junior partner Attila had been restricted by the treaties with Rome to small-scale expansions along the Danube. It is possible that Attila was unhappy with this state of affairs and wished to break with Rome so that he could have a target to also display his military skills and thus gain glory and plunder equal to that of his brother.

War

Consequently, it was in the year following the loss of Africa that Attila was to get his break on the international stage. At some point in 440 he sent ambassadors to Constantinople stating that the Romans had broken their treaty with the Huns. Allegedly, and under the leadership of the bishop of Margus, errant Romans had robbed the graves of the Huns situated across the Danube from that city.[18] Sadly, this is probably true since a law had to be written in 437 dealing with bishops ordering the robbing of Christian graves: if Christian graves were seen as suitable targets, those of Pagan Huns would be even more viable.[19] On this occasion, the Hunnic envoys received no satisfactory answer, yet Attila appears to have made no overt move against the empire. Although the Vandals had seized Africa, East Rome was militarily unaffected by the loss and so remained a force to be reckoned with.

As a further spur, it is possible that from 436 Theodosius had refused to send the annual payment agreed at Margus to Attila. Yet although this aggravated Attila, Hunnic policy towards the vastly stronger empire was to attack the Eastern Empire only when the Eastern Empire was vulnerable. Consequently, despite the lack of payment, Attila took no action since the Eastern armies were on station, the frontier posts were fully manned, the Danube was carefully patrolled by the ships of the Danubian fleet, and the fortresses that had been planted on the lower reaches of the river a quarter of a century before remained formidable.[20]

It was events in the following year that gave Attila his chance. In the spring of 441 the East dispatched a major expeditionary force to retake Africa from the Vandals, using Sicily as a forward base. The army was probably formed around the core of one of the *praesental* armies ('in the presence': one of the two armies retained in Constantinople to serve the emperor directly) with additional units being taken from Thrace.[21] Alongside the previous factors, the move may have been inflammatory, especially as far as Attila's personal standing was concerned. Firstly, in effect the East was declaring that Attila and his Huns were a far lesser threat than Gaiseric and his Vandals.[22] If this interpretation is correct, then it would have been taken as an insult by Attila, who would then need to restore his image as a successful and dominant warlord. Secondly, and far more provocatively, the Eastern army had now been weakened by the deployment of the troops to Sicily. The East had become a tempting target for Attila. Although several factors doubtless affected Attila's decision, a combination of those outlined above probably dominated his policy. The most obvious way for Attila to establish a military reputation equal to Bleda's was to invade the East. On the other hand, it should be noted that this analysis may be faulty and it may simply be that when the East removed troops from Thrace Attila saw a chance to extort better terms from the East than those agreed in the Treaty of Margus.

It is impossible to trace with certainty the events during the war between the Huns and Rome that occurred between 441 and 442. The sources are very fragmentary, consisting mainly of snippets of information contained in the *Chronicle* of Marcellinus *Comes* and the surviving fragments of the works of Priscus. Obviously, the relevant remnants of Priscus' work are largely devoid of context so the contents could relate to any of the Hunnic wars. Instead, it is necessary to contrast and compare what he states with the contents of Marcellinus in the hope of finding a feasible description of the course of the war.

This is not as simple as it sounds. Marcellinus' *Chronicle* has many of the failings of similar works by contemporary authors. In the context of the Hunnic War of 441–2 one of these conventions could affect understanding of the information. Although in theory a chronicle consists of events recorded on a year-by-year basis, ancient chroniclers had a tendency to include information that happened at a different date in an entry containing other information relating to the contents, especially if this gave greater weight to the underlying aims of the author.

A major example concerns the vital entry for 441. In this, Marcellinus has documented the invasion of the 'Persians, Saracens, Tzannes, Isaurians, [and] the Huns'.[23] However, from other sources it becomes clear that the Persians actually went to war in 440, although the war did continue into 441.[24] In other words, Marcellinus has apparently conflated the Persian War of 440–441 with the Hunnic War of 441–2 in order to emphasize the plight of the empire. In the same entry he then states that 'Naissus, Singidunum and other cities, and many *oppidae* ['fortresses'] of Illyricum have been devastated.'

Although a seemingly simple entry, following the same logic used above it is possible that he has also collected the named cities attacked over the course of both years under the entry for 441, again in order to emphasize the plight of the empire. However, in the separate entry for 442 he notes that Bleda and Attila devastated both Illyricum and Thrace.[25]

Despite these problems, it is necessary to use the context of Marcellinus' statements in order to arrive at a feasible course for the war. The fact that Marcellinus records the attack on Thrace in a separate entry suggests that the campaign of 441 attacked Illyricum only, and it was only in 442 that Thrace was devastated. If this assumption is correct, it has a major impact on the analysis of the campaigns. An examination of Maps 6 and 7 show that any attempt to include Naissus and Singidunum after the capture of Margus has the Huns crossing and re-crossing their path to reach all of their destinations. This is unusual, as in most accounts of military campaigns of this era an invading force forages on enemy territory in order to minimize the amount of supplies they need to carry. Passing back through the same region means that foragers will have difficulty, since they may have already used all of the available supplies on the way out. Therefore it is necessary to review the common description of the two campaigns in order to reach a viable and consistent conclusion.[26]

If, as noted above, Marcellinus has conflated the attacks of 440, 441 and 442 into the entry for 441, while almost in passing noting that Thrace was only attacked in 442, a solution appears. Although part of the Eastern army – possibly one of the *praesental* armies and a large part of the army of Thrace – was abroad in Sicily to face the Vandals, and the majority of the remainder of the Roman army was stationed in the far east to fight the Sasanids (although peace would be agreed in June 441, this was too late for the army in the Orient to affect events in Illyricum), there were still potentially strong forces in the nature of a second *praesental* army available for deployment in the region.

In this context, it is possible to conclude that Attila may have decided that in 441 he would raid the empire but remain distant from Constantinople in case of a Roman counter-attack. This may have caused a breach between Attila and Bleda, as up to now Bleda had remained friendly with Rome. It was only when Attila became aware of the lack of a Roman military response during the raid of 441 and the ensuing Roman political response that he determined to attack further to the east in 442. Therefore, in theory the Hunnic campaigns can be split into a first, western campaign and a second, eastern campaign.

The 'Western' Campaign of 441

Due to the above considerations, what follows is a clear and logical outline of the two Hunnic campaigns of 441 and 442. However, readers are reminded that this is hypothesis and other suggestions concerning events remain equally valid.

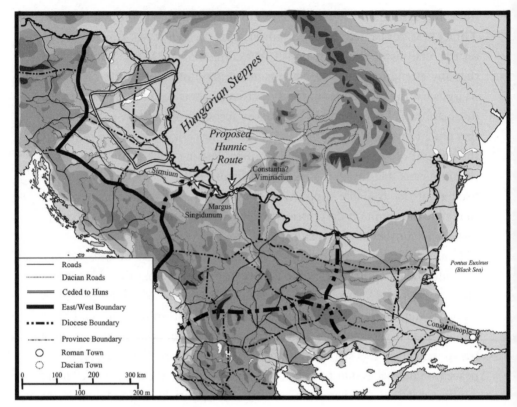

Map 7: The Hunnic Attack in 441.

The sources attest to the Huns attacking and capturing 'at least seven major cities' in the war.[27] Six of the cities were Sirmium (Sremska Mitrovica), Naissus (Niš), Singidunum (Belgrade), Viminacium (Kostalac), Margus (Orašje) and Ratiara (Archar).[28] Strangely, Constantia, which was only a fortress and trading post, is included in the list of seven 'cities': this anomaly is discussed in detail in Chapter 6. Using the concept of a 'Western' and an 'Eastern' campaign outlined above it is here assumed that Sirmium, Singidunum, Viminacium and Margum took place in 441, whereas the attacks on Naissus and Ratiaria are assumed to have taken place in 442.

Almost certainly it was only after news had reached Attila that the eastern armada had set sail for Africa that Attila launched his invasion. Dismissing Roman attempts to negotiate, and reiterating that it was the Romans who had breached the earlier peace treaty, the Huns moved against the fortress of Constantia, situated on their side of the Danube.[29]

Having started on the border with Constantia, it seems logical to suppose that Attila used the Roman roads to move his troops once he had crossed into the Roman Empire: although he would have had a good knowledge of the region from spies and local information, the fact that the raid was intended to capture as large an amount of slaves and booty as possible would mean that the best means of transporting the captives and treasure home would be by using the major Roman roads, including those still usable on the Hungarian Steppes (see Map 4).

If true, it is likely that from Constantia the Huns crossed the Danube and moved on Margus. Recognizing his danger, the bishop of Margus left the city unseen and joined the Huns before he could be handed over. At this point he agreed to betray the city. Returning, he convinced the troops in the city that they should attack the Huns, but as the Roman forces advanced to battle, Attila ambushed them and then went on to capture the defenceless city.[30]

Having captured Margus, Attila may still have been wary about the possibility of a Roman attack on his loot-bearing troops and so may have sent a proportion of his men to scout the regions to the east. It was these forces that accounted for the 'ravaging' of Viminacium. Their task was to keep any garrison of Viminacium occupied, as well as scouting and reporting to Attila the arrival of possible Roman reinforcements from the east.

Attila and the main body of the troops then moved west, with Attila himself leading the assault on the city of Singidunum. When it became clear that he still had freedom of action due to Roman inactivity, Attila advanced further into Roman territory and ravaged the region around the major city of Sirmium. Although it has been suggested that the 'capture' of Sirmium resulted in the Huns' 'annexation' of Pannonia II, this is not mentioned elsewhere so must remain a remote possibility.[31]

At an unknown point an embassy from the East arrived, led by the Eastern *magister militum* Aspar, at this time commanding the army in the Balkans.[32] A cease-fire was quickly negotiated.[33] Doubtless this was welcomed by Attila, as it allowed him to return home unmolested with all of his captured booty, probably taking the shortest route possible under the supervision of the agreement with Rome.

Unknown to Attila, an event occurred that would lead to increased tension with the West in later years. When Sirmium was laid under siege the bishop of the city entrusted the church's collection of silver vessels to Attila's secretary Constantius, with instructions that it be used to pay the ransom for the bishop himself or, if he was dead, to ransom other citizens of the city. Constantius absconded to Rome and used the vessels as security against a loan of gold from a banker, only later returning to serve Attila.

The 'Eastern' Campaign of 442

Although the truce had allowed Attila to leave the empire unmolested, the treaty was only valid for the year 441. Consequently, when the campaign season for 442 opened and there was still no sign of the troops that Theodosius II had sent to invade Africa, Attila determined upon a second campaign.

However, there was doubtless more to his decision than simply the absence of the expeditionary army. Possibly the most vital factor in his

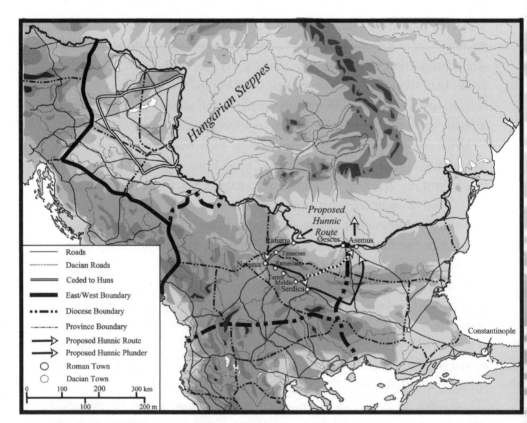

Map 8: The Hunnic Attack in 442.

decision was Constantinople's actions in the previous year. Rather than sending all available troops to face the Huns, the East had simply sent a military commander to sue for a cease-fire. This was not the action of an empire willing to face the Huns in battle.

Accordingly, Attila launched a second invasion. Following the proposal above that the first attack was on the western fringes of the East's dominions in the Balkans, this time – and with no obvious opposition to his attack – Attila struck east. Again, the little information in the surviving sources does not allow the tracking of a definitive campaign route, but by comparing the places listed to their location on the map it is possible to suggest an itinerary for the assault. However, it should be remembered that as usual this is hypothesis, not documented fact.

Attila and Bleda – who had in theory been forced into joining the attack due to Attila's actions the year before – crossed the Danube at Ratiaria before attacking and ravaging the city.[34] However, this was not the main focus of the assault. Probably moving on from Ratiaria and bypassing the small settlement of Timacum, the Huns arrived at the city of Naissus.[35] Here they employed all of their ingenuity – and possibly the service of captive engineers – to lay siege to the city. Priscus takes up the story:

The Scythians were besieging Naissus, a city of the Illyrians on the River Danuba.[36] ...Since the barbarians were destined to take this populous and well-fortified city, they made progress with every attempt. Since the citizens did not dare to come out to battle, the Scythians, to make the crossing easy for their forces, bridged the river from the southern side and brought their machines up to the circuit wall. First, because their access was easy, they brought up beams mounted on wheels, upon which men stood who shot across at the defenders on the ramparts. At the other end of the beams stood men who pushed the wheels with their feet and propelled the machines wherever they were needed, so that one could shoot successfully through the openings made in the screens. In order that the men on the beam should fight in safety, they were sheltered by screens woven from willow covered with rawhide and leather to protect them against other missiles and whatever fire darts might be shot at them. When in this manner a large number of machines had been brought up to the wall with the result that the defenders on the battlements gave in because of the clouds of missiles and evacuated their positions, the so-called 'rams' were brought up also. This is a very large machine. A beam is suspended by slack chains from timbers which incline together, and it is provided with a sharp metal point and, for the safety of those working it, screens like those described. With short ropes attached to the rear men vigorously swing the beam away from the target of the blow and then release it, so that by its force all the part of the wall facing it is smashed away. From the walls the defenders tumbled down wagon-sized boulders which they had prepared for this purpose when the machines were brought up to the circuit. Some they crushed together with the men working them, but they could not hold out against the great number of machines. The barbarians entered through the part of the circuit wall broken by the blows of the rams and also over the scaling ladders which were set against that part which was not crumbling and the city was taken.

Priscus, fragment 6.2, trans. Blockley.

The 'beams' mentioned in the story are reminiscent of the 'cranes' described by Thucydides.[37] Although the Huns may already have known of similar methods of siege-craft, due to this apparent imitation and the probability that a group of nomadic tribes from the east will not have been conversant with Thucydides, it may be that the episode adds weight to the suggestion that either captured or 'renegade' Romans were being used to design and build the siege engines used during the assault on Naissus.

Whatever the origin of the machines, the city fell and was put to the sack. The severity of the destruction was such that seven years later (449) when travelling as an envoy to the Huns, Priscus 'found the city empty of people … [only] …In the Christian hostels there were some people suffering from disease'.[38] Naissus was effectively wiped off the map for a century.[39]

The manner in which the Huns disposed of the booty and captives from Naissus is unknown, but it is unlikely that large numbers of wagons containing the loot from Naissus followed the Huns as they moved further into the Roman Empire. As a result, it is more sensible to see the Huns dispatching their plunder back to the Hungarian Steppes under the guard of a detachment from the main force. The route it took is unknown, but it may not have been using the same route past Naissus and Ratiaria: during their advance, and relying upon foraging for supplies to keep their 'pre-sack' baggage to a minimum, it is likely that these areas would not feed the Huns or their captives on their return journey.

In this context a puzzling entry in Priscus' account may be explained. After the conclusion of the war Attila 'demanded that the people of Asemus hand over the prisoners in their hands, both Roman and barbarian.'[40] Priscus then goes on to explain that the garrison of Asemus

> inflicted much damage upon the enemy, for they did not merely fight from their walls, but gave battle outside the ditch against an overwhelming force ... [and] ... the Huns, their numbers melting away, slowly withdrew ... [and the Asemuntians followed and] ... set out to attack them [the Huns] a good distance from their [the Asemuntians'] home, and falling upon the enemy unawares, they made the Hunnic spoils their own.
>
> *Priscus, fragment 9.3.42–50, trans. Blockley.*

The difficulty of correctly assembling the isolated fragments of Priscus into the correct chronological order is nowhere more problematic than here. Due to the lack of any context the resistance of Asemus has been dated to 433, 441, 442, 443 and 447.[41] Yet at least three of these dates can be eliminated. In 433 Attila was not yet king and so did not have the ability to make demands. It is clear from other evidence that by 443 the war was over and the Huns had gone from the empire (see below). In addition, 441 can also almost certainly be discounted: if the Hunnic army had suffered a reverse in 441 it is more than likely that the campaign of 442 would have targeted Asemus in revenge for the loss. Consequently, 433, 441 and 443 have been removed from the equation.

Although in theory the event could have been at the end of the main conflict in 447, this would be an odd addition to the resulting treaty, as Asemus was within the boundaries of the Roman lands to be evacuated in that treaty, so making the demand redundant. Therefore, it was in the treaty negotiations of 442–3 that the Huns demanded that captured Romans who had escaped captivity when the Asemuntians attacked them should be returned unless 12 *solidi* was paid per person in ransom.[42] As a result, the *magister militum per Thracias* (Master of the Troops in Thrace) and the imperial ambassador both wrote to the people of Asemus to demand a ransom. The Asemuntians refused, as they claimed the prisoners had gone.[43]

Consequently, it is here assumed that the Huns attacked by the Asemuntians were a detachment passing the city with their prisoners and spoils – probably from Naissus – when the garrison, realizing that the Hun guards were not strong enough to attack the city themselves, made a foray in strength and defeated the Huns, releasing the captives and retaking a large amount of booty. Realizing that the defeat was a stain on his reputation, since doubtless it was following Attila's orders that the Hunnic column had used that route, Attila was later forced to negotiate with Theodosius in order to restore his status.

In the meantime, Attila and Bleda continued down the Morava River valley towards Serdica. Although Priscus also attests that Serdica was ravaged, this was in no way to the same level as the sack of Naissus: after their attack Serdica remained a functioning city, so it is more likely that only the region surrounding the city was devastated, not the main urban centre itself.[44]

This may have been because of new information: in the spring of 442 the expedition to recover Africa from the Vandals, which had got no further than Sicily, was recalled and landed at Constantinople. Aware that they were again encumbered by wagon-loads of treasure from their exploits and that this could hamper them if they needed to fight a battle, the brothers decided that discretion was the better part of valour and withdrew from the empire.[45]

The war appears to have been over – at least for most of the affected regions – by 21 August 442, as a law was passed concerning affairs in Illyria and the neighbouring regions.[46] It may be at this point, as the main Hunnic army passed Asemus, that the Asemuntians emerged to release the Huns' captives as they passed the city, but as Priscus does not mention Attila or Bleda by name this has been deemed unlikely: the defeat of either of the two Hunnic leaders in person would almost certainly have been mentioned by Priscus.

443: The New Treaty

Unwilling to face a third Hunnic invasion, despite the return of the army from Sicily, Theodosius entered negotiations with Attila and Bleda. Although usually seen as a sign of weakness, the use of money to 'buy off' an enemy was to become a standard method of dealing with aggressive foes. To an empire whose wealth was infinitely more vast than that of the Huns and their successors, the payment was less than the cost of funding a large military campaign and of recruiting new troops to face those lost in battle, whether the fighting ended in a defeat or a victory.

Accordingly, Anatolius, the *magister utriusque militiae per Orientem* (Commander of all Troops in the Orient), was sent to the Hunnic court.[47] The Treaty of Horreum Margi was revised in favour of the Huns: 'fugitives' were to be handed over to the Huns; a payment of 6,000lb of gold was to be paid to cover arrears; tribute was to be set at 2,100lb of gold per annum; for any Roman prisoners who had escaped a ransom of 12 *solidi* was to be paid, and if not then the 'fugitive' was to be handed over; and the Romans would not give sanctuary to any 'barbarian' who fled to them.[48]

Priscus then goes on to claim that the payments were so large that the citizens of the East were brought to penury, 'selling on the market their wives' jewellery and furniture' and that as a result 'many killed themselves either by starvation or by the noose'.[49] Clearly this is an exaggeration. According to one early fifth-century source, aristocratic families in Rome might have an annual income of 1,000–1,500lb of gold: and the very wealthiest around 4,000lb: it is difficult to argue that a mere 2,100lb constituted a crippling amount.[50]

As a consequence, the demands of Attila should not be interpreted as being extortionate, since in this respect his demand was probably a well-computed amount demanded from Rome to demonstrate his power to his subordinates but also not to force the Roman emperor to deny the treaty due to loss of political face.[51] In addition, the fact that the amount demanded was now at the same level as that paid to the Persians will also have greatly enhanced Attila's prestige.[52] On the other hand, the East was at this point probably short of immediate funds due to the vast expense of the (failed) expedition to retake Africa from the Vandals, so although this description should not be taken at face value it is likely that an immediate demand for taxes was made to pay the tribute.

The last two points have resulted in at least one historian suggesting that the peace treaty here assigned to 443 should instead be dated after the war of 447, noting that if the treasury had been so denuded of funds that the aristocratic families were forced into supplying money then it is odd that in

444 the empire reduced its taxes and in 455 would finance the restoration of the Danubian fleets and frontier defences.[53] This must remain a possibility, but the law applies only in the eastern prefecture of Oriens and it is only the arrears of tax that have been negated, not the taxes themselves. Furthermore, as the region had recently been attacked by the Sasanids the reduction may have been a recognition that the taxpayers needed time to recover rather than reflecting the wealth of the East. In addition, the law may also have been aimed at improving loyalty to the empire in the region and of thus producing a more regular stream of income, rather than accepting that the empire had no need of the money.

Whether Eastern citizens committed suicide or not, for Attila and Bleda the treaty was an overwhelming success: at a stroke they had humbled the East and acquired a vast amount of booty, gold and enhanced personal reputations that would ensure their positions for a very long time in the future.

The West[54]

With a new peace treaty in place with the East, in 443 Attila turned his attentions to the West. There is no doubt that Attila wanted the West to offer him the same sort of conditions that the East had offered. Yet he was a realist: his uncles had been close friends of Aetius, and he respected the Western general as an opponent. He also knew that the West was not in the same financial condition as the East, and so he was willing to demand less money.

With these realities in mind, Attila sent envoys to Aetius demanding the opening of negotiations. Aetius, wary of Attila and half-expecting an attack, sent Cassiodorus and Carpilio, his son from his first marriage, to the court of the Huns to arrange a treaty with Attila.[55] It may also be now that a man named Orestes, who was to feature in the last decades of West Roman imperial history, was sent as *notarius* (secretary) to Attila to replace the now-deceased Constantius.[56] With large parts of Hispania in the hands of the Sueves, Africa under the control of the Vandals, large areas of Gaul being controlled by the Goths, with an ongoing war with the Franks and with other areas of Gaul in rebellion, Aetius knew that he could not afford a conflict. On the other hand, Aetius may have felt that a new treaty was necessary, since he had always employed Hunnic troops both as *bucellarii* and *foederati* and would not want the source of these troops cut off. Failure to deal with Attila could have resulted in large numbers of Hunnic warriors being recalled. Although many of these troops would have no reason to join Attila, since they were serving in the Roman army under their own independent leaders, Attila could easily use their failure to leave the West as a pretext for war, or at least a devastating raid.

An agreement was quickly reached. Sadly no details have survived, but it is likely that, mirroring Hunnic practice at other times, the Romans agreed to pay 'subsidies'. Although this is nowhere explicitly stated, it is possible that a *novel* issued by Valentinian in 444 relates directly to the need to pay money to the Huns.[57] Finally, and hopefully to ensure adherence to the treaty, hostages were exchanged. According to the later Cassiodorus in his *Variae*, his forebear, the envoy Cassiodorus, succeeded in agreeing a peace treaty with Attila, as part of which Carpilio remained at the Hunnic court as a hostage for some time.[58] It has been suggested that it was at this time that Aetius ceded territory in Pannonia to the Huns.[59] Given the fractured nature of the sources, this must remain a possibility. However, as the West had relinquished control of Pannonia to the East in 337 (see above) and so were no longer in a position to cede the region, this has been deemed unlikely.

With peace assured along the Roman borders, in theory the Huns could continue their expansion to the north of the Roman Empire. Instead, events took a dramatic and unexpected turn.

Chapter Six

Sole Rule

444/5

For the next two or three years little is heard of the Huns in Roman sources. Elated with their success and with their reputation as invincible warlords secure, doubtless Bleda and Attila spent these years in strengthening and expanding their positions in *barbaricum*. Yet despite Attila probably leading the way in the campaigns against Rome, Bleda undoubtedly remained the Huns' principal leader.[1] Under the joint rule of Bleda and Attila the Hun Empire reached the height of its power, with all Hunnic tribes being brought under the control of a centralized authority based on the Hungarian Steppes: there is no longer any mention in the sources of Hunnic kings other than Bleda and Attila.[2]

Yet there was obviously some festering tension between the brothers. Whether this was caused by the proposed opposition of Bleda to the attacks on the Roman Empire, or due to Attila's jealousy concerning Bleda's successful military campaigns, or because Attila wanted control, or was part of an internal tribal/clan-based conflict is unknown.[3] In either 444 or 445 tensions had become so unbearable that Attila took drastic action: he had Bleda assassinated.[4]

It has been suggested that the 'dwarf' Zercon was in part responsible for the estrangement between Bleda and Attila. Zercon, who had been presented to the Roman commander Aspar during his campaign in Africa against the Vandals (430–34), had been captured by the Huns during one of the attacks on the Balkans and had become Bleda's 'jester'. He was able to throw 'all except Attila into fits of unquenchable laughter by his appearance, his dress, his voice, and his words, which were a confused jumble of Latin, Hunnic, and Gothic.'[5] The falling-out of the brothers has been attested as due, at least in part, to the advice Zercon was giving to Bleda.[6] This must remain a possibility. Zercon, who was apparently a Moor in origin, may have counselled Bleda not to attack the empire, in direct contrast to Attila's strategy. Since Attila found Zercon immeasurably repulsive, the concept that the senior leader of the Huns was taking advice from a disgusting foreigner would certainly have caused strain in Attila's relationship with Bleda.

There is another fact which, although of dubious accuracy, may have been an ingredient in the brothers' falling-out. Jordanes, who is not the most reliable source for Hunnic history, tells the story of 'The Sword of Mars':

> The historian Priscus says it was discovered under the following circumstances: 'When a certain shepherd beheld one heifer of his flock limping and could find no cause for this wound, he anxiously followed the trail of blood and at length came to a sword it had unwittingly trampled while nibbling the grass. He dug it up and took it straight to Attila. He rejoiced at this gift and, being ambitious, thought he had been appointed ruler of the whole world, and that through the sword of Mars supremacy in all wars was assured to him.'
>
> *Jordanes*, Getica, *35 (183).*

Whether the story is true or not is impossible to determine. However, the tale may record a claim made by Attila in order to justify his decision to assassinate Bleda: Attila could hardly be destined to be 'ruler of the whole world' and 'supreme in all wars' if he was second in precedence to Bleda and obviously he was the chosen one of the gods.

Whatever the cause and justification for the killing of Bleda, that Attila ordered the killing appears to be beyond dispute. Yet the death of Bleda was not accepted by all of the Huns' tributaries. For example, the Akatziri revolted from Hunnic rule when news of the assassination arrived, and part of Attila's political agenda from this point forward was the return of 'imperial' relatives who sought sanctuary in the Roman Empire.[7]

Obviously one of the most important actions Attila took after the death of Bleda was to send embassies to both the East and the West to inform both halves of the empire that he was now sole ruler. In return, it has sometimes been suggested that it was in 445 that Aetius in the West sent his son Carpilio and the 'Tribune and Secretary' Cassiodorus as envoys to Attila.[8] As usual with undated events, this must remain a possibility; however, it is here assumed that the date of this embassy was 443 due to the factors outlined in

Chapter 5. However, it should be noted that there is no evidence to suggest that at this point Attila attempted to change the terms of the treaties with Rome, so any Western envoys would appear to have had little to do except to confirm that Attila was accepted as the sole king of the Huns.

446

Unlike the Western envoys, those from the East soon had to face stronger demands. Although uncertain, this is the most likely date for the account of Priscus in which he states that

> Attila again sent envoys to the Eastern Romans demanding the fugitives. They received the envoys, honoured them with many gifts and sent them away saying they had no fugitives. Again, he sent others, and, when they had been enriched, he sent a third embassy and a fourth after it. For the barbarian, mindful of the Romans' liberality, which they showed out of caution lest the treaty be broken, sent to them those of his retinue whom he wished to benefit.
>
> *Priscus, fragment 10, trans. Blockley.*

Although seen by Priscus as simply a means of enriching his envoys, it is likely that Attila was serious in his demands for the return of members of the 'royal dynasty' who had fled after his assassination of Bleda, as well as of subject peoples who had crossed into the empire in the hope of escaping Hunnic dominion. The possibility that these individuals or peoples could be financed by the East in an attempt to overthrow him appears to have been one of Attila's most enduring fears.

Attila's worries may not have been helped by the fact that by 446 Theodosius was in a far stronger position than he had been in early 443, when he had signed the earlier treaty. In September of 443 he had issued orders to strengthen the Danube flotilla, repair the damaged and destroyed military camps along the Danube frontier, and set in motion steps to bring the garrisons up to full strength.[9] In addition, a new wall was constructed across the Thracian Chersonese near Agara to protect the region from marauding bands of raiders, and it may be that the Hexamilion wall across the Isthmus of Corinth was also begun at this time.[10] Over the ensuing three years Theodosius' orders had been fulfilled, meaning that he was no longer as fearful of Hunnic attack as he had been.

In addition, the East was now at peace with both Sasanid Persia and the Vandals. When the latest envoys arrived, probably in 446, Theodosius rejected the envoys' demands, but suggested further negotiations. Sadly for the East, Attila refused.[11] Instead of further negotiations, he ravaged Roman territory in the region of Ratiaria, the headquarters of the Danubian fleet, and ravaging bands of Huns spread across Thrace.[12]

In response, Theodosius ordered Senator, 'a man of consular rank', to negotiate with Attila. Wary of being killed or of being captured and then of not being accepted as an ambassador by the roving bands of Huns along the Danube frontier, Senator instead sailed along the Black Sea coast to Odessus, from where he set out overland to Attila's court.[13] The date of Senator's embassy is uncertain, but it may be that it was sent either late in 446 or early in 447.[14] The fact that his embassy is not mentioned again could be due to a drastic change in circumstances.

With tensions once again rising along the Danubian frontier, on 26 January 447 an event occurred that altered the dynamic between Attila and Theodosius. Early in the morning a severe earthquake damaged the Walls of Constantinople: stretches of the wall fell into heaps of rubble, and fifty-seven towers collapsed.[15] Believing it to be a sign of God's wrath, Theodosius II dismissed his carriage and refused to wear either his jewels or his diadem. Instead, he walked in penitence for 7 miles from the Great Palace to the Hebdemon, the military parade ground outside the city walls.

Attila had already proved by his attack on Ratiaria that the new defences organized by Theodosius after the war of 441–2 were not as effective as the Romans had hoped. When news arrived of the earthquake, Attila appears to have taken this as a divine sign and ordered a full-scale assault on the Balkans.

The War of 447

A mighty war, greater than the previous one, was brought upon us by King Attila. It devastated almost the whole of Europe and cities and forts were invaded and pillaged.

Marcellinus comes, *447.2, trans. Croke.*

Crossing the Danube in the region of Ratiaria again, the Huns followed the upper reaches of the River Margus before turning south-east and bludgeoning their way down the valley of the River Hebrus. Once inside the empire they ravaged the provinces of Illyricum, Thrace, both Dacias, Moesia and Scythica.[16] They reached as far as the shores of Pontus and Propontis and possibly Thermopylae, and allegedly every city except for Heracleia/ Perinthus and Adrianople was captured.[17] It should be noted, however, that the 'Europe' listed by Marcellinus is not the modern continent but 'Europa', the name of one of the provinces in the Balkans.

Using all of the place names listed in the sources it is possible to propose a route and hence a strategy for Attila's assault, but it should be noted that this is hypothesis: the place names given in the sources may by no means be exhaustive but simply those used by the authors to highlight the plight of the regions under attack. The list includes the cities of Ratiaria, Serdica, Philippopolis (Plovdiv), Arcadiopolis (Lulebergas), Calliopolis (Gelibolu), Sestus (Eceabat), Athyras, Adrianopolis and Heracleia (Marmara Ereğli).[18]

As they had in 442, it is likely that the large Hunnic army used the territory of their allies on the north of the Danube as a stepping-stone towards the main objective of Constantinople. Crossing the Danube and ravaging the territory around Ratiaria, it would appear that the Huns then used the main Roman roads to head towards the capital. Bypassing the ruined city of Naissus, the Huns damaged the area around Serdica in the search for supplies and booty before advancing past the minor settlements of Bagaraea, Lissae and Burdipta and reaching Philippopolis. Although it is likely that the three smaller towns were sacked, it is by no means certain: Attila's main target was Constantinople and he would have known that speed was essential if he was to reach the city before the walls damaged in the earthquake could be repaired.

Learning of the attack, and knowing that the main target was almost certainly Constantinople, '[Theodosius] sent Aspar and the force under his command, along with Areobindus and Arnegisclus. The generals were badly beaten in the battles they fought, and Attila advanced to both seas, the Black Sea and that which washes Calliopolis and Sestus.'[19]

Although Priscus claims that the generals were 'badly beaten', he does not list any of the battles they allegedly fought. As a consequence, it is possible to assume that the three commanders were given orders to block, or at least

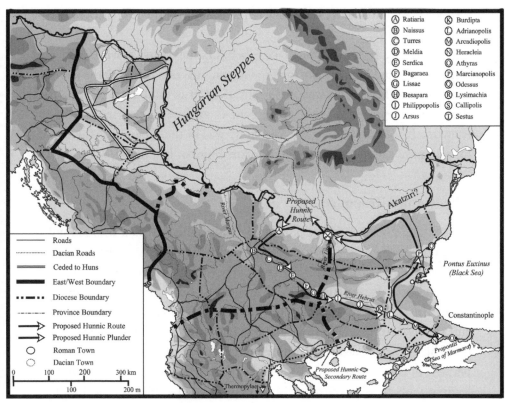

Map 9: The Hunnic Attack in 447.

slow, the passage of the Huns while avoiding a major battle if at all possible. The easiest way of doing this was to garrison the major cities on Attila's route, slowing him down and threatening his rear once he had passed.

Ignoring the Roman armies, leaving Philippopolis the Hunnic army bypassed Arsus and Burdipta before reaching the next major city on their route. It is probable that one of the Roman armies attested as blocking the 'route' to the capital was a small force stationed at Adrianople. This was one of the major cities in the Balkans and its position astride the main road towards the capital allowed it to act as a bastion against attack. However, as the city wasn't Attila's objective it was simply side-stepped, with the forces inside being deemed by Attila as of no consequence: Attila simply needed to reach Constantinople before the walls were repaired. It is also unlikely that the Huns would devastate the surrounding region to the extent of other cities under fear of a surprise attack by the Roman garrison. This accounts for the claim noted above that Adrianople was one of the few cities to escape devastation.

Leaving the heavily-fortified city behind, the Huns marched on past Arcadiopolis and Heracleia before moving on Athyras. Although the territory surrounding these cities was again ransacked, it is unlikely that Attila took the time to capture the main urban centres as time was on the side of the Romans. It was almost certainly while he was in the region of Athyras that his advanced scouts returned and informed him of bad news.

The Roman Response

Despite the presence of the *praesental* armies, the East had decided not to risk a decisive battle.[20] This had become standard policy, since the payment of subsidies was usually cheaper than replacing the losses in men and equipment brought about by a major battle, whether the outcome was a victory or a defeat. Instead, it appears that the Roman troops were divided into three and sent out to cover all of the possible land routes to Constantinople. It is quite likely that at least two of the major cities that 'resisted' the Huns did so because of the presence of a large body of troops under one of the empire's leading generals as a garrison. Although these troops failed to halt the attack, their presence had one major impact.

As soon as news arrived of the Huns' invasion, it would have been known in Constantinople that Attila's main target was the imperial capital, where the damaged walls had left the city vulnerable. In response, Flavius Constantinus, the *praetorian prefect*, organized the racing factions of the capital, the Blues and Greens, to repair the walls, giving sections of the wall to each group and then organizing a competition to see who could repair the wall the fastest.[21] Slowed by the Roman armies in the Balkans, by the time Attila's scouts arrived at the city they found the walls repaired and the city no longer open to attack. How Attila took the news is not known, but frustration would have been the least of his emotions.

Attila could not risk attacking Constantinople as he had little hope of provisioning a 'stationary' army in a 'region ruined by invasion and earthquake, and threatened by the outbreak of disease': plus he had no fleet to complete the siege.[22] However, one thing now appeared certain: the Romans were unwilling to face the Huns in the field, preferring to cower behind the walls of their cities. In these circumstances it is likely that Attila took the decision to send out at least one major sub-army from his main force to ravage the previously untouched regions to the south of the main road between Naissus and Constantinople. Such a large raiding party would explain the inclusion in the sources of attacks on Lysimachia, Calliopolis, Sestus and possibly even an attack on Thermopylae, although the latter is uncertain. The Huns finally reached the Propontis, a stretch of water now known as the Sea of Marmara.

In the meantime, Attila took advantage of the Romans' unwillingness to fight by targeting a major city that did not have the strong garrisons found on the route towards Constantinople. Turning north, and so avoiding having to travel over ground already ransacked by his troops, Attila and the main Hunnic army headed towards Marcianopolis, so coming within sight of the Black Sea, known in Roman times as the Pontus Euxinus. Knowing he was not being followed by a Roman army and aware that the Roman forces had been positioned to protect Constantinople, it is possible that Attila launched a major assault upon Marcianopolis. This would account for the 'devastation' of Marcianopolis as recorded in the sources.

The Battle of the River Utus

Having finally sacked a major city, Attila and his Huns took the roads to the north before following the Danube west. However, he was not to have things all his own way. The Roman *magister militum* Arnegisclus, probably learning of the vast amounts of booty and large numbers of captives taken by the Huns, ignored the orders to avoid battle and headed to cut off Attila's route home. At the River Utus, west of Marcianopolis, Arnegisclus and his men blocked the crossing. Attila had little choice but to fight a battle. Sadly, no detailed record of the course of the conflict survives. All that is known is that the battle was hard-fought, with heavy casualties on both sides, but eventually the Huns won the crossing and Arnegisclus was killed.[23] Despite the 'Phyrric' nature of the battle, the course of the conflict provided a major political victory for Attila.[24] He had devastated large parts of the Roman Empire and proved that the Roman army was unable to defeat him.

The Balkans: Cities and Population

The war in the Balkans was seen as a devastating calamity for the region by (near) contemporaries. The Huns are said by a Gallic chronicler to have devastated no fewer than seventy cities, and the monk Callinicus in his *Vita Hypatii* (*Life of Hypatius*) records the murder and enslavement of so many people that 'Thrace could never possibly have been repopulated as it was before.'[25] In the face of these claims, it is surprising that the region continued to operate as an economically viable unit. A close scrutiny of the available evidence, plus an analysis of the methods and aims of the contemporary writers, suggests that the claims are not as straightforward as they appear.

Cities

Map 10, which has attempted to show all of the known major settlements in the region attributable to the Romans, has in excess of 100 towns and cities. However, that seventy of these could have been sacked by the Huns in a single year is difficult to accept. If nothing else, the time needed to sack each city would limit the number that could be taken in one campaign season. On the other hand, there are two ways in which the report in the *Gallic Chronicle* can be accepted as possible 'fact'.

The first of these relates to the use of the term *civitas* or *polis* ('city', 'town') in ancient sources. Although this is now applied to a heavily-urbanized region, in antiquity the phrase *civitas* or *polis* 'comprehended not just the urban centre, but also the surrounding territory, the fields, villages and towns that belonged to the city'.[26] Indeed, it has been postulated that of a total Roman population of c.50 million, only around 6 million lived in urban centres.[27] Consequently, when ancient sources mention the 'sack' of cities it is necessary to remember that in many cases the central, fortified settlement may have been left untouched, with only the surrounding region being pillaged.

If this is then applied to the Hunnic War, then the number of 'cities' attacked by the Huns could easily rise to a far higher number than first expected, since a Hunnic 'attack' on any of the surrounding territory and villages of a city could qualify as a 'sack'. Since roving Hunnic cavalry in search of supplies would have travelled great distances to obtain them, this would account for a large number of the cities recorded as ravaged by the *Gallic Chronicle*.

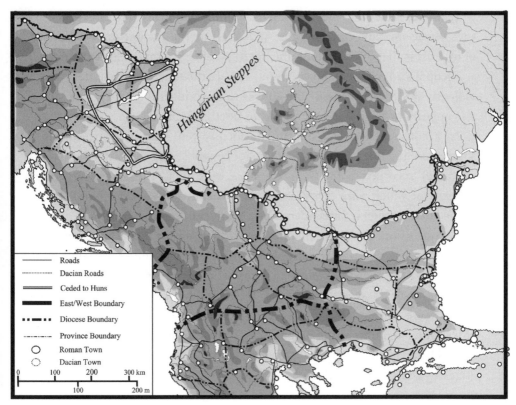

Map 10: The Balkan Cities.

The second explanation also relates in some ways to the use of the term *civitas*. From the end of the fourth century – possibly due to the major war with the Goths between 376 and 382 – there came into existence in Thrace a large number of non-urban sites that were fortified. These can be grouped into two types: 'quasi-urban centres' with an area of 1 hectare or above, and 'fortified villages' of less than 1 hectare. Most occupied highly-defensive positions, and although some appear to have been built of dry stone walls by local people, the majority were constructed under imperial aegis of stone and mortar.[28]

Although the majority were probably built for strategic considerations – not least to slow down barbarian raiders who had penetrated the frontiers – some are 'best considered as fortified iron-working centres'. The implication here is that for the 'barbarians' at least one reason for ravaging the region was to source iron ingots for their own use once they had returned home.[29]

Yet there is one other piece of important information in this context. These sites were sometimes called 'cities' (*civitates*) by the ancient sources.[30] Also of interest is that excavations at the 'fortress' of Iatrus on the lower Danube, at Nicopolis ad Astrum, and at Novae – where the town's headquarters were violently destroyed – all date the attacks to the mid–fifth century. The same also appears to be true of excavations in Scythia Minor.[31]

As a consequence, and due to the inconsistent way in which ancient sources use the term *civitatis/civitates*, it is possible that the vast majority of the 'cities' recorded by the *Gallic Chronicle* were in fact these small forts, the majority of which were either simply overwhelmed by superior numbers of Huns or were quickly surrendered by a vastly outnumbered garrison.

In conclusion, the above demonstrates the need for care when assessing the sources. Such large–scale destruction of cities is almost certainly too much for a single year's campaign, even when the alleged mobility of the Hunnic attacks is taken into account. It is far more likely that many of these 'sacks' were simply large raiding parties ravaging the countryside around cities rather than besieging and sacking the metropolitan centres listed, or were the overrunning of a small 'fortlet' that was never intended to withstand attack by a large invading army.

Population

During the invasions that Attila launched against the East it has been suggested that the Huns killed or took captive 'large numbers of provincials', and that Hunnic actions 'denuded Rome's Danubian provinces'.[32] This may be true, and the fact that the Balkans had been 'bled dry' may have been one factor in Attila's decision to turn west in 451. Yet although it must be accepted that the attacks would have had a severe effect on the region, it may be that this has been overestimated by both the ancient sources and modern historians using them.

The Hunnic attacks obviously had a major impact upon the population of the Balkans. Modern historians have attempted to calculate how many people were taken into captivity by the Huns in the 440s. These estimates begin with the claim in the sources that the Huns who invaded Anatolia in 395 took 18,000 prisoners.[33] It is then suggested, following later sources, that as the attacks on the Balkans were nearer to the Huns' homes, more prisoners could be taken. To support this theory, it is noted that in the late

530s the Huns, Sclaveni and Antae are recorded as taking 200,000 prisoners and in 539 the Huns on their own allegedly took 120,000 prisoners.[34]

In addition, using basic maths it has been suggested that the attack of 447 that captured seventy cities actually took ten major cities and sixty lesser ones. Therefore calculating that the larger cities would have yielded 7,000 prisoners and the smaller cities 1,000 prisoners each, plus 'one-fourth as many' from the countryside, then the attack of 447 took '10 x 7,000; plus 60 x 1,000; plus one-quarter of this total', resulting in 70,000 plus 60,000 giving 130,000 for the cities, plus 32,000 for the countryside, giving a total of 162,000 prisoners in one attack.[35]

It is hard to believe that the Huns would either need such a large number of slaves in one year – especially as, even were they to trade most of them to tribes far away from Rome, such a large number would inevitably lead to a collapse in the price – or more importantly have the logistical ability or the number of men needed to organize and supervise the trek from the Balkans back to the Hungarian Steppes for such a vast number of people, especially when under the threat of a possible Roman attack.

As to the numbers, it should be accepted that slaves were used by the Huns to manage their herds of livestock, act as household servants, cup-bearers, orderlies and bath attendants, as well as to be presented as gifts to the allied Goths, Gepids, Heruls, Sciri and Rugi. This is true, but the sheer number implied by these calculations makes it hard to believe that these societies could have accepted so many Roman slaves without it having a major internal effect. In the first century BCE the Romans had captured such vast numbers of slaves that they had to quell several major slave revolts using large numbers of regular troops.

Although ancient peoples appear to have accepted slavery as 'the norm', this does not mean that individuals would be happy to be enslaved, especially when being taken from a 'civilised' society to one classed as 'barbarian'. In the specific case of the Huns, slaves' unhappiness may have been increased by the fact that they were forced to participate in Hunnic religious ceremonies.[36] To Christian captives, such ceremonies would have been seen as an abomination.

On the other hand, it should be remembered that 'pastoral societies often … tend to integrate their captives'.[37] This is certainly the case with the Huns, where Priscus records that on one of his embassies he was surprised to find a 'Hun' speaking Greek. On enquiring, it turned out that the man in question had begun life as a captive, but after serving his master well and fighting alongside the Huns – even in their campaigns against his fellow Romans – the man had been given his freedom and preferred a life among the Huns to his old life as a Roman.[38] Obviously this man was one of the lucky ones; the skilled and educated among the captives who were used as secretaries, accountants and architects.[39] Yet for the vast majority of slaves, life would be hard and thankless. Therefore the concept of 162,000 captives being absorbed into the Hunnic 'polity' is difficult to believe.

The capture of slaves was almost certainly one of the reasons for the attack, but possibly a more financially rewarding process would be the taking of captives for ransom, a payment repeatedly asked for by Hunnic envoys to the East throughout Attila's reign. Once the ransom had been paid – and in many cases it certainly was – the captives would be allowed to return to their former lives in the Balkans.

As a result of the above analysis, it is possible to suggest that, although the attack of 447 was the most devastating ever launched on the Roman Empire by the Huns, its severity, and in some cases the effects of the assault, have been overplayed. The number of urban centres captured and the number of slaves taken has certainly been exaggerated. As a consequence, although the war certainly devastated large areas of the region, in most cases this would have been temporary and with the infrastructure remaining intact and a ransomed population being allowed to return, regrowth would have been far easier and faster than is usually accepted. On the other hand, the presence across the Danube of a political entity able to attack at a moment's notice certainly acted as a disincentive to people thinking of living in the region.

Aftermath

The swift penetration of the theoretically strengthened defences along the Danube, the ravaging of a wide area of land, and the defeat of a Roman army at the Battle of the River Utus would have been a great shock to Theodosius in Constantinople. He quickly took action in an attempt to prevent a recurrence of the attack. Before the end of the year the surviving *magister militum* Aspar had been removed from his post, ostensibly as a scapegoat for the defeat but possibly part of the internal political machinations at the court of Constantinople.[40] Theodosius also dispatched envoys to Attila, who in 447 were Anatolius, who had been consul in 440, for a second time and the *magister* Theodulus.[41] In return, Attila sent Scottas, a leading Hun warrior, as his envoy to the empire.[42] For Attila, everything would depend upon the terms he was able to extract from the empire in order to guarantee freedom from further attacks.

The Treaty of 448

Over the winter of 447–8 negotiations continued, until in the New Year a new treaty was agreed between Attila and Theodosius.[43] From his position of strength Attila was able to humiliate the East, so proving to his followers and subjects that resistance to his commands was pointless. The treaty has not been recorded in its entirety, and due to the fragmentary nature of the sources it is unclear which recorded 'treaty' belongs to which year. This has led to confusion and disagreement among modern historians. What follows is a hypothetical reconstruction of the treaty using the few sources that exist, but taking into account the earlier analyses of the previous treaties, especially that of 442.

There were a few 'standard' provisions in the treaty. For the East, the major clause was that the Huns were not to attack the Balkans again. This may not have been a problem for Attila: although the Huns had been victorious at the Battle of the River Utus, Hunnic losses had been high and a repeat would weaken Attila's military arm. For Attila, the standard inclusions were agreements that the East would return 'Hunnic' refugees, especially any of his political opponents who could be capable of causing problems should they return to the Hungarian Steppes financed by the empire. In addition, there was probably a financial clause, but the nature of this clause may have confused both ancient and modern historians.

The financial demand by Attila may have been a repeat of the treaty of 433 and the demand for 2,100lb of gold per annum. The fact that this may have been imposed twice is not usually accepted, since it is assumed that the Huns demanded ever-greater amounts of gold every time they forced the empire to sign a treaty. This may be true, and it is possible that any demand for money has either been overlooked by the ancient sources, or this provision only applies to this treaty, not that of 443. However, it may also have been effectively disguised by Theodosius.

It is usually accepted that Attila was made an honorary *magister militum* by the Western Empire, since the fact is mentioned by Western ambassadors on a mission to Attila.[44] As the political implications of him being appointed prior to 434 are nowhere mentioned, it is assumed that the appointment was after the death of Bleda. Yet while the latter is probable, the former is debatable: although the post of *magister militum* was appointed separately by both East and West, and so there was a distinction in the operational command between East and West, the rank associated with the post was recognized by both. In addition, there may be an excellent reason for the East to bestow the title on Attila which is greater than those proposed for the West. Not only would this theoretically make Attila less eager to invade the East, but in this way the East could disguise what would otherwise be seen as 'tribute' as simply the normal payment of a Roman official. This hypothesis would explain both why there is no mention of tribute by contemporary sources and also give reasonable grounds for Attila being made *magister*.[45]

Whether the 2,100lb of gold refers to the treaties of both 443 and 448 or whether the tribute was disguised by the appointment of Attila as *magister militum*, it must be accepted that Attila made further demands that humiliated the empire more than ever and simultaneously elevated his own status to new, unbelievable heights, although it should be noted that these may not have been part of the treaty agreed in 448.

These stipulations are only recorded by Priscus as having been demanded in 449 prior to his own participation in the embassy of that year. Both are included in the letter carried by the Hunnic envoy Edeco to Constantinople in 449. One is that the 'market in Illyria was not on the bank of the Danube, as it has been before, but at Naissus, which he had laid waste and established as the border point between the Scythian and the Roman territory.'[46] That a city so deep inside Roman territory was needed as a trading centre was due to the second part, and the main claim made by Attila. This was that the Romans should 'stop cultivating the land which he had won in the war … a strip of territory five days' journey wide and extending along the Danube from Pannonia to Novae in Thrace'.[47] Assuming that travel in one day would equal 20 miles, this would mean that an area 100 miles deep would need to be relinquished.

It has been suggested that the main aims of this claim would be the protection of the Huns from surprise Roman attacks and the deprivation of the defensive line of the Danube from the Roman army. This may indeed have been one of the main purposes, but there are two further factors that have been overlooked. One is that it would humiliate the empire to an even greater degree than the capture of Carthage by the Vandals. In the latter, the need of the Romans to mount a major overseas expedition to retake the territory was certainly a mitigating factor in the acceptance of the Vandal takeover. In the case of the Danube, there were no such extenuating circumstances: the territory taken was only a few days' journey overland from the capital of East Rome. Theodosius II was facing the most humiliating capitulation since his predecessor Theodosius I had been forced to allow the Goths to remain within the empire under their own leaders in 382.

The second is political. At a stroke, by forcing Rome to accede to the abandonment of its own territory, Attila would raise his profile above that of Theodosius: there could be little doubt in the eyes of his contemporaries, and especially of his followers and the subject peoples of the Hunnic Empire, that Attila was the supreme political and military commander of the age. In addition, it is possible that at least in part Attila's demand was in order to gain land on which to settle vassals, so establishing a form of 'buffer state' between himself and the empire, although this is speculation.

In the same year as signing the treaty Attila received a little-known refugee from Gaul whose importance is little understood. At some point in 448 a *bacaudic* rising in Gaul was crushed and one of the leaders, a 'doctor and an able man' named Eudoxius, fled to the Huns.[48] His arrival may have helped Attila come to a decision on what actions to take over the coming years.

Yet that was in the future. With his political position secure, for a short time Attila appears to have focused upon settling dependent tribes around the periphery of his empire to protect his rule. As a consequence, his aims changed from conquest to ensuring that the leaders of his protective ring were not allowed to defect to Rome, and to the continued extortion of tribute from the empire to maintain his own financial position.[49] His reign had reached its apogee.

Chapter Seven

Undisputed Rule

449

Although Attila had reached the height of his political and military power and had defeated the Roman East, events conspired to maintain the tension between both halves of the Roman Empire and the Huns. With the East, this concerned the embassy in which Priscus was to play a large part. With the West, it was in part due to events in 441, eight years earlier.

The West

Priscus of Panium describes the affair when meeting the Western ambassadors during his own diplomatic journey to Attila in 449:

Here we met with some of the 'western Romans', who had also come on an embassy to Attila – the Count Romulus, Promotus governor of Noricum, and Romanus a military captain. With them was Constantius whom Aetius had sent to Attila to be his secretary, and Tatulus, the father of Orestes; these two were not connected with the embassy, but were friends of the ambassadors ...The object of the embassy was to soften the soul of Attila, who demanded the surrender of one Silvanus, a dealer in silver plate in Rome, because he had received golden vessels from a certain Constantius. This Constantius, a native of Gaul, had preceded his namesake in the office of secretary to Attila. When Sirmium in Pannonia was besieged by the Scythians, the bishop of the place consigned the vessels to his (Constantius') care, that if the city were taken and he survived they might be used to ransom him; and in case he were slain, to ransom the citizens who were led into captivity. But when the city was enslaved, Constantius violated his engagement, and, as he happened to be at Rome on business, pawned the vessels to Silvanus for a sum of money, on condition that if he gave back the money within a prescribed period the dishes should be returned, but otherwise should become the property of Silvanus. Constantius, suspected of treachery, was crucified by Attila and Bleda; and afterwards, when the affair of the vessels became known to Attila, he demanded the surrender of Silvanus on the ground that he had stolen his property. Accordingly Aetius and the Emperor of the Western Romans sent to explain that Silvanus was the creditor of Constantius, the vessels having been pawned and not stolen, and that he had sold them to priests and others for sacred purposes. If, however, Attila refused to desist from his demand, he, the Emperor, would send him the value of the vessels, but would not surrender the innocent Silvanus.

Priscus, fragment 8, trans. Blockley.

This passage is interesting in two ways. The first is that, although Sirmium was a Roman city and therefore the people and goods in it were theoretically 'Roman', the Western court accepted that the vessels that could have been taken in an assault belonged to Attila. A more modern viewpoint would be that the silver plates would remain 'Roman' and that Attila's request would therefore amount to 'theft'. Secondly, it would appear that Attila was using any available pretext to put pressure on the West. Having humiliated the East, and in control of most of *barbaricum* north of the Danube, Attila's remaining areas for conquest were either further to the east or the west; Attila was keeping his options open.

Sirmium had been captured in 441, but it was probably only in 448 that Attila had learned of Constantius' disloyalty, almost certainly from informants after the treaty of 448 gave the Huns nominal control of Sirmium. Once informed, Attila had Constantius crucified. From sources in the West he had then discovered that the vessels had been sold to a Roman church by the banker and probably in late 448 had sent envoys demanding that either the vessels or the banker be handed over.[1]

The envoys sent by the West to defuse the situation were members of the local civil and military elite of Pannonia and Noricum:[2] Promotus, governor of Noricum, and the *magister* Romanus,[3] plus Attila's secretary Orestes and Orestes' father Tatulus, and father-in-law the *comes* Romulus.[4] Orestes was from the part of Pannonia that had been ceded to Attila in 435.[5] The embassy included a new secretary for Attila, another man named Constantius, provided by Aetius.[6] Interestingly, the appointment of secretaries by Aetius for Attila was almost certainly double-edged: it gave Attila the service of men accustomed to dealing with the bureaucratic needs of a large empire, but at the same time it gave Aetius men at the heart of Hunnic politics who could both influence and simultaneously keep an eye on Hunnic affairs.[7]

Confusion surrounds this embassy: it may be that at this time Attila was given the title *magister militum*, plus the concomitant salary, by the West rather than the East.[8] If true, the offer was almost certainly made as a means of deflecting Attila's claims to the Sirmium treasure since, as has already been noted, the West had refused to accede to Attila's demands for the vessels or the banker. Interestingly, no further mention is made in the sources of the dispute. This may be because an unexpected messenger from the West arrived and altered the balance of political power in an alarming manner. It was probably late in 449 that events in Italy gave Attila his chance to go on the political offensive against the West. Immediately prior to this, he had to deal with a multitude of Eastern envoys.

The East

Before the Western envoys had arrived, in the spring of 449 Attila sent Edeco, one of his personal bodyguards, and Orestes as envoys to the East.[9] These talks continued through the summer, when Eslas, who had represented Rua in 435, was twice sent to the East.[10] The last of the return embassies to Attila included Priscus, whose description of the embassy is the only detailed eye-witness account that has survived of Attila and the Huns. Although his description has often been analysed solely from the viewpoint of those interested in Attila and the Huns – as in Chapter 2 – the fact that Theodosius was prepared to go to any lengths to remove his shame is often minimized: for the East the main difficulty remained the extreme loss of face caused by the treaty of 448.

In addition, Theodosius was attempting to divide the Huns by the use of the East's massive financial resources:

> Onegesius had been sent together with Attila's eldest son [Ellac] to the Akatziri, a Scythian people that had submitted to Attila for the following reason. This people had many rulers according to their tribes and clans, and the emperor Theodosius sent gifts to them to the end that they

might unanimously renounce their alliance with Attila and seek peace with the Romans. The envoy who conveyed the gifts did not deliver them to each of the kings by rank, with the result that Kouridachus, the senior in office, received his gifts second and, being thus overlooked and deprived of his proper honours, called in Attila against his fellow kings. Attila without delay sent a large force, destroyed some and forced the rest to submit ... Kouridachus remained amongst his own folk and saved his realm, while all the rest of the Akatzirian people submitted to Attila. He, wishing to make his eldest son king of this people, sent Onegesius for this purpose.

Priscus, fragment 11.241f, trans. Blockley.

This passage is interesting for several reasons. Firstly, Theodosius was clearly more proactive in his dealings with the Huns than is usually recognized. That he was attempting to subvert 'allied' tribes from their alliance with Attila is rarely mentioned by either ancient or modern historians, both of whom tend to portray him as a weak ruler willing to pay Attila whatever was necessary to avoid a conflict.

A second is that although by 448–9 Attila was the sole ruler of the Huns, his control over his empire was not as absolute as is sometimes perceived. If Priscus' account is to be trusted, the Akatziri would have transferred their allegiance to Rome had the Roman envoys followed the correct procedure for the allocation of 'gifts'. On the other hand, it should be noted that Priscus may have been following a traditional Roman practice of ascribing failure to individual treachery or mistake. In this case, the mistake was made by the envoys.

It has been suggested that the Akatziri were actually part of the core Hunnic polity, and were the dominant Eastern half of a Hunnic empire divided in the same manner as the earlier Xiongnu, and that they were 'rebelling' against Attila's sole dominance.[11] This is a possibility, but without further evidence the hypothesis is difficult to prove.

Finally, there is the political aspect to the event. Following the reinstatement of his rule, Attila could possibly have placed Kouridachus as the sole ruler of the Akatziri. However, this may have caused renewed conflict, since many of the tribes would have resented one of their clans being placed in a superior political situation by an alien force. Consequently, Attila took a sensible decision by appointing his eldest son as the ruler of the Akatziri. In this way, he regained control of the situation without the need to cause internal conflict among the tribes.

This was not the only method attempted by the East to regain their supremacy. A sub-text of Priscus' narrative is a plot hatched at Constantinople to assassinate Attila. When the Hunnic ambassador Edeco, who was one of Attila's personal guards, arrived at Constantinople in spring 449 he brought with him letters demanding that the Romans evacuate part of the Balkans as theoretically agreed in the treaty of 448 and use Naissus – now theoretically on the Romano-Hun border – as a trading post. In the letters Attila also demanded that 'highest ranking' ambassadors be sent in return, offering to move to Serdica to receive them.[12]

That the empire still had people living in the disputed region is to be expected. When major cities were ceded in treaties – such as Nisibis in 363 after the death of the Emperor Julian – the limited number of people in an easily-defined area who needed to be evacuated meant that the Roman authorities were able to impose their will. An area of the size that Attila wanted to be depopulated was a different matter: the necessary logistics and the inability of the recently-defeated and demoralized army to control the large and dispersed population doubtless resulted in many simply ignoring any order to leave, hence the demand made in 449.

After the interview Edeco met with Chrysaphius, the emperor's chamberlain. When he expressed admiration for the wealth of the Romans, Chrysaphius promised him wealth of his own if he would desert Attila. Shortly afterwards Edeco appeared to agree to take part in a plot to assassinate Attila. Although offered money immediately, Edeco responded that he needed to return to Attila and instead asked that Vigilas, the official interpreter in the discussions, be sent as part of the return embassy to Attila and that Edeco would give Vigilas instructions as to how the money should be paid; Attila would be suspicious if Edeco was to be found carrying large amounts of money when he returned. This was agreed.[13] Interestingly, it was only at this point that Chrysaphius informed the emperor of the plan and it was approved. Shortly afterwards an embassy led by Maximinus – at this time possibly *comes rei militaris*[14] – set off to meet Attila. Priscus was asked by Maximinus to accompany the mission, with neither man knowing of the plan to kill Attila.

The embassy was put in danger simply because Edeco had returned home and gone straight to Attila and informed him of the plot. The fact that Edeco immediately told Attila can be seen as proof that Attila was able to foster intense loyalty among his subordinates. In response, Attila ordered that the envoys should not be allowed to buy anything other than food 'until the disputes between the Romans and the Huns had been settled', but organized things so that Vigilas was sent back to Constantinople to obtain the money to pay Edeco for Attila's assassination.[15] When Vigilas returned with the money he was accompanied by his son. Interrogated by Attila, Vigilas declared that the money was to buy provisions, horses and baggage animals, as well as to ransom captives. At this point Attila reminded Vigilas that he had ordered that only food was to be bought, before threatening Vigilas' son with death unless Vigilas told the truth about the money. At this point Vigilas broke down and confessed about the assassination plot. Attila now placed Vigilas in chains and sent his son to Constantinople for a further 50lb of gold to pay for the release of his father.[16]

Attila next sent Orestes and Eslas as envoys to Theodosius, exposing his knowledge of the plot and demanding that unless Chrysaphius was handed over he would lay all of the blame on Theodosius.[17] Thankfully for the East, either in 449 or more likely spring of 450 Theodosius again sent Anatolius and Nomus as envoys, and at first Attila 'negotiated arrogantly, but he was overwhelmed by the number of gifts and pacified by their conciliatory statements'. At around the same time Vigilas' son returned with enough money to buy Vigilas' freedom, and a small matter concerning Attila's secretary Constantius was also concluded. Earlier Constantius had been part of a Hunnic embassy and had struck a bargain with Theodosius involving a marriage to a wealthy and well-connected woman. The arrangement had fallen through, but now Constantius was offered a different bride of equivalent wealth and status. The envoys had managed to maintain peace between the Huns and Rome.

However, that was not all: surprisingly, Priscus records that Attila made an agreement with the East that he would 'keep the peace on the same [agreed] terms [and] that he would withdraw from the Roman territory bordering the Danube.'[18] Attila had apparently relinquished his claims to the large region in Pannonia he had claimed in 448. The reasons for the withdrawal are uncertain, simply due to the lack of information in the sources. Priscus includes in his text the description of a discussion in which he was involved with the envoys who had arrived at Attila's court from Ravenna. According to Romulus, 'an ambassador of long experience':

> [Attila's] very great good fortune and the power which it had given him had made him so arrogant that he would not entertain just proposals unless he thought that they were to his advantage. No previous ruler of Scythia or of any other land had ever achieved so much in so short a time ....He was aiming at more than his present achievements and, in order to increase his empire further, he wanted to attack the Persians.
>
> *Priscus, fragment 11.2.585f, trans. Blockley*

Although this is in some respects feasible, the length of the journey outside territories he controlled, plus the fact that he would have to take a very large number of troops with him, would make such a campaign extremely risky.[19] Not only would it destroy his reputation if he failed, but the absence of Attila and a large proportion of the Hunnic army in Persia could easily result in internal revolt, both among any relatives who wanted to claim the throne as well as the large number of subordinate tribes, as proved by events after his death.

However, the most likely explanation is that in between Priscus' embassy and the arrival of Anatolius and Nomus a messenger had arrived from the West with unexpected information. Rather than concentrate on the East, which he had already humiliated, Attila had decided to change the focus of his attention.

Iusta Gratia Honoria

Honoria was the older sister of the Western Emperor Valentinian III. Born in either 417 or 418, in 425 she had been acclaimed as *Augusta* but had been forced to follow imperial policy with regard to the behaviour of an imperial 'princess'.[20] Unfortunately for the empire, it would appear that she was unwilling to accede to these imperial standards:

> Honoria, the sister of the Emperor Valentinian, was defiled by her *procurator* [manager of her estates] Eugenius and conceived. She

was expelled from the palace and sent off from Italy to the emperor
Theodosius.

Marc. com. s.a. 434, *trans. Croke.*

As punishment, Eugenius was tortured and executed, but Valentinian and
his advisors unsurprisingly took a different approach with Honoria. The
latter part of Marcellinus' account, claiming that Honoria was 'expelled',
has usually been discounted. The most common assessment is that the affair
happened c.448, allowing no time for the exile in Constantinople. However,
it is more likely that Marcellinus is correct in his statement. In 434 Honoria
was found to be pregnant by Eugenius and was sent to Constantinople before
this became common knowledge or her pregnancy became obvious.[21] The
little information available suggests that following Valentinian's wedding in
Constantinople in 437 there was a reconciliation between brother and sister
that allowed her to return to Ravenna. What happened to the prospective
child is unknown.

However, this was not the last time that Honoria's actions would cause
problems for Valentinian. Relations between the siblings appear to have
slowly deteriorated again, until in either 448 or 449 she was forcibly betrothed
to Flavius Bassus Herculanus, a wealthy senator, who shortly afterwards,
in 452, was to become consul. Apparently at the same time Honoria was
divested of her title of *Augusta*, although the reasons for this are unknown.[22]
What happened next was to be a factor in relations between the West and the
Huns for the next three years. Priscus tells of the whole affair in an extract
used by John of Antioch that has a surprising twist at the end:

> [Honoria was]…caught in a clandestine affair with a certain Eugenius
> …He was executed for the crime, and she was betrothed to Herculanus,
> a man of consular rank and of … good character. [In response, she] …
> sent the eunuch Hyacinthus to Attila offering him money to avenge her
> marriage. She also sent her ring as her pledge to the barbarian.
>
> *Priscus, fr. 17 = Joh. Ant. fr. 199.2* = Exc. De Ins. *84*.[23]

The exact dating of Hyacinthus' journey is uncertain. It has been suggested
that Honoria sent Hyacinthus in spring of 449 and that both the Eastern and
Western embassies described by Priscus were in response to Attila's return

envoys. In this hypothesis, only an event of this magnitude would explain the seniority of the envoys – especially of the Western diplomats – and the convoluted negotiations involved. The fact that the Hyacinthus affair is not mentioned by Priscus is allegedly due to the high-stakes political game being played, as well as the embarrassment the whole affair was causing the West, which resulted in the negotiations being secret.[24] This may be true, but can almost certainly be dismissed due to the fact that Priscus was writing at a later date when the whole incident had become common knowledge, so would have no need to omit the truth from his account. In addition, it is likely that his 'friends' who had been involved in any 'secret negotiations' would have told him about it.[25] Consequently, it is assumed here that the betrothal probably took place after the embassy from the West concerning the Sirmium gold plates, analysed above, and Hyacinthus' journey dates to at least the summer of 449.[26]

Although the whole story has been dismissed by some historians, it is almost certain that the event happened.[27] Several explanations are possible, but probably the correct interpretation of the passage is that Honoria was betrothed to Herculanus, a man deemed to be safe from imperial pretensions, but a man in whom she had no interest and probably loathed. As a result, she petitioned members of the court for help. When this was not forthcoming – since the courtiers were either supporters of Valentinian or of Aetius, both of whom appear to have agreed upon her marriage – she sought elsewhere for aid. The only other individual of any political or military standing who could possibly help her was Attila, who was an 'honorary' *magister militum*. As a result, she offered him gold to take her side in the disagreement at court.

By those who accept the story as fact, the act of attempting to enlist the aid of a barbarian is usually interpreted as a betrayal, since in hindsight the effects of her request were to be calamitous. This is a mistake. In the first place, Attila was an imperial officer and her last resort. Secondly, this was not the first time that a member of the court had appealed to the Huns for help against their opponents at court: Aetius owed his career to that ability. Finally, Honoria's mother had actually been married to a 'barbarian': Alaric's brother-in-law and successor Athaulf.[28] There was a family tradition of dealing with 'barbarian' individuals only indirectly connected with the court.

As proof of her identity, Honoria sent her ring with the messenger. This gesture mirrored a common act of giving a specific personal item to a messenger as proof that the bearer was acting on the sender's behalf. In return, Honoria would have expected Attila to simply make a threat and then the engagement would be annulled: after all, Aetius had been returned to power in a similar manner. Honoria, however, gambled and lost.

Once the affair became known, Valentinian was obviously furious. Hyacinthus was tortured and beheaded, and Honoria allegedly only survived due to prolonged pleas for clemency from Placidia, the mother of the warring siblings. Finally coming to a decision, Valentinian banished Honoria from court and she was surrendered to the custody of Placidia.[29] Circumstances now hinged upon Attila's response to Honoria's request.

Attila

As noted, Attila's reason for change of policy concerning the conquered territories is unknown, but maybe Honoria's message had resulted in Attila's decision to turn west. On the other hand, there may have been one further reason why Attila gave up Pannonia. Priscus records that when he was informed of Honoria's 'treachery', Theodosius sent messengers to Valentinian to recommend that he surrender Honoria to Attila.[30] It is feasible, although impossible to prove, that Attila had sent envoys to Theodosius demanding that the latter add his weight to Attila's demands concerning Honoria. This would probably not present a problem for Theodosius: although the senior emperor, he would have known that Valentinian did not need to heed his advice, so for little effort he was able to regain the Danube frontier and ease tensions with Attila. In addition, it has been suggested that simply by sending envoys to Valentinian he would divert Attila's attention to the West, plus 'redeem himself' with Attila for complicity in the plan to assassinate the Hun ruler.[31] The combination of these theories is probably accurate: the East needed time to recover from Attila's assaults, and up to now the main difficulty remained the relationship between Theodosius and Attila, a relationship damaged by the assassination attempt. At little cost to himself, Theodosius had 'atoned' for the assassination attempt and recovered lost territory.

Attila and the West

Despite Theodosius' actions, Attila's decision to change his focus from the East to the West had probably already been made prior to Theodosius' embassy to Ravenna. At the same time as sending an embassy to Theodosius, he certainly sent envoys to the West demanding that Honoria be handed over, although these do not seem to be recorded. The fragmentary nature of the sources means that the different embassies mentioned have to be carefully assessed and placed in a reasonable chronological order, and the result is that those embassies recorded are described here as being sent after the death of Theodosius and the accession of Marcian.

In a short period of time, not only had Attila demanded that the West accept a marriage between himself and the emperor's sister along with half of the Western Empire as a dowry, he had also managed to obtain the East's acquiescence in the proposal. It has been suggested that the sending of these two embassies demonstrates that Attila wanted a peaceful conclusion to demands; probably because he had concluded that he had already shown that the East could not defeat him and consequently the weaker West had no chance against him.[32] It is indeed possible that Attila was hoping that he could reach a 'peaceful' solution to his demands, and believed that the Roman Empire would simply negotiate a settlement. Yet he could not really have expected the West to accede to losing half of its territory as a dowry, so if he was looking for a peaceful solution there is no knowing what terms could have been reached with the West that would have been acceptable to Attila, and vice versa.

Despite the attention of historians being focused upon the (possible) letter from Honoria and the ensuing political fallout, as well as Attila's relinquishing of territory inside the Eastern Empire, there were other factors affecting Attila's decision upon what course to take. The most important of these were two major developments that have not necessarily received the attention they deserve.

Franks

The first, and most important, was the news that the king of the Franks had died. Previously, the king's younger son had been sent on an embassy to Rome where he had been adopted by Aetius and had been promised support in his claim to rule.[33] When the Frankish king died, the younger son seized the throne. The support of Aetius had proved to be decisive, so the elder son of the Frankish king decided to appeal to Attila, the only alternative, for aid in his claim to the throne.[34] Obviously, any attempt to support the elder son would break Attila's agreement with the West and precipitate war. It is possible that it was Attila's decision to support the elder son which was the cause of the break between Attila and Aetius, and that the 'Honoria' affair was just court politics with no real repercussions, later embraced by Roman writers intent on using the *topos* (a standard historical theme) of an individual's betrayal of the empire as the cause for the war.[35] Sadly, it is impossible to know whether or not this is the case.

Eudoxius

Possibly of similar importance, though not receiving its due attention, was the earlier arrival of Eudoxius, the exiled leader of the *bacaudae* in Gaul, at Attila's court.[36] Eudoxius' fate is nowhere mentioned, but if he was to follow the example of the majority of political exiles then it is likely that he bombarded Attila with stories of how the peoples of Gaul were unhappy with Roman rule and how they would rise against the empire if a strong man arrived to lead them. As the tales of the multiple *bacaudic* revolts would now be circulating, it is possible that Attila became convinced that if he marched on Gaul then the majority of the population would rise up and support him.

Gaiseric

The later historian Jordanes, along with the *Chronicle of Fredegar*, claims that at least part of the reason why Attila contemplated the attack on Gaul was because he was 'bribed' by Gaiseric to attack the Goths.[37] Allegedly this is because Gaiseric was afraid that Theoderic would try to avenge his daughter, who had been married to Gaiseric's son Huneric but was then mutilated and sent home for allegedly planning to poison Gaiseric. Obviously, if Theoderic was already at war with the Huns, Gaiseric would be safe. In addition, Priscus claims that Attila attacked Gaul and the Goths partly because he was 'laying up a store of favour with Gaiseric'.[38]

These statements are usually dismissed by historians; however, there is one additional piece of information that may hint that at least some of this story is true. In 450 Eudocia reached the age of 12 and according to Roman custom she was now allowed to marry. In theory, she should have gone to Carthage to marry Huneric. The fact that she did not may hint at strained relations between Gaiseric and Valentinian, possibly caused by the knowledge that Gaiseric had suggested to Attila that he invade Gaul.[39]

In conclusion, although the two claims concerning a Vandal-Hun 'alliance' remain a possibility, they must be classed as of doubtful reliability, largely because Gaiseric had little influence over events on the Continent and, despite his control of the sea, would be unable to help Attila in central Gaul. In theory, Gaiseric could halt the grain shipments to Rome, but this would both invalidate the treaty of 442 and simply annoy the Romans rather than damaging the Goths. Further, any reasons for Attila wishing to retain Gaiseric's friendship and alliance are not made clear by Priscus. It is perhaps best to assume that in the confusing times of late 450 and early 451 envoys were travelling throughout the Western Empire and to Attila in the east, including those from the Vandals. What was really said at these meetings was unknown, even at the time, but gossip within the empire may have suggested that the Vandals wanted Attila to invade the West and that Attila agreed with the Vandal envoys who suggested that the softest target for Attila was Gaul. The truth will never be known.

Death of Theodosius: Marcian Assumes the Throne

Before Attila could take any action, events in the East again intervened. The Emperor Theodosius injured his spine after falling from his horse.[40] Despite the best efforts of his physicians, on 28 July 450 he died in Constantinople at the age of 49.[41] The only surviving male member of the House of Theodosius was now Valentinian in the West. In the East the dynasty was represented by Pulcheria, the elder sister of Theodosius and Augusta. As the empire could not be ruled by a woman, Pulcheria chose to marry a man named Marcian, who was then crowned emperor. Interestingly, Pulcheria quickly convinced Marcian to execute Chrysaphius, the man who had orchestrated the failed assassination attempt on Attila. Although this could be seen as a conciliatory gesture to Attila, in reality it was part of the internal political upheaval that took place in Constantinople after Theodosius' death.

With the elevation of Marcian there was an immediate change in policy in the East. Unlike his imperial predecessors, who had been forced to rely from a young age upon ministers and generals, Marcian was a mature individual who had spent his career rising through the ranks of the army. His confidence in his military abilities was high, and despite Aspar's political and military strength, Marcian had no fear that a strong *magister militum* would force him to relinquish the reins of power, as had happened in the West.

On learning of the change of regime, Attila sent envoys to Constantinople. It has been plausibly suggested that these were 'intended to test the commitment of the new imperial regime to the peace settlement renegotiated by Anatolius and Nomus eight months earlier'.[42] Marcian refused to ratify the agreement: Attila may have been raising the stakes by his use of the word 'tribute' and Marcian may have been angered by the phrasing of Attila's demands. Rome paid 'subsidies' or 'gifts', not 'tribute'.[43] The first Eastern envoys sent by Marcian in return, led by the *magister* Apollonius, carried the message that 'if he [Attila] remained at peace they would give him gifts but if he threatened war they would bring against him men and equipment no less powerful than his own.' Attila refused to meet them.[44]

The net result of these events was that, probably in mid-450, Attila had received two pieces of news in quick succession. The first was that the West had rebuffed his envoys and refused to surrender Honoria, despite Theodosius' intervention. The second was that Theodosius had died and that Marcian, the new, more militant emperor of the East, was not going to pay the 'subsidies' that Attila expected.

Winter, 450–451

The difficulties in establishing a chronology of events is nowhere as evident as for the period prior to Attila's invasion of Gaul. Consequently, the multitude of embassies described here could have taken place any time between autumn 450 and spring 451; however, the description of events given below is believed to be the most logical.

Probably in late 450 Attila sent ambassadors to Ravenna: 'To the ruler of the Western Romans he sent envoys to declare that Honoria, whom he had engaged to himself, should not be wronged at all and that, if she did not receive the sceptre of sovereignty, he would avenge her.'[45] Attila had used Honoria's inclusion of her ring to change Honoria's request into something far more alarming for the West. Although it was common practice to use personal items as a sign that a message was from an individual, Attila had chosen to interpret the inclusion of the ring as a proposal of marriage. From the West came a denial that Honoria could be married to Attila, since she was already either engaged or married to another; the wording is imprecise but the overall meaning is clear. Furthermore, the envoy reported that the West had refused Honoria any regal rights to the throne, 'since the rule of the Roman state belonged not to females but to males'.[46]

At around the same time Attila also sent envoys to Marcian in Constantinople concerning the 'appointed tribute'.[47] Marcian replied that he 'would not consent to pay the tribute agreed by Theodosius and that if he [Attila] kept the peace he would give him gifts, but if he threatened war they would bring against him men and weaponry equal to his own.'[48] From a position of strength and security, in a very short space of time events had conspired to increase the tension along Attila's long border with the Roman Empire.

In response, Attila decided to up the stakes. Probably still in 450, but possibly in early 451:

> [Attila] ... again sent men of his court to Italy that Honoria might be handed over. He claimed that she had been betrothed to him and as proof sent the ring which she had despatched to him in order that it might be shown. He also said that Valentinian should resign to him half of his empire, since Honoria had received the sovereignty of it from her father and had been deprived of it by her brother's greed. When the Romans maintained their earlier position and rejected all of his proposals, Attila pressed on more eagerly with his preparations for war, and mustered all of his fighting force.
>
> *Priscus, fragment 20.3.8f, trans. Blockley.*

Sadly for Attila, the change of regime in Constantinople and the West's refusal to grant his demands now meant that he had been denied his 'rights' by both emperors. Calmly accepting this state of affairs would have encouraged his rivals to see him as weak and so have precipitated a civil war among the Huns and their subjects: Attila was the leader of a 'vast military machine which demanded action and an influx of rewards, otherwise it could easily turn on him.'[49] He had to declare a war. He now had to decide which option to take. If, as Priscus claimed, Attila was thinking of invading

Persia at some point, any such plan was now abandoned: there could be no possibility of him leading his troops to Persia with a potentially hostile empire on his southern border.[50]

Attacking the East remained feasible, but there were three major problems with this. Possibly the most important was that the provinces that were within easy reach had been plundered on several occasions in previous years, so the amount of booty available would be minimal. Furthermore, ravaging already ravaged areas was unlikely to put enough pressure on Marcian to force him to agree to Attila's terms. More importantly, Marcian was not Theodosius II: he was a mature, strong-willed individual who would not yield to pressure from his courtiers. The political contacts that Attila had fostered in Constantinople and that had almost certainly helped to hinder imperial policy-making had been rendered powerless. Finally, Marcian was a military man. If Attila invaded, unlike his predecessors – who had used the army sparingly to avoid having a 'military dictatorship' such as existed in the West – Marcian could gather as many troops as he needed and personally lead them against Attila.[51] Attila had led successful raids, but although the only 'set-piece' battle at the River Utus had been a victory it had been a costly one. A larger army led by the emperor in person was a much greater threat to the Huns.

In conclusion, the East had always been stronger than the West and it was now led by a military emperor who was prepared to marshal the forces of the whole East to defeat Attila. Attila knew when to cut his losses. Accordingly, Attila's envoys in Constantinople agreed a treaty with the new emperor that was 'surprisingly favourable to Rome': the concept that this was due to the 'wisdom of his East Roman interlocutors' is mistaken.[52] Attila simply wanted a peaceful border in the East.

On the other hand, the letter from Honoria changed the political dynamics with the West. If he so desired, Attila now had a 'valid' reason to invade the West, in effect claiming Honoria's hand in marriage and thus, at least in theory, becoming overlord of a sizeable section of the Western Empire.[53] On their part, the West actually believed that Attila now wanted half of the empire, whether as a dowry or as conquest.[54] Obviously, the West now offered a far more tempting and realistic target than the East. Furthermore, and according to Jordanes, Attila had 'long thought' about a campaign in the

West.[55] In reality it was only Aetius' relationship with Attila's predecessors that had saved the West from Hunnic attack.

There then remained the question of where to invade. Attila knew that attacking Italy would be problematic, since Aetius would be ready to defend the Alps against any attempt to enter Italy, and theoretically Aetius had enough forces to enable him to block the passes. Gaul, on the other hand, was a different proposition. The West was in the process of fragmenting and Attila could use this to his advantage. On the northern border, the Franks were in turmoil as the younger son of the recently-deceased king cemented his power, but if Attila attacked the elder son could assume the throne and so give Attila an allied power-base on the Rhine. In fact, as already noted, it has been suggested that the Frankish succession crisis was the main cause of the war. Obviously both Aetius and Attila now believed the Franks to be in their sphere of influence, but if the hypothesis of the succession being the main cause of the war is correct, the question remains as to why Attila advanced as far south as Orléans.[56]

Away from the Rhine, in the interior the repeated risings of *bacaudae* plus the proposed urgings of Eudoxius suggested that the Huns could receive a surge of popular support that would overthrow Roman rule in the north of Gaul, and the Goths in Toulouse had recently been at war with Rome so there was a good chance that the Goths would ally with the Huns and divide Gaul between them. Bearing all of this in mind, as a wily political leader Attila knew that there was a good chance that he could play the various factions in Gaul against each other by the use of intelligent diplomacy.

Despite the apparent weakness of the West, Attila apparently believed that Aetius, who he may have known from childhood, was a capable adversary and a more than competent commander. As a result, it is possible that before he decided to attack Gaul Attila attempted to have Aetius removed.[57] Whether true or not, the fact that the story had at least a limited circulation clearly demonstrates that Aetius was held in high esteem by contemporaries and it was at least feasible that Attila would not want to face the Roman in battle. Despite these possible reservations, Attila prepared for war.

Chapter Eight

The Invasion of Gaul

Opening Moves

At the opening of the campaign season in 451 Attila gathered his armies ready to travel west. It was probably at this point that Attila's diplomacy changed tack:

> Attila ... sent ambassadors into Italy to the emperor Valentinian to sow strife between the Goths and the Romans, thinking to shatter by civil discord those whom he could not crush in battle. He declared that he was in no way violating his friendly relations with the empire, but that he had a quarrel with Theodorid, king of the Visigoths. As he wished to be kindly received, he had filled the rest of the letter with the usual flattering salutations, striving to win credence for his falsehood. In like manner, he despatched a message to Theodorid, king of the Visigoths, urging him to break his alliance with the Romans and reminding him of the battles to which they had recently provoked him. Beneath his great ferocity he was a subtle man, and fought with craft before he made war.
>
> *Jordanes*, Getica, *36 (185–6)*.

The embassy to Ravenna also claimed that in his new role as co-emperor and 'guardian of Roman friendship, he would wage [war] only against the Goths'.[1] No doubt he asserted that in this he was only doing his duty, both as the prospective husband and co-ruler of Honoria and also as honorary *magister militum*. He may have also referred to past history, as this was not the first time that an army of Huns had destroyed Germanic intruders in the West: in 437 they had annihilated the Burgundians.

That Attila had also sent a similar message to Theoderic in Toulouse demonstrates the aim of his new political policy. It was doubtless intended to create division and turmoil in both the Western court and the court of the Goths, ensuring that the two would not cooperate against him. A joint

Romano–Gothic force would present serious competition for Attila's forces. Yet, given the nature of his coming campaign, it is possible to suggest that Attila was hoping that the Goths really would join him, dividing Gaul between the two powers.

However, Attila had underestimated Aetius. Following his advice, Valentinian stood firm and rejected the claim. In part this was almost certainly thanks to the fact that Aetius had his own spy network both within Gaul and within the Hunnic court. Aetius may have been receiving information from several sources in Attila's court, not least those men he had sent to serve as Attila's secretary, as well as other similar officials. It is even possible that Aetius' son Carpilio was still a hostage with the Huns at this time and able to inform Aetius of Attila's possible plans.[2] It is also a remote possibility that many of the older Huns (who were contemporaries of Aetius and knew him from his days as a hostage) did not support Attila in his attack on the West and did all they could to stop the invasion.

From this multitude of sources, it is likely that Aetius was able to inform the emperor and senate that Attila was also sending envoys with the stated aim of forming a 'barbarian coalition' of Huns, Goths, Franks and Alans in Gaul. Attila's message to the Franks was quite simple: it was a call to arms for supporters of the older son of the dead king, and an attempt to gain support against the younger brother, the adopted son of Aetius. Attila also sent envoys to Sambida, the leader of those Alans who had been settled in the region of Valence by Aetius. According to Jordanes, Sambida now considered the possibility of joining Attila, although if so this was no doubt out of fear of Attila rather than disloyalty to Aetius.[3] Attila's strategy appeared to be beginning to work.

Amid all this frantic political activity it was the Hunnic envoys to the Goths that were the main thrust of Attila's policy. In a direct contradiction to the message to Rome, Attila had sent a message to the Gothic king Theoderic urging him to break his treaty with the Romans, and remember instead the recent defeats he had suffered at the hands of Aetius.[4] At the same time, Aetius was using Attila's duplicity for his own purposes, sending embassies to Theoderic to request an alliance and informing him of Attila's claim that he was going to attack the Goths. Unsure of whom to trust and of what Attila's intentions actually were, Theoderic initially decided to remain neutral and follow his own policies.[5]

The Western Alliance[6]

For his part, Aetius began an attempt to build a 'Western Alliance' to face the alliance being attempted by Attila. Apart from envoys to the Goths, Aetius also sent embassies to all of those peoples who had signed treaties to serve as *foederati* when called upon. Obviously, he could rely on at least a large percentage of the Franks, the supporters of the deceased king's younger son who was his own adopted son.[7] At the same time he sent messengers to the 'Sarmatians', which is an alternative and poetic name for any of the nomadic tribes from the east, but in this case denotes the Alans of Sambida around Valence and those who had settled under Goar further north (see Map 11). Despite the appeal from Attila to join with the forces from the east, Sambida now bowed to Roman pressure and agreed to fight against the Huns.[8]

In his bid to join together the military powers of the whole of the West, Aetius also sent messengers to several distinct political entities that had formed in the West.[9] One of these was the *Armoriciani*, the semi-independent natives of Armorica, by this date possibly under 'British' leadership. Another was the *Liticiani* or 'Liticians', of unknown origin but perhaps the remnants of old units of *laeti* now living on the extreme edges of the empire but still willing to serve the Romans.[10] Also included are the *Ripari* (Riparians), Franks from northern Gaul, and the *Olibriones*, 'once Roman soldiers and now the flower of the Allied forces'.[11] It has been suggested that the *Olibriones* were old Roman units of *riparienses* from northern Gaul, now serving the Franks. By this time these units were probably largely manned by Franks, although the new recruits may have been trained in traditional Roman fighting techniques by the Roman officers and their 'descendants' in command of the units.[12] An unexpected addition to the list was the Saxons, which would appear strange given their isolation from events, unless they had established otherwise-unknown enclaves in North Gaul, possibly around the regions of Bologna (Boulogne) and Bessin (see Map 11).[13] Jordanes also notes the inclusion of several tribes of 'Celts' and 'Germans', although these are not individually named. Finally, Aetius managed to convince the Burgundians who he had settled in Gaul to also join the alliance. Despite the agreements of all of these people, the main concern for Aetius remained enlisting the aid of the most powerful force in Gaul: the Goths of Theoderic.

Immediately prior to the invasion of Gaul, the envoys from both Ravenna and Toulouse appear to have returned. Now aware that Ravenna would never

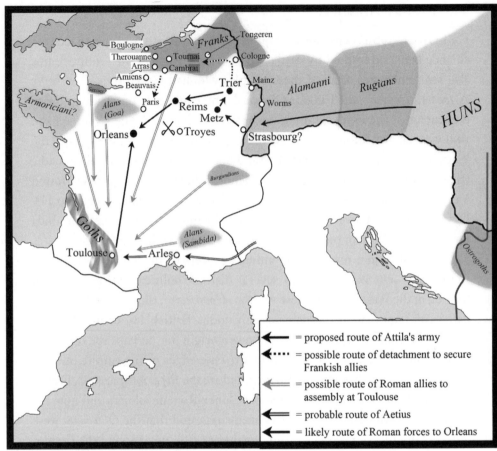

Map 11: Attila's invasion of Gaul.

accept his demands, Attila's response was to become more aggressive, and he appears to have changed the nature of his envoys. Rather than sending Huns as ambassadors, Attila sent two embassies, both composed of Goths, to Constantinople and to Italy. It may be that Attila was intent on keeping his military leaders close to help in the upcoming war rather than sending them away as envoys. According to the *Chronicon Paschale*:

Attila, who was from the race of the Gepid Huns, marched against Rome and Constantinople with a horde of many tens of thousands. And by means of a certain Goth ambassador he declared to Valentinian emperor of Rome, 'My master and your master Attila commands you through me to make ready a palace for him. And likewise also to Theodosius the emperor he made the same declaration in Constantinople by means of a certain Goth ambassador.'

> *Chronicon Paschale*, s.a. 450, *trans. Whitby and Whitby.*[14]

If accurate, the text implies that before crossing the Rhine Attila had ordered that at least some troops were to ravage the borders of the Eastern Empire, although the claim by the chronicler that the embassy took place in 450 and was sent to Theodosius, plus other anachronistic difficulties, suggests that the chronicler himself was a little confused about events. On the other hand, the fact that immediately after the embassy the *Chronicle* reports that Aetius sent to the Goths to ask for an alliance suggests that these events took place in 451 as Attila led his men West, rather than 450 as attested in the *Chronicle*. Of equal importance, the extract demonstrates that Attila had given up on Valentinian and Aetius and was now solely intent upon gaining an alliance with the Goths against Rome.

The passage further hints that Attila had not neglected his homeland: at the same time as his main force moved west, another group of Huns skirmished in the Balkans, probably in an attempt to pin down the Eastern forces and prevent cooperation between the two empires.[15] The envoys sent to the East had, in effect, declared war and Attila would have known that with the main Hun army in Gaul there was a chance that the new and aggressive Eastern emperor Marcian could take advantage and cross the Danube to attack the Huns' homeland.

In early 451 Attila arrived on the Rhine. He immediately set his men to building boats using wood from the German forests, before crossing the Rhine and entering Gaul 'as if he had the right to ask for a wife that was owed to him'.[16]

The Invasion of Gaul*

Despite being called a 'Hun' army, Attila's army was actually composed of many different tribes. Sidonius provides a list of those tribes allegedly

---

* The main thrust of this text was first proposed in *Aetius: Attila's Nemesis*, Barnsley, 2012. What follows here is an attempt to analyse the invasion of Gaul from the viewpoint of Attila, rather than that of Aetius.

joining with Attila's attack, yet it should be remembered that in some cases the poem may be following traditional literary motifs, rather than accurately enumerating the tribes involved.[17]

The tribes listed include the Geloni from the region of the Volga, the Neuri and Bastarnae from the Ukraine, the Sciri from the region of modern Odessa, the Rugi from Pomerania, the Bructeri from the Weser and the Thuringi from Bavaria.[18] Although possibly following literary traditions rather than being an accurate list of the tribes involved, the fact that such a wide variety of tribes is listed implies that this was a major coalition under the Huns. Also included is a contingent from those members of the Burgundians who had remained in their original homeland around the Vistula, rather than taking up Aetius' offer of land in Gaul. Finally, those Franks who supported the claim of the deceased king's elder son appear to have joined Attila en route. However, the main allied contingents were provided by the Ostrogoths, under their leaders the brothers Valamir, Thiudimer and Vidimer, and the Gepids under their king Ardaric. In fact, Valamir and Ardaric were even recognized by Attila himself as being of far higher value than the other kings.[19]

The course of the Hunnic attack on Gaul is sparsely attested and open to different interpretations. The main problem is the fact that medieval ecclesiastical chronicles exaggerated the effects of Attila's attacks. The medieval chronicles include a list of towns that claimed to have been attacked by Attila, yet many of these towns are now known to have escaped unscathed.[20] What follows is a list of the towns noted as being attacked, taken largely from the *Acta Sanctorum* (*Acts of the Saints*), a collection of minor *hagiographies* (biographies of saints), which include in the text stories concerning the behaviour of religious leaders as their towns were attacked by the Huns, plus an analysis of the accuracy of the claims.[21] Along with the accounts of Gregory of Tours, Sidonius Apollinaris and Jordanes, among others, these help to expand on the course of the war.

It is obvious that Attila marched through Germania towards Gaul, although the fact that the Alamanni are not mentioned in any of the sources concerning the invasion suggests that they either simply bowed to the inevitable and let him pass unhindered, or that the Huns passed to the north of Alamannic territory.[22]

Reaching the Roman frontier, it seems that the invading forces crossed the Rhine near Koblenz.[23] The first city that Attila is known to have attacked was Metz, on 7 April (Easter Eve).[24] Metz was quickly taken and sacked.[25] Following this early success, Attila 'ravaged a great number of other cities'.[26] The meaning of the term 'ravaged' is open to question. Most authorities assume that the towns were stormed and sacked, but this would have taken time and the speed of the Hunnic advance suggests that this was not the case. In the context of the war and of the late Roman Empire it is more likely that, as in the Balkans in 442–3 and 447, in reality a large proportion of the towns 'ravaged' were not themselves attacked; rather their supporting territories would have been scoured by the Huns for provisions for their large army, while the inhabitants cowered behind the city walls.[27] After this the areas 'ravaged' would have needed a large amount of time to bring them back to full productivity. However, some of the more strategically-important towns, and any towns that were inadequately defended, were no doubt attacked and sacked in the traditional manner.

Several towns are described in the *Acta* as being attacked. Reims was captured and sacked, with its bishop (Saint) Nicasius being killed, and Tongres (Tongeren) was also sacked, although its bishop, (Saint) Servatius, escaped to die shortly thereafter.[28] According to the *Gesta Treverorum* (*Deeds of the Treveri*), Trier was also attacked, an event possibly supported by excavations in the twentieth century.[29] Other towns alleged to have been attacked during Attila's invasion are Strasbourg, Worms, Mainz, Cologne, Cambrai, Arras, Tournai, Thérouanne, Amiens and Beauvais.

It is possible that either Strasbourg or Worms were attacked and sacked, as they were on the route towards the centre of Gaul. Yet the claims that Cologne, Tournai, Cambrai, Thérouanne and Arras were also sacked would appear to be unlikely. Instead, it is probable that a small picked force was separated from the main army and sent north in an attempt to force the Franks to submit to Attila's nominee for the Frankish throne. The Frankish king would in return be expected to establish a firm base, organize supplies for the invading army, and recruit troops for the upcoming campaign (see Map 11). As Attila was expecting a military reaction from the Romans, the 'Frankish' detachment would have been given orders to move quickly, so it is likely that these towns had their territories 'ravaged' by the invading Huns as they marched to rejoin the main force and in their search for supplies for their large army, rather than being captured and sacked.

Yet there is another possible explanation for the widespread 'devastation' of northern Gaul. Attila may have moved his army in separate columns to help with foraging, which strategy would also explain how the Huns were able to 'sack' so many towns. The main force may have moved from Metz to Orléans with two or more contingents operating on its flanks. This would have been difficult for the Romans to oppose because there were many threats and the Roman commander of the Gallic army may not have been strong enough or mobile enough to do more than withdraw ahead of Attila.[30]

However, on reflection this would appear to be unlikely. Attila would not have known how the different groups within Gaul were going to respond to his invasion. Nor did he know of the likely deployment of potential enemies. The chances are that, apart from the 'Frankish' detachment, he would have wanted to keep his troops concentrated to meet any threat from the Romans. The majority of damage not caused by the main force is probably attributable to either the troops sent to the Franks or to the activities of the Hunnic scouts as they scoured the countryside for supplies and information.

In addition, thankfully for the future capital of France, Paris was bypassed. Although its safety is normally attributed to the intervention of (Saint) Genevieve, in reality at this period the 'city' was small and insignificant. What is more likely is that the city itself was ignored by the Huns – who were intent upon rejoining Attila – rather than being saved by divine intervention: as usual, only the surrounding territories were scoured in the search for supplies.[31]

The Roman Response

One factor emerges from the Huns' attacks on the cities of Gaul: all of the 'sacked' cities were taken quickly before the Huns pressed on to new targets. This can be contrasted to the siege of Aquileia in the following year.[32] From this evidence it would appear that the towns and cities of Gaul did not have large garrisons, in which case the men who had once been expected to defend them may have been removed to reinforce the Gallic 'field army'. This may have been according to Aetius' orders: no doubt he wanted to concentrate as many troops as possible to face the Huns. By contrast, that he decided to abandon the cities to their fate implies that Aetius was desperate for recruits and had not yet come to an agreement with the Goths, the main military force in Gaul apart from the empire.

Apart from this there is no evidence for the activities of the Gallic army when Attila invaded Gaul. Despite the possible withdrawal of troops from the majority of cities, it remains likely that Aetius left garrisons for the more important cities. However, the main body of the Gallic army appears to have been ordered by Aetius to retreat in front of the advancing Huns, heading for either Toulouse in the hope of a Gothic alliance, or to Arles to join with Aetius when he crossed the Alps into Gaul with part of the Italian army.

While the Huns were ravaging the north-east of Gaul, Aetius crossed the Alps from Italy with 'a thin, meagre force of auxiliaries without legionaries (*tenue et rarum sine milite ducens robur in auxiliis*)'.[33] It would appear that he had either been anticipating a Hunnic attack on Italy after their diplomacy had neutralized the Goths, or that he had realized that the Goths would not help to defend Italy so he needed to leave a strong force behind in case of a Hunnic assault.[34] Once across the Alps Aetius would have been expecting to meet the Gallic field army before joining the Goths and advancing to face the Huns.[35] With the Goths remaining neutral, Aetius travelled to Arles and pondered his next move. The remainder of the Italian army was left in Italy, partly to guard the emperor from attack across the Alps, but possibly also to deal with any unrest in Italy: at this moment of crisis the crops in Italy had failed and the region was threatened with the prospect of famine.[36]

In desperation, Aetius made a final attempt to win the support of Theoderic against Attila. Despite the gravity of the situation, and contrary to expectation, Aetius did not travel to Toulouse in person. Instead, Aetius, intent on using the best man for the job, sent Avitus. Avitus was a 'favourite' of King Theoderic I, having first visited the Gothic court in either 425 or 426. After this he had been involved with the education of Theoderic's son Theoderic. Avitus had also had a military career, serving under Aetius in the campaigns of 430, 431 and 436. Following his successful career under Aetius, Avitus was promoted to be *magister militum per Gallias* in 437, and had helped raise the siege of Narbo by Theoderic. In 439 he had become *Praefectus praetorio Galliarum*, during which tenure in 439 he negotiated the peace treaty with Theoderic. After this, Avitus had retired to his estates.[37] With his prolonged activity in Gaul and his personal contacts with Theoderic, Avitus was the ideal man for the task at hand.

After a brief but intense bout of diplomatic manoeuvring, Avitus succeeded where Aetius had failed. He convinced the Goths that their interest would be best served by an alliance with Rome against the Huns, although it must be acknowledged that the fact that the Huns had instantly begun to ravage Gaul probably had at least some influence on the negotiations.[38] Furthermore, it is possible that rumours concerning the possible attempts by Gaiseric to influence Attila to attack had some weight in Theoderic's judgement: Theoderic would never forgive Gaiseric for what had happened to his daughter.

Abandoning his policy of self-reliance, Theoderic prepared for war, taking with him his two eldest sons, Theoderic and Thorismund.[39] His other sons were left in Toulouse. In the meantime, it is likely that Aetius called for reinforcements from Italy prior to advancing further into Gaul as it was now clear that the Goths would not attempt to invade Italy. It is probably at this point that news reached Aetius' wife Pelagia that Aetius was in great difficulty in Gaul. She now began praying for his safety and the success of the war.[40]

It may also have been at about this time that news arrived in Orléans that the Huns had invaded. Anianus, the bishop of the city, realized that Orléans would be a target for the Huns, since it was the last major city denying the Huns access to the Goths in Aquitania. Anianus therefore travelled to Arles to meet Aetius and request aid for the city.[41] With Aetius' assurance that he was now advancing to join with the Goths and face Attila in battle, Anianus left Arles and returned home.

Although Attila was roaming Gaul unhindered, there was one major factor that was to prove to be his undoing. Aetius had the advantage of interior lines of supply, as well as the logistical support of the Western Empire. Early in the year, or possibly even in 450, Aetius had ordered Ferreolus, the *praefectus praetorio Galliarum* (Praetorian Prefect of Gaul), to organize the collection of supplies and equipment at pre-designated locations.[42] With supplies assured, the allies joined their forces, almost certainly at Toulouse to help the Goths with their late mobilization. This is the most logical place for them to collect, since the Huns were threatening locations in the north or east of Gaul, and it is almost certain that Aetius had ordered that supplies be collected at the city ready for the upcoming campaign. The move would also allow the Goths and Burgundians to be supplied by the imperial government: as they gathered and began the march to confront the Huns, Ferreolus' logistical abilities kept the Romans and their allies supplied with the necessities needed for the campaign.[43]

In direct contrast, Attila's coalition was forced to rely on plundering the local areas for supplies. Although a viable means of support, they did not have large reserves of supplies and so could not afford to either be blockaded or to have their lines of retreat cut off. Any such occurrence would result in the army quickly being reduced to starvation and having to surrender to Aetius. Attila could not afford to be surrounded. Speed was essential, and Anianus' fears came to be realized. Even as Aetius travelled to Toulouse to join with Theoderic, Attila's forces arrived at Orléans and began to lay siege to the city.[44]

Attila and the Invasion

Having described the course of Attila's invasion of Gaul, there remains the question of Attila's overall strategy. As most historians have focused upon the Roman response, little attention has been paid as to why Attila advanced as far as Orléans. The uncertainty revolves around Attila's reasons for invading Gaul. If, as posited earlier, his aim was to enforce his choice of king upon the Franks, there is no reason for him to advance so deep into enemy territory: a strong force imposing the elder son of the deceased Frankish king would almost certainly have sufficed to achieve this aim. The Roman army was unlikely to interfere in favour of Aetius' adopted son since Rome was already stretched in its attempts to maintain the borders. It may be that Attila was indeed intent upon claiming a large part of the Roman Empire and ensure his marriage to Honoria, but the question then remains as to why his invasion in no way threatened Italy and the emperor in Ravenna.

However, the direction of his advance may give a clue as to at least part of his aim. Although speculation, it is interesting to note that Attila's course was taking him directly towards the Goths in Aquitaine. The implication here is that Attila was intent on linking with the Goths prior to a joint campaign against Aetius. In this way a large part of Gaul would easily be detached from Rome and divided between Attila and Theoderic. It may even be that a region in the north would be given to the new Frankish king to help cement his position against his younger brother. From a position of strength in Gaul Attila would have the upper hand in negotiations regarding Honoria and Attila's claim to half of the West, yet it should be noted that no information regarding Attila's overall strategy either with regard to the position of Honoria or of his invasion of Gaul is given. He might not have known of the recent alliance between Theoderic and Aetius, since any spies in the region could have trouble locating Attila as he forged his way through Gaul: any delay in receiving the information could prove crucial.

The Siege of Orléans

Deploying battering rams and doubtless other siege engines, Attila's men began their assault.[45] There are two different accounts of the siege, and by combining them it is possible to gain a clearer view of the event. The city was under heavy siege, and the Huns were preparing their forces, when 'four-days' storm of rain' hampered their attempts to take the city.[46] However, after the rain had cleared on 14 June they launched an attack that breached the walls and they prepared to take the city.[47] At this moment, the armies of the West arrived.[48] With his forces dispersed for the attack on the city, and doubtless concerned about his supplies and line of retreat, Attila immediately called off the attack and retreated from the city.[49]

Although the story has undoubtedly been embellished by the ancient chroniclers and the end of the siege dramatically embellished to enhance the story, it is clear that the siege of Orléans was a close-run thing. It is only thanks to the speedy arrival of the allies that the Huns were stopped from entering and plundering the city. Moreover, Hunnic success would have left the route into the Gothic heartlands open. With the Huns at large in his own territories it is uncertain whether Theoderic would have remained loyal to Aetius or changed sides and joined Attila in order to spare his people from attack. Whatever the case, the siege of Orléans proved to be the high point of Attila's attack on the West. Unwilling to chance being cut off from his way home and blockaded, Attila retreated towards the Rhine with the allies in hot pursuit. It may only have been now that Attila learned of Theoderic's alliance with Aetius: his worst fears for the campaign had now become reality.

The Pursuit

Having been forced to raise the siege, Attila retired in front of the Romans and their allies. The direction his forces took implies that he was aiming to retreat from Gaul, or at least outdistance the pursuit in order to re-form and prepare a fresh plan for the campaign. Unfortunately for Attila, this was not to be. Five days after the end of the siege of Orléans Attila arrived at Troyes. The city was unprotected and could be easily taken and sacked by the Huns. It is claimed in the *Acta Sanctorum* that it was only through the saintly actions of Lupus, the bishop of Troyes, who pleaded with Attila to spare the city, that Troyes was saved from destruction. However, although Lupus probably met Attila outside the city, it was not the bishop's pleas that saved the city. Attila would have been more intent on the actions of the pursuing allies than on the plight of Troyes. Although Troyes was undefended and easy to attack, the allies were in close pursuit and Attila could not spare the time for sacking the city, which would have resulted in large numbers of his men – especially the allied Ostrogoths and Gepids – losing discipline and no doubt getting drunk. The loss of time in reordering his forces after the sack might have been a worry, but even more was the prospect of his disorganized and dispersed forces being attacked by the Romans and their allies as the Huns sacked the town.[50]

Yet there was one other factor. Troyes was on the River Seine. As Attila's forces gathered on the nearby plains known as the Campus Mauriacus and awaited the daybreak, Attila himself was no doubt aware that there was little chance of him escaping with his troops unhindered across the river.[51] Furthermore, he needed to safeguard the plunder he had already taken. Leaving the spoils behind would have demoralized his men and damaged his prestige. He could afford neither.

Crossing the river by bridge would take a very long time, and there was a good chance of his forces being attacked by the pursuing allies as they crossed the river. This would be a disaster, so Attila decided that this was the place where he was going to stand and face the allies. Possibly the allied force outnumbered the Huns slightly as Attila, who had shown himself perfectly happy to take aggressive action in the past, acted very defensively as soon as the combined Roman-Visigoth army came close.

Chapter Nine

The Battle of the Catalaunian Plains

On the afternoon of 19 June 451 Attila's Gepid rearguard reported that the 'Roman' army had come into view, marching fast. In fact, the speed at which the allies were moving was so great that Aetius' Frankish allies clashed with the Gepids before darkness fell. In a brief but savage engagement, neither side could gain the advantage and the onset of night brought the fighting to a halt. Although Jordanes claims that 15,000 men died in this encounter, it is certain that these figures are vastly inflated.[1] However, the clash was proof to Attila that on the following day Aetius would not balk from fighting a set-piece battle.

On the morning of 20 June 451 the two armies prepared for battle.[2] The location is unknown, although many suggestions have been proposed. The difficulty lies in the vague terms used by the sources. Jordanes, Hydatius and the *Chronica Caesaraugusta* note that the battle was fought on the 'Catalaunian Plains'.[3] However, the *Gallic Chronicler of 511* locates the battle on the Mauriac Plain which is echoed by the *Consularia Italica*, Gregory of Tours and the *Lex Burgundionum*.[4] Theophanes writes simply that Attila was defeated at the River Lygis (Loire).[5] On the other hand, the claim by Malalas that Attila was defeated on the River Danube is certainly mistaken.[6] The net result of this confusion has been a debate over the possible sites for the battle, although nothing has yet been proved decisively.[7]

Soothsayers

The account written by Jordanes has an interesting passage prior to the battle: allegedly, Attila was in doubt as to the outcome of the battle, so decided to 'inquire into the future through soothsayers'. These men examined the entrails and bones of cattle and foretold disaster for the Huns, possibly using scapulimancy, as had happened when the Roman commander Litorius had fought the Goths in 439.[8] Yet alongside the Hunnic defeat they also announced that the leader of the enemy would fall, and Attila took this to mean that Aetius would be killed.[9] Taking everything into consideration, it is likely that Attila sought the advice of soothsayers, as this was a common feature of non-Christian societies as forecasting the future could often influence the morale of the army. Yet the description given is of doubtful accuracy, as it is unknown how Jordanes could have obtained this detailed information. Instead, its inclusion in the text may be Jordanes' method of emphasizing Attila's barbarity, since he took part in a Pagan ritual that was no longer relevant to the Christian Romans. Unfortunately, without corroborating evidence, it is unlikely whether the truth will ever be known.

The Deployment

The only detailed description we have of the battle is that given by Jordanes.[10] It has been noted that there are similarities between the account given by Jordanes and that of Themistocles' account of the Persians.[11] This may be true, but if the battles were in any way similar then the two accounts are also bound to be similar. In conclusion, although in most cases Jordanes needs to be used with care, the fact that this is the only description of the battle forces reliance on his account.

Yet even here the end result can be confusing. For example, the traditional account followed by most modern historians has the Visigoths attacking a hill on the right flank and dominating the battle from there.[12] This is mirrored in other writers and has become an accepted norm. Its origins are unclear, but the following extract may give a clue as to its source. It is a translation of Jordanes:

> Now this was the configuration of the field of battle. It rose [on one side] into a decided undulation which might be called a hill.
> *Hodgkin, 1892, Vol. 2, 127.*

As shown by the use of closed brackets, the phrase 'on one side' was added by the translator. It is this that leads to the interpretation upon which the majority of the modern accounts of the battlefield are based, yet the author does not state his source for the addition and so it cannot be traced further back. Both the original Latin and a more literal translation of Jordanes' account do not support this reconstruction, so is worth quoting:

Convenere partes, ut diximus, in campos Catalaunicos. Erat autem positio loci declivi tumore in editum collis excrescens. Quem uterque cupiens exercitus obtinere, quia loci oportunitas non parvum benificium confert, dextram partem Hunni cum suis, sinistram Romani et Vesegothae cum auxiliariis occuparunt, relictoque de cacumine eius iugo certamen ineunt.

Jordanes, Getica, *39 (196–197).*

The armies met, as we have said, in the Catalaunian Plains. The battle field was a plain rising by a sharp slope to a ridge, which both armies sought to gain; for advantage of position is a great help. The Huns with their forces seized the right side, the Romans, the Visigoths and their allies the left, and then began a struggle for the yet untaken crest.

Trans. Mierow, C.C.

Therefore, discounting the earlier interpretations, the battlefield appears to have been a plain dominated by a ridge across its centre, not by a hill, although the ridge was higher in some places than others. Having reached this conclusion, the rest of the passage from Jordanes is easier to interpret, although there are still one or two points that are uncertain.

As already noted, Jordanes claims that the Huns 'seized the right side, the Romans, the Visigoths and their allies the left'. If Jordanes is writing from the Roman perspective then his use of 'right' and 'left' refers to 'south' and 'north' respectively, a conclusion from both his phrasing and from the allies' line of advance in a 'east-north-eastern' direction. Therefore the Huns won the battle for the southern end of the crest, whereas the allies won on the north. The centre of the ridge thus became the focus of the battle.

Yet the same sentence gives us evidence that Jordanes' account needs to be treated with caution. The Huns are the enemy, and the appearance of other tribes as their allies – especially the Ostrogoths – is unwelcome to Jordanes. In direct contrast, Jordanes focuses on the Visigoths almost to the exclusion of the Romans. This clearly demonstrates Jordanes' bias: the work is a history of the Goths, both branches, and so the appearance of the Ostrogoths on the side of Attila is downplayed, and that of the Visigoths overplayed, in order to boost their status. This needs to be borne in mind throughout the analysis of the battle.

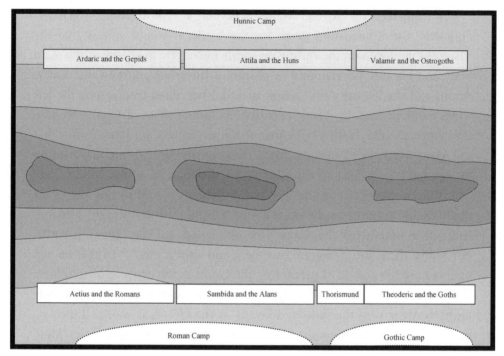

Deployment for battle.

Attila arrayed his forces with himself and his Huns in the centre. The Ostrogoths, and possibly some of the minor allies, were placed on Attila's left wing specifically to face the Visigoths, as Attila had faith in their king Valamir and his brothers Thiudimer and Vidimer. The Gepids, and possibly some other allied troops, appear to have been on the right wing under the Gepid King Ardaric.

The tactics of Attila are nowhere outlined and so have to be deduced from his deployment. They appear to be based on the assumption that Aetius would adopt the traditional Roman deployment of cavalry on the flanks and infantry in the centre. If this assumption is correct, Attila's plan was that the whole army was to advance and seize the top of the hill, at which point the two flanks – under his most trusted subordinates – would charge and defeat the enemy cavalry. In the meantime, the Huns would use their traditional tactics to pin the enemy infantry in the centre, causing as much confusion as possible with a hail of missiles. At the point where one or both flanks of the alliance broke, the victorious wing(s) would be able to follow the retreating Romans and eventually turn on to the flanks of the centre. The enemy would then collapse, leaving the Huns to pursue; a tactic at which they excelled.

Unfortunately for Attila, Aetius was not a typical Roman general. Following the information given for the battle, it would appear that the Visigoths deployed on the right wing, with Theoderic in charge of the main body and his son Thorismund in charge of the troops next to the centre. Aetius and the majority of his Roman and other allied troops took the left wing. Sambida and the Alans – possibly including those of Goar – were in the centre, possibly with a stiffening of Roman troops: Jordanes claims that the Alans were placed in the centre, 'thus contriving with military caution to surround by a host of faithful troops the man in whose loyalty they had little confidence. For one who has difficulties placed in the way of his flight readily submits to the necessity of fighting.'[13] Interestingly, Jordanes had earlier noted that the Alans were 'the equals [of the Huns] in battle, but unlike them in civilisation, manners and appearance'.[14] In this he was maintaining his agenda of promoting the Goths at the expense of all others. By portraying the Alans as 'ready to run' he was contrasting the potentially faithless Alans with the skills and loyalty of the Goths, as well as drawing a major distinction between the 'disloyal' Alan leader Sambida and the 'loyal' Gothic King Theoderic.[15]

Although the claim of potential Alan perfidy is usually accepted at face value, in reality it has little to recommend it.[16] The major difficulty is that the Alans were not 'surrounded'. Once battle began, the troops on either side of the Alans would be more concerned with the opposition than with the Alans, as would any troops stationed to support the Alans. On the contrary, the deployment suggests that Aetius was unworried, as otherwise by placing the Alans in the centre Aetius was taking a great risk. Should they rout, the Roman lines would be divided and each sector easily dealt with piecemeal. As will be seen, Aetius' trust was vindicated.

The question then remains concerning Aetius' use of the Alans. It is often forgotten at this point that Aetius was a man with a deep knowledge of Hunnic strategy and tactics due to his time among them as a hostage and his continuing employment of Hun troops as *foederati* and *bucellarii*. Although speculation, the chances are that Aetius foresaw that the Huns would deploy using a standard formation, especially since they were being assisted by large numbers of subject troops and such a deployment would help to avoid confusion. Therefore it is more reasonable to assume that Aetius was using his knowledge of the Huns against them. Knowing that the Huns would deploy their own forces, comprised mainly of horse-archers, in the centre, Aetius deployed the Alans to face them, troops which used roughly the same tactics themselves. Rather than being faced by a solid block of relatively immobile infantry in the centre, Attila found himself faced by the mobile and highly-skilled Alans. Furthermore, these men had been fighting alongside the Romans for many years and knew how to fight effectively as their allies, advancing to harass the enemy and retreating behind the cover of the supporting infantry when threatened. If the hypotheses concerning deployment are accurate, then it would appear that both sides had adopted the same strategy: pin the centre and attempt to destroy the opposition's wings.

With a ridge between them, both Attila and Aetius would have known the tactical advantage of possession of the crest. With this in mind, it is surprising that the battle began 'about the ninth hour of the day' (early to mid-afternoon). The late start is allegedly due to the fact that Attila was scared by the omens and decided to wait: if the battle should prove to be a disaster, in this way darkness would cover the retreat of the Huns and allow many of them to escape.[17]

This does not, however, explain why Aetius did not make the first move. The likelihood is that both generals realized that a pre-emptive attempt to attack without a proper deployment could lead to disaster. Both sides had troops capable of making fast attacks on isolated and unsupported troops. Therefore a well-timed 'combined assault' would be necessary to win the battle. In addition, any aggressive move by small groups could easily lead to confusion among their own armies. Both sides comprised large numbers of troops with little experience of working together, and without a common language. Deployment would take a long time. In addition, there were troops on opposite sides who spoke the same language, so care and accuracy of deployment would avoid the risk of troops attacking their own allies. As a result, both generals chose to slowly deploy their troops ready for battle. The deployment was crucial: thanks to language difficulties and the lack of joint training, both sides would find it difficult to change their strategy during the battle as the majority of the troops did not have adequate training in working together.

The Battle[18]

It would appear that the opposing forces began the battle at roughly the same time, both attempting to seize the crest and so dominate the battlefield. Again, Jordanes' account is open to debate: 'The Huns with their forces seized the right side, the Romans, the Visigoths and their allies the left, and then began a struggle for the yet untaken crest.'[19] As noted earlier, all depends upon the interpretation of Jordanes' 'right' and 'left'. In the majority of modern accounts it is assumed that the battle is seen from the Huns' perspective, as they are depicted seizing the hill to their right, opposing Aetius himself, while the Visigoths beat the Ostrogoths to the crest and so dominate the battlefield on their flank. Yet this analysis is almost certainly mistaken. The real course of events can be seen by arranging Jordanes' account into a chronological course of events.

As already stated:

> The Huns with their forces seized the right side, the Romans, the Visigoths and their allies the left, and then began a struggle for the yet untaken crest.
>
> Jordanes, *Getica, 38 (197).*

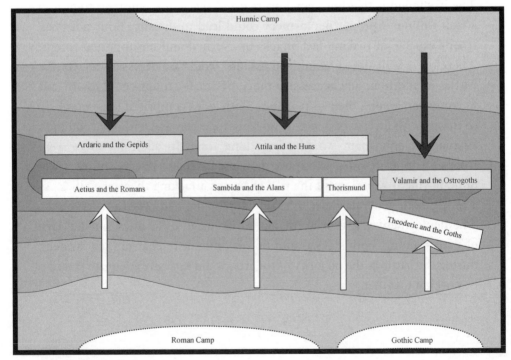

Stage 1: The battle for the crest.

This is followed by a description of the deployment of the Romans and their allies, following which:

> So then the struggle began for the advantage of position we have mentioned. Attila sent his men to take the summit of the mountain, but was outstripped by Thorismund and Aetius, who in their effort to gain the top of the hill reached higher ground and through this advantage of position easily routed the Huns as they came up.
>
> *Jordanes*, Getica, *38 (201)*.

What has happened is clear: Jordanes is describing the battle from the Roman lines. Attila's forces had occupied the crest on the right of the Romans, facing the Visigoths. At least part of Attila's plan to defeat the Romans' wings, as hypothesized above, looked to be succeeding. In contrast, Aetius had seized the left side of the crest facing the Gepids, who were no doubt weakened by their 'skirmish' of the night before. In a 'joint operation', Aetius' troops – including the Alans – had then taken the centre of the ridge, helped by the Visigothic forces under Thorismund. Attempting to dislodge the allies from this strong position, the Huns were easily beaten back as they climbed the slope.

The Huns now became demoralized by their failure and Attila was forced to make a speech:

> Now when Attila saw his army was thrown into confusion by this event, he thought it best to encourage them by an extemporaneous address ...
>
> *Jordanes*, Getica, *39 (202)*.

The text of the speech need not be analysed in detail, since it is extremely unlikely that Jordanes would have been able to write, word-for-word, a speech made by Attila. In fact, it is unlikely that Attila made any speech at all, since in the din and confusion of the battle his words would have been lost to all but a few.[20] The whole episode is a rhetorical piece invented by Jordanes, but one small part of the speech is useful, as Jordanes gives clues as to the nature of the battlefield:

> They seek the heights, they seize the hills and, repenting too late, clamour for protection against battle in the open fields.
>
> *Jordanes*, Getica, *39 (204)*.

The use of the plurals 'heights' and 'hills' reinforces the concept suggested earlier that there was not just one single hill on the right-hand side of the Romans' deployment area, but rather a long crest, with some parts being higher than others, especially in the centre.

(Allegedly) encouraged, the Huns and their allies renewed their assault on the crest:

> And although the situation was itself fearful, yet the presence of their king dispelled anxiety and hesitation. Hand to hand they clashed in battle, and the fight grew fierce, confused, monstrous, unrelenting – a fight whose like no ancient time has ever recorded. There such deeds were done that a brave man who missed this marvellous spectacle could not hope to see anything so wonderful all his life long.
>
> *Jordanes*, Getica, 40 (207).

On the other hand, the Visigoths on the extreme right of the Roman line appear to have been unable to take the ridge in front of them. At this point a potential disaster happened to the Roman allies:

> Here King Theoderic, while riding by to encourage his army, was thrown from his horse and trampled under foot by his own men, thus ending his days at a ripe old age. But others say he was slain by the spear of Andag of the host of the Ostrogoths, who were then under the sway of Attila. This was what the soothsayers had told to Attila in prophecy, though he understood it of Aetius.
>
> *Jordanes*, Getica, 40 (209).

By way of contrast, both Malalas and the *Chronicon Paschale* claim that Theoderic was killed by an arrow.[21] Since Malalas and the *Chronicon* are much later, their evidence is probably less likely than that given by Jordanes; however, there remains the remote possibility that it is accurate.

It is interesting to note that Jordanes, writing the history of the Goths, does not mention the Ostrogoths during the course of the battle anywhere but at this point. The reason is almost certainly that he wanted to minimize the fact that the Ostrogoths fought against the Romans alongside Attila, a man later reviled as 'The Scourge of God'. Yet it should be noted that

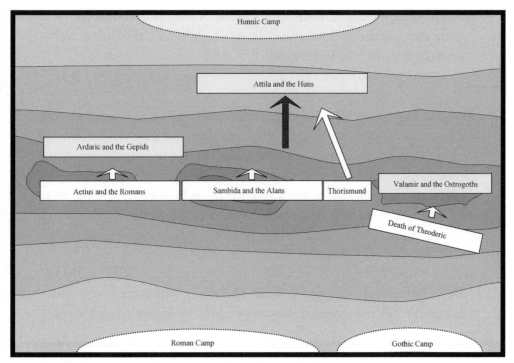

Stage 2: The death of Theoderic; Thorismund routs the Huns.

Jordanes may have had access to the descendants of Andag and so may have recorded a family tradition that may in fact have contained the true course of events. Theoderic had been killed as he led his men uphill against the Ostrogoths. Yet the news did not immediately spread.

Unaware of his father's death, as darkness was beginning to descend, Thorismund, from the top of the ridge, saw that the Huns to his front were beginning to lose heart, and that they were trapped between their own wings and their camp. He also located Attila's position in the battle. Thorismund seized the opportunity and led his forces in a downhill charge at the Huns opposing them, trying to reach Attila. Unable to use their traditional hit-and-run tactics, the Huns disintegrated and began to rout, in the process exposing Attila to danger:

> Then the Visigoths, separating from the Alans, fell upon the horde
> of the Huns and nearly slew Attila. But he prudently took flight and
> straightway shut himself and his companions within the barriers of the

camp, which he had fortified with wagons. A frail defence indeed; yet there they sought refuge for their lives, whom but a little while before no walls of earth could withstand.

Jordanes, Getica, *40 (210)*.

When Attila fled the field his army, including his allies, also seems to have lost heart. As the sun set, what was left of the Huns and their allies attempted to retire to their camp and await the dawn. Others wandered lost in the darkness. Many of these men were killed, and no doubt large numbers of them forgot their alliance to Attila and fled the field and attempted to make their way back to their homes, especially the Franks. Yet Attila's decision to postpone the battle now paid dividends. In the darkness confusion quickly spread:

But Thorismund, the son of King Theoderic, who with Aetius had seized the hill and repulsed the enemy from the higher ground, came

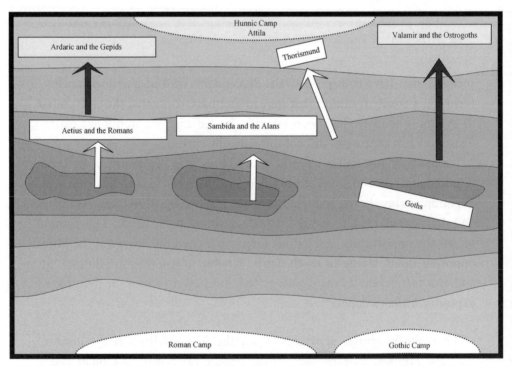

Stage 3: The end of the battle; the Gepids and Ostrogoths retire, and Attila is pinned in his camp.

unwittingly to the wagons of the enemy in the darkness of night, thinking he had reached his own lines. As he was fighting bravely, someone wounded him in the head and dragged him from his horse. Then he was rescued by the watchful care of his followers and withdrew from the fierce conflict. Aetius also became separated from his men in the confusion of night and wandered about in the midst of the enemy. Fearing disaster had happened, he went about in search of the Goths. At last he reached the camp of his allies and passed the remainder of the night in the protection of their shields.

Jordanes, Getica, *40 (211–212).*

With a high level of confusion, and expecting the worst, the allies awaited the dawn, with Thorismund receiving treatment for his head wound. Much to their surprise, when daylight came:

At dawn on the following day, when the Romans saw the fields were piled high with bodies and that the Huns did not venture forth, they thought the victory was theirs, but knew that Attila would not flee from the battle unless overwhelmed by a great disaster. Yet he did nothing cowardly, like one that is overcome, but with clash of arms sounded the trumpets and threatened an attack. He was like a lion pierced by hunting spears, who paces to and fro before the mouth of his den and dares not spring, but ceases not to terrify the neighbourhood by his roaring. Even so this warlike king at bay terrified his conquerors. Therefore the Goths and Romans assembled and considered what to do with the vanquished Attila. They determined to wear him out by a siege, because he had no supply of provisions and was hindered from approaching by a shower of arrows from the bowmen placed within the confines of the Roman camp. But it was said that the king remained supremely brave even in this extremity and had heaped up a funeral pyre of horse trappings, so that if the enemy should attack him, he was determined to cast himself into the flames, that none might have the joy of wounding him and that the lord of so many races might not fall into the hands of his foes.

Jordanes, Getica, *40 (212–213).*

Determined to capture or kill Attila, the victorious allies now deployed troops to contain the Huns, but at the same time began the task of dealing with the dead and wounded on the battlefield. Foremost in their minds was the absence of Theoderic:

> Now during these delays in the siege, the Visigoths sought their king and the king's sons their father, wondering at his absence when success had been attained. When, after a long search, they found him where the dead lay thickest, as happens with brave men, they honoured him with songs and bore him away in the sight of the enemy.
>
> *Jordanes*, Getica, *40 (214).*

Aftermath

With the Huns remaining in their camp and the Visigoths having recovered Theoderic's body, Aetius allegedly made a strange decision: fearful that 'if the Huns were totally destroyed by the Goths, the Roman Empire would be overwhelmed', Aetius disbanded the alliance, advising the new king Thorismund that he should return home, as otherwise he 'would be cheated out of his father's kingdom' and also giving the same advice to his foster-son, the reinstated younger son of the recently-deceased Frankish king.[22]

When the allies withdrew and dispersed, Attila was at first fearful of a trick and that they would attack him as he left his camp. As a result, he waited in his camp for a long time.[23] When he was certain that he was safe, he gathered the remnants of his forces and began the long march home. As he marched his thoughts would have been busy with plans to negate the negative political ramifications of his defeat.

Victory and Defeat

Jordanes' account of Attila considering suicide implies that the Romans had the upper hand and can be seen as being the victors, but not all historians agree with this.[24] However, taking into account Jordanes' report, plus the fact that no source mentions the Huns retreating along with large amounts of booty and great numbers of captives, it is probably more accurate to see this as a Romano-Gothic victory, but a narrow one. Indeed, the Romans themselves accepted that they had only won the battle with the help of the Goths, as demonstrated by the Roman chroniclers.[25] The value of the Gothic alliance is also stressed by Sidonius in his poem in praise of Avitus, the man who made the alliance possible, although this may also have been an attempt to ingratiate himself with his new overlords, the Goths.[26]

The writings of the chroniclers and Sidonius clearly emphasize that the battle was seen as important shortly after it had occurred, but it is possible that at the time the battle was seen as just yet another barbarian raid. For example, Prosper, who was hostile to Aetius, ignores the battle, but even he could not have overlooked it if it had been instantly recognized as one of the most important events of the fifth century.[27]

Yet in retrospect many historians have seen this battle as one of the pivotal incidents that shaped modern Europe. It was suggested that had Attila won the conflict, a new, non-Christian empire would have come into existence between the Atlantic and the Black Sea.[28] Yet early in the twentieth century doubts began to be raised about this concept. The main objection must remain that Attila's 'empire' only existed while he was alive. Upon his death it fragmented. Even had he conquered Gaul, upon his death his sons would still have been unable to maintain their empire and it would quickly have fallen apart.[29] Gaul might have been damaged, and the specific history of France changed, but Christianity would have been maintained and the impact of the Huns been only fleeting.

Chapter Ten

Final Years

I n late summer or early autumn, Attila returned home to find that contrary to his expectations, the East had been fighting 'vigorously against the Huns in the Balkans'.[1] However, his grievances against the East were small; his focus was still on the West, as allegedly he was 'enraged' by the 'unexpected defeat in Gaul'.[2] Over the winter of 451 and 452, Attila spent his time consolidating his position at home and preparing for a return to the fray. He would have been encouraged by the information from his spies that the Western allies had gone their separate ways, and may have known that there was – or appears to have been – little contact between the victors. Attila began to look at the options for the New Year.

The Invasion of Italy

Attila was determined to avenge his defeat and regain his aura of invincibility, as the fact that he had been defeated could easily lead to internal unrest in the Hunnic Empire. Furthermore, there was also the remote possibility that Aetius in the West and the new regime of Marcian in the East would cooperate to oppose Attila. Yet in one respect Attila had a great advantage: he realized that the alliance between Aetius and Theoderic had been forged only thanks to his own invasion of Gaul. Intelligence from the West, possibly from Franks unhappy with their new young king, may have informed Attila of how close the Goths had been to remaining neutral during his invasion of Gaul. Attila correctly assumed that if he attacked Italy the Goths would not join in the defence, and so he would only have to face the forces of Aetius, plus possibly a few of the less numerous allies, such as the Burgundians.[3] Yet it took Attila a long time to gather his troops together for another invasion of the West. This was doubtless in part due to the losses he had suffered in Gaul, a hypothesis reinforced by the fact that, for this second invasion, he did not leave troops behind to pin down the forces of the East.[4]

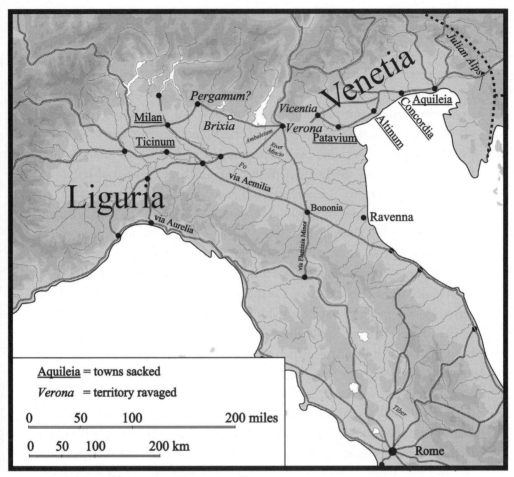

Map 12: Attila's Invasion of Italy, 452.

In the early summer of 452, Attila launched his invasion:

King Attila … in the 451st year of Our Lord's birth, coming down from Scythia, entered Pannonia with a mighty force and, putting the Romans to flight, took the realm and made a royal residence for himself beside the Danube above the hot springs, and he ordered all the old buildings that he found there to be restored and he built them in a circular and very strong wall that in the Hungarian language is now called Budavár and by the Germans Etzelburg.[5]

Gesta Hungarorum 1, *trans. Rady.*

Although the *Gesta Hungarorum* is usually seen as being less than reliable, on this occasion it may be recording an item of interest. Whether the information is accurate and this really was an invasion of Pannonia is open to question, as the region may have been part of the territory allotted to the Huns in 435. In that case, it is more likely that Attila had ordered his troops to muster in the region of Aquincum (Budapest, see Map 5) and that he had set his headquarters in the remains of the Roman amphitheatre. Once his men had gathered, certainly well before mid-June 452, he led them through Pannonia and across the Julian Alps into the north-east corner of Italy.[6]

In the previous year, Aetius had been expecting Attila to invade Italy, yet Prosper claims that this invasion was a 'complete surprise'.[7] This has usually been accepted but analysis has disputed the claim.[8] The main reason why the claim has been accepted is the statement that Aetius 'failed to make use of the barriers of the Alps'.[9] In some ways this makes sense militarily; a determined defence of the passes at the mountains would have caused Attila serious losses and may have caused him to turn back. Yet the impression is actually false: although applicable to high mountain ranges, this theory does not apply to the Julian Alps, which are lower and easier to traverse than their northern counterparts.[10] In the past, attempts to defend these passes had ended in defeat, especially as the defences that were in place, the *Claustra Alpium Juliarum* (Fortifications of the Julian Alps), were lightly-held and mainly intended to halt barbarian raids that had penetrated into Illyricum from the east.[11] Knowing that in the height of summer the mounted and fast-moving Huns would easily outflank his positions, Aetius probably decided not to attempt a forward defence, but rather to retreat and call on reinforcements from the East. In the meantime he probably reinforced the garrison of Aquileia, which would be the first city reached by the Huns.

Towards the end of June Attila arrived at Aquileia. More than fifty years earlier, in 401, the Gothic leader Alaric had invaded Italy and, having no knowledge of siege warfare and believing that Aquileia was too strong to attack, had simply bypassed the city.[12] In contrast, Attila had the ability to capture cities and he appears to have thought it unwise to bypass Aquileia, possibly since the garrison would be in a position to threaten his lines of communication, his rear, and to block his return home.

Attila immediately began a siege using a variety of siege engines.[13] He would have hoped for a quick siege, much as had happened to many cities in Gaul the previous year.[14] If so, he was to be disappointed: Priscus writes that 'He pressed the siege there long and hard … from within the bravest of Roman soldiers withstood him.'[15] Attila's need for a very fast campaign was thwarted by the defenders of Aquileia. Instead of a speedy advance, Attila found himself besieging the city for three months in the middle of a famine in Italy.[16] In addition, an unknown epidemic had broken out in the region.[17] Eventually his army began to lose heart and think of home but, again according to Priscus, Attila noticed that the storks that nested in the city were carrying their young away.[18] Seeing this as an omen, he ordered his troops to renew the assault, and either in late August or early September, the city fell to the Huns.[19] In anger at its resistance, Attila and his troops savagely plundered the city; however, it should be noted that Jordanes' claim that no trace of the city was left is false.[20] Surprisingly, despite the fact that Attila was at large in the north-east of Italy, Aetius continued to address the problems of famine, issuing an edict to ensure the arrival of animals in Rome to feed the population.[21]

Once the scale of Attila's invasion became known, Prosper claims that Aetius 'believed his only hope lay in a full retreat from Italy', but a 'sense of shame' stopped this proposal.[22] Prosper does not state where Aetius would have retreated to, and indeed, there were very few places left in the West where the Roman emperor would be safe. The only possibility is that Aetius intended to take Valentinian to Constantinople and there to seek the support of the Eastern Emperor Marcian to provide an expedition to 'retake' Italy.

Although Prosper's claim is usually dismissed or ignored, given later events it is clear that Aetius was in contact with Marcian, and the episode would make sense if Aetius was convinced that he would be unable to face Attila in battle without external help; the Goths were focused upon their own affairs and made no effort to support Aetius. Consequently, it is possible to suggest that Aetius did in fact send messengers to Marcian asking for help, and mooting the possibility of exile for himself and Valentinian should Attila overrun Italy. Fortunately for Aetius, Marcian agreed to send help as soon as he could.[23] Even more fortunately, the defenders of Aquileia gave Aetius the breathing space he needed to organize his forces.

While Aetius was negotiating with the East, which given the distances involved probably took up to at least two months, Attila successfully stormed Aquileia and then led his forces deeper into Italy. Advancing further into Venetia and Liguria, Attila besieged and sacked Mediolanum (Milan) and Ticinum (Pavia).[24] According to Paul the Deacon, at the same time – the actual chronology is unknown – Attila also sacked Concordia, Altinum (Altino) and Patavium (Padua). Paul goes on to say that the Huns in addition attacked Vicentia (Vicenza), Verona, Brixia (Brescia) and Pergamum (Bergamo?).[25] It is unclear whether these cities were actually sacked, since Paul's phrasing is somewhat ambivalent; however, it is possible to conclude from the wording that Concordia, Altinum and Patavium were sacked, and that the territories of Vicentia, Verona, Brixia and Pergamum were ravaged, although the cities themselves remained untouched. This would not be a surprise, as with Italy in the middle of a famine the Hunnic forces would need to range far afield to find the supplies they needed, especially as they would have used most if not all with which they had started the invasion during the siege of Aquileia.

After the capture of Milan it is claimed by Priscus that Attila saw a painting of the Roman emperors on golden thrones with 'Scythians lying dead before their feet', over which he ordered a painter to paint 'Attila upon a throne and the Roman emperors heaving sacks upon their shoulders and pouring out gold before his feet.'[26] Although the origin of the story is unknown, it is probably true, as it would accord with what we assume of the temperament of Attila from the sources.

No source describes the actions of Aetius in response to the Huns' advance across northern Italy, or where he had positioned the Roman forces. As he was awaiting reinforcements from the East, it is possible that he was in one of the ports on the eastern coast of Italy. If this is the case, it was almost certainly Ravenna. The other option was that Aetius, recognizing that he could not defend the valley of the River Po against the mobile Huns, resolved to defend Rome. This concept may be reinforced by the fact that the ongoing famine would have made supplying one large army difficult. Holding the supplies in Rome and other well-defended cities would deny food to the Huns. He may also have hoped that the Huns would be demoralized by the long siege of Aquileia and withdraw.[27] As a final note, it was traditional Roman tactics to attack large enemy forces within the empire when the barbarians were on the way home laden with loot and so more likely be forced to fight at a disadvantage, so it is quite possible that Aetius was simply waiting for the right moment to move.

If any of these scenarios are applicable, then it is possible that Aetius positioned his forces at Bononia (Bologna). This not only covered the major routes to the south of Italy, it also covered the crossing of the Apennines using the *Via Flaminia Minor*, a road that headed directly for Rome. In addition, if Attila decided to attack Ravenna, Aetius would also be in a suitable position to fall on Attila's unprotected rear. In this way Aetius could ensure that Attila's activities were confined to the north of Italy. Finally, once the Huns began their retreat from Italy, he was in a good position to harass them as they left the peninsula.

Despite Aetius' inactivity, Attila and his men were not having everything their own way: 'The Huns ... were victims of divine punishment, being visited with heaven-sent disasters: famine and some kind of disease.'[28] Attila had made the mistake of invading Italy when the region was suffering from a failure of the harvest. Outside the walls of Aquileia his men had been suffering the effects of the siege, mainly hunger due to a shortage of provisions and probably a disease, such as dysentery, which affected armies that were stationary for too long a time.[29] Attila's strategy had no doubt been aimed at a very quick campaign, as had happened in Gaul: he had not organized the 'substantial logistic support' needed to supply the army during what, in the event, turned out to be a series of sieges.[30]

Passing into the valley of the River Po did not help in any significant way. Although provisions for the horses would have been easier to secure, with the inhabitants having little food of their own the Huns were unable to secure provisions without sacking cities and looting the imperial granaries. After they had penetrated as far as Ticinum, Attila faced a dilemma: at this point the lack of supplies was probably being very keenly felt. The only options were to either return home or attempt to cross the northern Apennines and so march down the *Via Aurelia* to Rome. According to Priscus, Attila's followers pointed to the fate of Alaric after he had sacked the 'eternal city' in 410, fearing that Attila, like Alaric, would die if he sacked Rome.[31] Although Attila was probably superstitious, if he had wanted to he could easily have ignored this advice. However, things were not that simple. The Huns were suffering from hunger and sickness. Furthermore, it is probably at around this time when news arrived that Marcian had sent forces out of Illyricum to attack the practically-defenceless homes of the Huns.[32]

Aetius and Aetius

At about the same time, Aetius himself had received reinforcements from the East. Unfortunately, there is confusion around the source of this information. Hydatius writes that:

> The Huns ... were victims of divine punishment, being visited with heaven-sent disasters: famine and some kind of disease. In addition, they were slaughtered by auxiliaries sent by the emperor Marcian and led by Aetius, and at the same time they were crushed in their settlements by both heaven-sent disasters and the army of Marcian.
>
> *Hydatius s.a. 452–3.*[33]

The wording of this statement could have been clearer. What makes it harder to interpret is the fact that by 452 there was a second Flavius Aetius, this time a general in the East. Some historians have conflated the two Aetiuses, seeing them as a single individual.[34] However, it is clear that there were two individuals named Aetius, one in the West and one in the East. The Eastern Aetius was Praetorian Prefect of the East in 425, when the Western Aetius was in Gaul.[35] Furthermore, the Eastern Aetius was present at the sixth session of the Council of Chalcedon on 25 October 451, when the Western Aetius was still dealing with the fall-out of Attila's invasion of Gaul.[36] The Eastern Aetius was clearly the East's nominee for consul in 454, possibly as a reward for campaigns against the Huns in the previous two years. Finally, there are two inscriptions referring to Aetius in Syria, one dating to after the death of the 'Western' Aetius.[37]

As a result, the identical names of the two generals have resulted in Hydatius' account being the cause of confusion. Yet Hydatius lived in Spain and his information coming from the East would have been late and possibly distorted. From Western sources he will have known that Aetius, the Western *patricius*, had received reinforcements from the East. He may have been told by individuals travelling from the East that Aetius had led troops into the Hunnic homelands. Due to the confused nature of the tale, and not being certain that the two men were separate individuals, it is likely that Hydatius' wording was ambiguous in order to cover his own confusion.

On the other hand, it may simply be that modern historians have attempted to read too much into this account. Taken individually it seems to be much simpler than at first appears: Marcian sent two armies out of the East. The first was a smaller force that was sent to reinforce Aetius in Italy. With these Aetius put pressure on the Huns as they retired across northern Italy. A second force invaded the homeland of the Huns in an attempt to weaken them and also to force them to leave Italy to defend their homes.[38] This second army may – or may not – have been led by the Eastern Aetius. If this interpretation is accepted, it allows for an easier reading of the passage and also a clearer interpretation of events, especially with regard to Attila's decision to leave Italy without fighting Aetius.

However, it should be noted that not all historians accept the hypothesis of there being two separate generals named Aetius.[39] Therefore, all that can be claimed with any chance of being accurate is that in Italy Aetius put pressure on the Huns as they left, possibly using some Eastern troops that had been sent in support, and that Marcian also sent troops to attack the Huns' homes across the Danube.

With the news that Aetius had been reinforced from the East, Attila was certain that his chances of negotiating with the emperor were over. Attila began the withdrawal from Italy, a move that was very slow due to the number of wagons carrying booty and the large number of captives being forced to march away from their homes. As they re-crossed northern Italy towards the east, Aetius and his men were in a position to harass their rear and destroy any stragglers that were lagging behind and to attack any foraging parties sent out from the main host.

Pope Leo

When Attila and his men reached the territory of Ambuleium in Venetia and were crossing the River Mincius, a tributary of the River Po, envoys arrived from Valentinian.[40] The nature and result of this embassy has been the subject of controversy ever since. The story begins with Prosper, who is supported by Victor Tonnensis, the *Chronicle of Cassiodorus*, and Priscus.[41] Accompanied by Trygetius, *Vir Praefectorius* – the same man who had negotiated the treaty with the Vandals in 435 – and Gennadius Avienus, who had been consul in 450, Pope Leo arranged a meeting with Attila:[42]

The king received the whole delegation courteously, and he was so flattered by the presence of the highest priest that he ordered his men to stop the hostilities and, promising peace, retired beyond the Danube.

Prosper, s.a. 452: trans. Maenchen-Helfen, 1973, 140.

During the course of the Middle Ages this story was magnified until now it is almost totally altered. For example:

When Attila marched on Rome, Leo went out to meet him and pleaded for him to leave. As Leo spoke, Attila saw the vision of a man in priestly robes, carrying a bare sword, and threatening to kill the invader if he did not obey Leo; Attila left. As Leo had a great devotion to Saint Peter the Apostle, it is generally believed the first pope was the visionary opponent to the Huns. When Genseric [*sic*] invaded Rome, Leo's sanctity and eloquence saved the city again.

http://saints.sqpn.com/pope-saint-leo-the-great/ (August 2010)

Interestingly Hydatius, who as bishop of Aquae Flaviae would be expected to make the most of this opportunity to promote Catholicism, makes no mention of the Pope.

The main objection to the later version of events is that, far from marching on Rome, Attila was in the north-east of Italy and marching away from Rome. However, if Leo was not attempting to save Rome, as is usually portrayed, the question remains as to the actual reasons for him being present. This was simply due to the fact that Valentinian, the emperor, requested him to lead the delegation. As a major religious figure he was of immense political stature and his presence added sincerity and grace to the meeting: it would have been expected that this would influence Attila's decisions concerning the embassy.

The origin of the story of Saint Peter and the flaming sword probably lies with Paulus Diaconus, who claims that one of Leo's attendants 'threatened the king with a drawn sword', a story later embellished by Isidore of Seville among others.[43] However, Leo's main purpose was not to 'order' Attila to withdraw. Fortunately, a letter from eastern bishops to Pope Symmachus, dated to 512 or 513, shows that Leo's task was to negotiate the release of captives, not only of the Christians, but 'if that can be believed, Jews and

Pagans'.[44] In return for a large sum of gold, which he had brought with him, Leo was able to obtain the release of many – but not all – of the captives.

Attila also 'agreed' to continue his retreat from Italy. However, he repeated his demand that Honoria be surrendered to him, threatening to invade again unless she was sent to him 'with her due share of the royal wealth'.[45] Realistically, he was not in a position to make good on his demands. Attila's invasion had gone some way towards repairing the damage to his reputation of the previous year, but it was still far from a complete success. Furthermore, the attack on the homes of the Huns demonstrated that Attila's boasts about controlling the Eastern Roman Empire were no longer true. Attila retired to his homeland, this time determined on vengeance against the East whose actions had helped to thwart his plans.

Conclusion

The major difference between the invasions of Gaul and Italy was the defence of Aquileia. In 451 Attila had taken a number of cities in quick succession, a fact that had allowed him to penetrate deep into Gaul. Recognizing that fact, Aetius may have stationed a strong garrison in Aquileia as soon as he heard of Attila's approach. As a consequence, the three-month siege of Aquileia caused Attila to lose a great part of the campaign season and, coupled with the heavy losses and the beginnings of disease, ultimately shortened the duration of the campaign in northern Italy.

Aetius' strategy is usually seen as poor, mainly due to the fact that he allowed Attila to enter Italy without attempting to defend the Julian Alps. However, as noted above, this is unrealistic. Having realized that he could not defend the Alps, Aetius had resorted to delaying tactics, reinforcing Aquileia in the hope that the city would hold out and give time for the East to organize a relief force for Italy. With famine throughout Italy, time was on Aetius' side.

Once the troops arrived from the East there can be little doubt that Aetius used his forces to harass the Huns as they retreated across northern Italy. This, together with the envoys sent by Valentinian, determined Attila that the West, although fragmented, was simply too strong while led by Aetius. Attila took the only course open to him. Having saved at least a little face by ransoming some of the prisoners in negotiations with Pope Leo, the Huns returned home to begin the rebuilding of their shattered homesteads and Attila's palaces. However, Attila's anger had now transferred to the East and he began to make plans for an invasion of the East in the following year.

453

It was only after the accession of Marcian and the emperor's refusal to pay tribute that events had conspired against Attila. In theory Attila's campaign in Italy and the refusal of the Roman army to fight him in battle had rectified the loss at the Catalaunian Plains. Consequently, Attila returned to his usual stance with the East. Early in 453 he not only demanded the payment of tribute, but also the arrears that had not been paid to him since before the death of Theodosius.[46] In response Marcian sent emissaries to meet with Attila to negotiate. Attila blankly refused to treat with them.[47]

Yet since the accession of Marcian the political and military landscape had changed. Marcian had concluded peace treaties with both the Persians in the east and the Blemmyes and Nobades who had been causing trouble in southern Egypt. With peace on his other frontiers, Marcian, although wary of the threat still posed by Attila, was no longer as fearful of the Huns and was prepared, if necessary, to fight.[48] Marcian's dogged refusal to pay was no doubt also reinforced by the fact that Attila had lost his aura of invincibility: if the weak West had defeated Attila, there was no reason why the much stronger East should be afraid of the Hunnic king. There may also have been increased tensions within Attila's empire as the subject nations considered the possibility of a rebellion against Hunnic rule following Attila's defeat in 451. In addition, although impossible to prove, Marcian may have sent agents into Hunnic territory with the specific intention of stirring up discontent and encouraging a rebellion.

With pressure mounting, it was imperative that Attila succeed in obtaining the tribute he demanded from the East, but with Marcian refusing to pay the only course open to Attila was war. Prior to leading his men against the East, Attila

> took in marriage according to the custom of his race a very beautiful girl named Ildico. At his wedding he gave himself up to excessive celebration and he lay down on his back sodden with wine and sleep.

He suffered a haemorrhage, and the blood, which would ordinarily have drained through his nose, was unable to pass through the usual passages and flowed in its deadly course down his throat, killing him.

Priscus, fr. 24.1.[49]

Although this is the cause of death accepted by most historians, it should be noted that other variations are recorded. Jordanes and Theophanes both claim he died because of an accident, whereas Marcellinus claims that he was killed either by Ildico or in an accident.[50] John Malalas records three different possible causes, including the two already mentioned, but also notes the rumour that Aetius had bribed Attila's *spatharius* (bodyguard) to kill him.[51] This is extremely unlikely, as it is not mentioned elsewhere and Malalas, writing so long after events, does not explain from where he obtained the information.

So passed the ruler of the Empire of the Huns, and possibly the single greatest external threat to Roman imperial security.

Chapter Eleven

Aftermath and Conclusions

Reaction

When the news arrived in Constantinople and Rome no doubt there was great relief: the individual who had welded the disparate tribes of the Huns into a major military force had died. Yet at the same time, there would have been great concern over what would happen to Attila's empire: after all, one of his sons could easily emulate – if not better – the acts of the 'Scourge of God'. It was not to be. Rather than closing ranks and ensuring that the Hunnic Empire remained one whole body, Attila's sons immediately began a civil war to determine which individual would inherit the whole empire.[1] This is not surprising: Attila had numerous wives, and although it is not known if all of them bore him children, he left his empire to be divided among his many sons, who 'themselves almost amounted to a people'.[2] Strife was inevitable.

In the West, Aetius may have hoped that at least one of Attila's sons would appeal to him for aid, so allowing a return to the former situation where Aetius and at least one section of the Huns were close allies. In the East, the relief with which the news of the Huns' implosion was received was tempered by some unhappy news, especially for Marcian. In July 453 his wife died, leaving her property for 'charitable purposes'.[3] Marcian now had to survive without her political support, so he was extremely fortunate that the death of Attila and the outbreak of the Hunnic civil war gave him and the East a breathing space in which he could cement his position as 'sole' ruler. He was to be helped by events that took place in 454.

454

With the death of Attila his treaties with other peoples became void, and the hostages given by Aetius – probably including Aetius' son Carpilio –

returned home. At the same time, the bureaucrats sent by Aetius to serve Attila when he was made honorary *magister militum*, including Orestes, also returned home. They would have brought the news that, if not before the New Year then almost certainly at the start of it, the Hunnic Empire, already in the grip of civil war, now faced internal revolt.[4] Ardaric, the king of the Gepids – one of Attila's most trusted allies and the same man who had fought at the Battle of the Catalaunian Plains – didn't give the same respect to Attila's sons as he had to their father and was angered that the sons were squabbling over Attila's empire. Allegedly they had 'allotted war-like kings and peoples like household servants'.[5] In response he raised the standard of revolt and other tribes emulated his actions and within a short time an alliance was formed against the Huns.

Although this is the standard account of events – based on Prosper's *Chronicle* – it has recently been questioned. A new analysis suggests that by 454 the leaders of all the subordinate tribes were part of a 'heterogeneous' Hunnic group, so rather than being the 'conquered' tribes demanding their freedom, the 'revolt' of Ardaric was not a rebellion but simply an extension of the Hunnic civil war.[6] This may be true, since the sources concerning events among the Huns after Attila's death are very poor and it is indeed possible that rather than leading a rebelling 'people', Ardaric may simply have been fighting for his share of the empire, rather like the Macedonian generals partitioning Alexander the Great's empire after his death. However, unless new information comes to light the accuracy of the two conflicting theories remains in doubt. Here, the traditional account is being followed, largely due to the fact that it is the one related in the ancient sources. On the other hand, the net result was to be the same whether the uprising was a revolt or simply an extension of the civil war.

The Battle of Nedao[7]

At an unknown date, but most likely in 454, in a great battle the two major opponents met at the River Nedao (Nedava). According to the traditional tale, the forces of the Huns were led by Ellac, the eldest of Attila's sons and Attila's personal favourite. Due to the nature of the rebellion it would appear that most, if not all, of Attila's other sons joined Ellac's forces in an attempt to defeat the rebels.

Ardaric and his Gepids had enlisted the help of the Ostrogoths, the Rugians, the Sueves, the Alans and the Heruls, among others. Although it may appear surprising that many of the tribes listed are to be found within the boundaries of the Roman empire – for example, the Sueves in Spain – it should be remembered that the peoples listed here represent those tribes who did not join the invasion of the Roman Empire, either preferring or being compelled to remain in their original homelands under the dominion of the Huns.

In a fierce battle the Huns, unexpectedly, were heavily defeated and Ellac himself 'died fighting so bravely that, had his father been alive, he would have wished for an end so glorious'.[8] After his death the Hunnic Empire disintegrated. So ended the Hunnic threat to Rome. The survivors of the Battle of Nedao separately followed those sons of Attila who were still alive. However, the modern conception that the Huns immediately passed from history is mistaken. This belief is in part due to the fact that the sources for the Huns now become extremely scarce, with only rare mentions of their activities. However, into the sixth century they are attested serving as mercenaries for the Eastern Empire. It would appear that the remnants of the Huns had retreated to the region of the River Dnieper:

> With Attila's death in 453 and the subsequent dissolution of the Hunnic tribal union after the Battle of Nedao, in 454 or 455 (in which Ellac perished), Hunnic remnants and closely allied tribes about whom we know only their names (Ultinzures, Bitgorres or Bittugures, Angisciri and Bardores) retreated to 'Scythia Minor', present-day Dobrudja and adjacent areas. Two Hunnic groupings remained, led by the surviving sons of Attila, Dengizikh ... [or Dintzic] ... and Hernac. The head of the former was brought to the Byzantine capital in 469 and the fate of the latter is unknown. His name, however, does appear in the Bulgarian Prince-List and it may well be presumed that either he or his 'charismatic clan', and most certainly elements of his tribal followers, mixed with tribes that were then entering the western steppe zone and would later form the Bulghar tribal union.
>
> *Golden,* The Peoples of the South Russian Steppes, *1990.*[9]

As a result, rather than disappearing without trace, it is likely that the blood of the Huns flows in the veins of many Eastern Europeans, and especially those tracing their ancestry to the ancient Bulgars.

The Hunnic War Machine

In the history of war there is nothing more prevalent than the image of the savage nomad riding his horse around the static, cowering infantry of his agriculturalist enemies, whether this be the Huns of Attila or the Mongol horde of Chingiz Khan. Yet there is one interesting feature to note about the Hunnic war machine. Although usually seen as being 'unstoppable' and capable of defeating the Roman army thanks to the deployment of large numbers of mobile horse-archers, this perception is almost certainly simply the result of a standard perception of nomadic warfare, coupled with the Huns' use of 'large-scale raids' to achieve their ends. In this context, the attacks on the East are the most obvious examples of Hunnic 'superiority'. During 441, 442 and 447 the Huns inflicted demoralizing 'defeats' on the East Roman Empire. The end result was humiliation and the relinquishing of a large region of Roman territory to Attila.

Yet when seen in context, in these examples the Huns were not facing large Roman armies and defeating them, but conducting raids on a scale scarcely seen in the ancient world, including the besieging and sack of Roman cities. For the most part the raids were effective simply because they were unopposed. On the other hand, when fighting 'set-piece' battles, the Huns were actually not very successful. In fact, of the few battles known from the sources – namely the Battle of Toulouse in 439, of the Utus River in 447, of the Catalaunian Plains in 451, and of Nedao in 454 – the only definite victory was that at the Utus, and even this is described as being 'Pyrrhic'.[10] Surprisingly, even where the Huns could be expected to be victorious, such as when fighting the garrison of Asemus, the Huns were defeated by the garrison.

It would appear that the Huns' reputation lies in their victories over the Alans, Greuthungi and Tervingi – long before their contact with Rome – and their conquest of the large numbers of 'barbarian' tribes that eventually constituted their empire. Their hit-and-run tactics were what won them their prominence, and this was easier against the tribes beyond the Rhine and the Danube who struggled to defend their 'urban centres' against the Huns. It even worked for a time against the East Roman Empire, who found it easier and cheaper to 'buy them off' rather than risk a battle, especially when the East's attention was focused elsewhere.

In fact, there is some credence to the claim that the Hun state was a 'protection racket on a grand scale'.[11] The perception is reinforced by the suggestion that the attacks on Gaul and Italy were 'typical nomadic attempts to gain a steady source of supplies and income ... [which] failed'.[12] In addition, the need of the Hunnic leaders – and especially Attila – to acquire and maintain a high level of prestige is noted.

As proof, it is highlighted that, despite their reputation:

> The political and economic damage inflicted by the Huns' attacks on the Roman Empire was significantly less than the damage that followed the permanent settlements of the Goths in Aquitaine, or the Vandal invasion of North Africa. Nor did the Huns ever inflict a major defeat on a Roman field army.
>
> *Kelly*, 'Neither Conquest Nor Settlement: Attila's Empire and its Impact', *207*.

In direct contrast, not only did the Goths inflict a damaging military and political defeat at the Battle of Adrianople in 378, but the Vandals decisively defeated the Roman armies in battle in Hispania in 422, in Africa in 431 and 432, and during the attempted Roman reconquests of Africa in 460 and 468. Also both the Goths and the Vandals sacked Rome (in 410 and 455 respectively). The Huns did not accomplish these feats.

Although accurate to a point, this model is rather simplistic and only applies to the Huns' dealings with Rome. It needs to be remembered that the Huns established their dominion over many tribes inside *barbaricum* – in this way possibly inheriting the mantle of the near-legendary Gothic king Ermanaric – and forced many others to flee rather than submit to Hunnic hegemony. This is the result of a military power, not simply a few warriors with an inflated reputation and with the limited aims of demanding loot. The Huns were an outstanding political and military power for around four generations, before their own success proved to be their downfall as they became ruptured by civil war and/or were defeated by their subjects. At the height of their power they could, in some ways, rival both Sasanid Persia and Rome. Their greatest failings included their lack of a monetary system for the raising of taxes with which to fund a large state and the lack of a comprehensive bureaucracy. However, the greatest single weakness was that their apogee was created by an individual who left no single successor. Again, the most obvious comparison from the ancient world is that of Alexander the Great, whose empire also fragmented after his death due to him leaving no obvious successor.

Attila

That the height of Hunnic power was reached under the leadership of Attila is beyond doubt. Yet uncertainty remains concerning Attila himself. The question is whether any specific aspects of Attila's personality and of his political and military abilities can be detected across the intervening centuries. Unsurprisingly, many modern historians tend to repeat the image portrayed in the ancient sources. For example:

> Beneath his great savagery, Attila was a subtle man, and fought with diplomacy before he went to war.
>
> *Jordanes*, Getica, *186.*

> [Attila was a] subtle and effective diplomat able to outwit the most powerful courtiers in Constantinople.
>
> *Kelly, 2008, 154–5,* The End of Empire: Attila the
> Hun & the Fall of Rome.

Attila was definitely sensitive to any sign of Roman weakness. This could be either military or political weakness. For example, as far as military weakness was concerned, his action in 441–2 demonstrates that he was determined to use the capture of Carthage by the Vandals and the subsequent deployment of Aspar and a large Eastern army to Africa to gain a political advantage from the East.[13] Politically, in 451 he was faced with disunity in the West, with Rome and the Goths disputing affairs in Gaul and the Franks disunited over the claimants to the throne. Attila took advantage of both by sending envoys to further the confusion and then actually invading. In the end it was only fear of the Huns that resulted in a coalition being formed to face the Huns on an equal footing. Furthermore, and despite the defeat of Attila in 451, the fact that there was little chance of the Goths of Toulouse supporting the Romans in Italy in 452 was almost certainly a major factor in Attila's decision to invade.

On the other hand, this is not the whole picture. The weaknesses inherent in the empire were obvious to many barbarian leaders, so in this respect Attila may not have been outstanding. Some recent historians have attempted to analyse the subtle differences between the more important 'barbarian warlords' and arrived at a different conclusion to that previously proposed. For example:

> The actions and attitudes of the Hun king Attila in the 440s and early 450s ... [demonstrate that] ... unlike the leaders of the Goths, Burgundians and Vandals in particular, he remained a barbarian warlord who never appreciated, nor fully engaged with, the dynastic and aristocratic mainstays of contemporary Roman politics and society. Therein lies the key to his ultimate political failure.
>
> *Croke,* Dynasty and Aristocracy in the Fifth Century, *98–9.*

It is possible to suggest that the description 'barbarian warlord' shows simply that the author is a traditionalist who sees a stark division between Roman and barbarian that didn't exist in reality. This may be an error. Both Euric, King of the Visigoths (466–84), and Gaiseric, King of the Vandals (428–77), appear to have been intensely aware of the political machinery of both halves of the Roman Empire and subsequently used this knowledge to the benefit of their peoples and the detriment of the empire. Despite his reputation of being a 'subtle and effective diplomat', when facing the West Attila was outwitted by Aetius – admittedly probably the most able individual of his generation – and in the East his bluff was called by Marcian, a capable military commander who replaced Theodosius II, the latter an emperor far more willing to use the vast imperial resources to halt Hun attacks rather than risk a battle. In both cases Attila's response was to revert simply to war, although in the latter he was to die before the war could be waged.

The conclusion seems to be that Attila was undoubtedly a man with political and military flair, capable of waging war and manipulating less able ambassadors. However, his methods sometimes displayed a distinct lack of delicacy and a lack of understanding of the complexity of Roman politics. For example, the demand for half of the West for Honoria and the sending of multiple envoys to Aetius in Rome and the Goths in Toulouse, although usually described as cunning political manoeuvres, in reality may be seen as counterproductive. There was no possibility of the West acceding to his demands concerning Honoria, so any claim that he was entering Gaul in defence of 'her realm' was a non-starter. In addition, it was obvious to all parties in Gaul after they had themselves exchanged envoys that Attila was attempting to 'divide and conquer'. The fact that Theoderic in Toulouse nearly remained neutral is not so much a sign of Attila's political genius as it is of Theoderic's desire to be free of Roman control. Indeed, Attila's plan may have succeeded had he not sent envoys to Italy but relied solely on those to the Goths. Yet this is all supposition: whatever the methods Attila used it is possible that eventually Theoderic would have acceded to Roman pressure, simply because the Huns were the 'great enemy' that had driven his people out of their homes in the previous century.

Conclusion

With so little established fact it is difficult to reach a sure conclusion on any aspect of Attila's life. He was either a descendant of the Xiongnu, or the offspring of an unknown lineage. He was either a military genius whose exploits helped to fatally weaken the West Roman Empire, or an average strategist who took advantage of Roman military weakness but did not have the skills needed to make the most of his opportunities. He was either a political mastermind who followed the maxim of 'divide and conquer', or again, simply an opportunist who failed to make the most of his political openings when they materialized. Or maybe he was a combination of all of these things: an individual of partial Mongol stock who had moments of political and military brilliance but who did not have them often enough to establish a lasting political and military state. It is extremely unlikely that the truth will ever be known. Yet whatever the reality, Attila's legacy will forever be the image of the marauding nomad sweeping down on a helpless Roman Empire: truly, the 'Scourge of God'.

Notes

Introduction

1. Thorsten Dunlap: http://germanhistorydocs.ghi-dc.org/sub_document.cfm? document_id=755&language=english
2. Kelly, 2008, 20–1.
3. Paul the Deacon, *Historia Romana*, 14.12.
4. Kelly, 2008, 17.
5. Heather, 1994, 5f.
6. For the chronicles of Prosper and Hydatius and the *Gallic Chronicles* of 452 and 511 Muhlberger is an invaluable introduction and commentary, from which much of this section is derived.
7. Muhlberger, 2006, 2.
8. Muhlberger, 2006, 147.
9. Whitby and Whitby, 1989, ix.
10. Muhlberger, 2006, 147; 213.
11. Muhlberger, 2006, 213.
12. Muhlberger, 2006, 73f.
13. Muhlberger, 2006, 98. More on Prosper's 'unhappiness' with Aetius, 99f. Muhlberger comments: 'one wonders what Prosper might have said if Aetius had not been ruling when he wrote.' However, Prosper wrote in 'editions', and in the last edition of 455 Aetius was dead, so we might be seeing Prosper's 'official' opinion.
14. Halsall, 2007, 237. n.78.
15. Oost, 1964, 23.
16. This section is based largely upon Clover, 1971, 7f.
17. PLRE I, *Merobaudes* 2.
18. Clover, 1971, 8f, esp. 8, n.6 and 11.
19. On the similarities between the existing fragments of Merobaudes and the works of Claudian, Clover, 1971, 32–3: citing Vollmer, *MGH*: AA 14, pp.3–6, 12–13, 16–20.
20. For a detailed analysis of these poems, along with a bibliography, see Clover, 1971, 16–28.
21. The dating of this piece is extremely difficult and several possibilities exist. The dating of 443–6 is that given by Clover, 1971, 32–41, where he also discusses the other hypotheses.
22. Wood, in CAH, 519–520.

23. *Cod. Th.* 1.1.5 (26 March 429).
24. Freeman, 1887, 423.
25. Gaiseric being spelt 'Zinzirich', *Chron. Pasch.* s.a. 439.
26. Kulikowski, 2002, 69, n.2.
27. Collins, 2006, 19.

Chapter 1

1. de la Vaissière, 2014, 175–6: 'Xiongnu' may mean 'ferocious/howling slaves'.
2. On the changes in thought, see e.g. de la Vaissière, 2014, 175–6; c.f. Gordon, 1960, 57. For an analysis of more recent discussions, see de la Vaissière, 2014, 180.
3. See e.g. Pritsak, 1982, 429, for a history of the arguments over the origins of the Huns.
4. C.f. Heather, 1995, 5: Pritsak, 1982, *passim*: the concept of the Huns speaking 'Ket' – a variation of the Yeniseian language – was proposed by Pulleyblank (1962) but has not received widespread acceptance, but c.f. Vovin, 2000.
5. Pritsak, 1982, 470: but c.f. Mangaltepe, 2011, 8.
6. Kim, 2016, 34.
7. de la Vaissière, 2014, 178: c.f. http://www.universalis.fr/encyclopedie/fahu-dharmaraksa
8. de la Vaissière, 2014, 179.
9. de la Vaissière, 2014, 179.
10. de la Vaissière, 2014, 179: date and association, Henning, 1948, esp. 613–615.
11. For a more detailed analysis of these problems, de la Vaissière, 2014, 181f: Atwood, 2012, *passim*.
12. The majority of their body in central Asia was a mix of Iranic speakers and Oghur speakers, the latter of which were a people conquered by the Xiongnu called the Dingling, later the known as the Tiele Confederation.
13. C.f. Maas, 2015, 7.
14. de la Vaissière, 2014, 176.
15. de la Vaissière, 2014, 176: c.f. Theophylact Simocatta.
16. de la Vaissière, 2014, 180; 2015, 182.
17. Walden and Mason, 2006, vol. 2, 393.
18. C.f. Golden, 1992, 86.
19. *Weishu*, 103.2290.
20. de la Vaissière, 2014, 187–8.
21. de la Vaissière, 2014, 185–6.
22. Kelly, 2008, 21, 32.
23. Kelly, 2008, 30.
24. de la Vaissière, 2014, 187.
25. Maas, 2015, 6–7: de la Vaissière, 2014, 189.
26. de la Vaissière, 2014, 189–90.
27. de la Vaissière, 2014, 190.

28. de la Vaissière, 2014, 176.
29. de la Vaissière, 2014, 183.
30. Kim, 2016, 38.
31. de la Vaissière, 2014, 177.
32. C.f. Walden and Mason, 2006, Vol. 2, 393.
33. AM 31.2.
34. Possibly comparable to the later story concerning Attila and the 'Sword of Mars': thanks to Evan Schultheis for this link.
35. Heather, 1995, 6.
36. Prisc. frg. 10.
37. Prisc. frg. 1.
38. Prisc.
39. Thanks to Evan Schultheis for providing this hypothesis.
40. AM 31.3.1.
41. AM 31.3.2.
42. C.f. Kim, 2016, 74.
43. C.f. Kim, 2016, 74.
44. Heather, 2009, 215.
45. AM 31.3.3.
46. AM 31.3.4–5.
47. C.f. Heather, 1995, 6.
48. Heather, P., 1998, 100.
49. Whether the Huns and Alans were allies is debated: it is possible that the Alans were simply serving as Hun vassals.
50. 'Caucalanda', AM 31.4.13: c.f. Heather, 1995, 8; Kelly, 2008, 38.
51. C.f. Heather, 1995, 6: but see Kim, 2016, 74–5 for the 'traditional' view of the Gothic collapse being swift.
52. 'Less than a generation', de la Vaissière, 2014, 177.
53. On the Huns' weaponry, see Hughes, 2009, 37.
54. Kim, 2016, 75.
55. AM 31.2.1; 3.1f: Eun. frg. 41.1; 42: Zos. 4.10.3ff: Soc. 4.43: Soz. 6.37: Ambrose, *Expositio Evangelii secundum Lucam*, 10.10.
56. AM 31.8.3.
57. AM 31.16.
58. AM 31.16.7; 25.10.9: c.f. Gračanin, 2006, 32.
59. Marc. *com. s.a.* 427: cf. Jord. *Get.* 32. 166: Gordon, 1960, 58–9: Gračanin, 2006, 34.
60. C.f. Gračanin, 2006, 34–5.
61. AM. 31.11.6.
62. Alans serving Gratian, Zos. 4. 35. 2.
63. On the Alpidzuri, Tongouri and other distinct 'Hunnic' tribes, see above.
64. Settlement, c.f. Gračanin, 2006, 34–5, although Gračanin himself disputes this: conversion attempt, Gračanin, 2006, 36.

65. Zos. 4.35.6.
66. Contra, Kim, 2016, 75.
67. Ambrose Ep. 24.8: the wording used by Ambrose is a little confusing: c.f. Gračanin, 2006, 37.
68. Gračanin, 2006, 37: Quintus Aurelius Symmachus, *Relationes ad Principes* 2.47.
69. AM 31.2.7. It should be noted, however, that Ammianus' accuracy on Hunnic affairs during this period in their history is open to some doubt.
70. Zos. 4.39, 5.36: date, Claud. *Cos. Hon* 4.633–37.
71. Kim, 2016, 75, suggests that these 'Huns' may in fact be Alpidzuri taking advantage of the Hun name.
72. C.f. Kim, 2016, 76: contra, e.g. Heather, 1995, 103.
73. C.f. Heather, 1995, 9: Gračanin, 2006, 39.
74. Maenchen-Helfen, 1973, 46: Zos. 4. 48–50: c.f. Eun. frgs. 58 and 60.
75. Bear arms, CTh 9.14.2: Theodosius, Zos. 4.50.1; Maenchen-Helfen, 1973, 46–7.
76. For a more detailed analysis of this model, Kim, 2016, 14f.
77. One kingdom, split into East and West, Kim, 2016, 76.
78. C.f. Amidon, 2007, 20, n.14.
79. Maenchen-Helfen, 1973, 54: Heather, 1995, 8–9.
80. Hughes, 2010, 81–5; but c.f. Zos. 5.7.3.
81. Joh. Ant. frg. 187.
82. C.f. Amb. *Ep.* 60.
83. Claud. *In Ruf.* 1.317: Zos. 4.51.
84. Ephrain the Syrian, *Ep.* 77.8: trans. and comments, Kim, 2016, 76.
85. Maenchen-Helfen, 1973, 55.
86. TU 89, 1, 1892, 104: C.f. Maenchen-Helfen, 1973, 55–6.
87. Claud. *In Eut.* 2; *praef.* 55; 2. 367: c.f. Kim, 2016, 76–7.
88. *Incerti auctoris Chronicon Pseudo-Dionysianum vulgo dictum*, vol. 1, ed. J.-B. Chabot, *CSCO* 91, Paris, 1927, pp.187.17–188.14: trans. G. Greatrex, M. Greatrex, 1999, 69–70: Eutropius and date of repulse to 397. Greatrex and Greatrex, 1999, 73: c.f. Maenchen-Helfen, 1973, pp.51–5: contra, dating the raid to 410–1, Blockley, 1983, 384–7, n-n. 66–8: Heather, 1995, 6.
89. C.f. Heather, 2015, 214.
90. Heather, 1995, 5.

Chapter 2
1. Khazanov, 1994, 2.
2. Khazanov, 1994, 12. For a greater analysis of nomads/nomadism see 14f, esp. 16.
3. Khazanov, 1994, 45.
4. Kim, 2016, 2.
5. Golden, 1992, 3.
6. Golden, 1992, 3.

7. Maas, 2015, 5; c.f. Kelly, 2008, 27.
8. Golden, 1992, 4.
9. Maas, 2015, 4.
10. Kelly, 2008, 24.
11. On the consequences of such exchanges, see Lindner, 1981, 4.
12. Golden, 1992, 7.
13. Golden, 1992, 10.
14. 'World's best', Kim, 2015, 82.
15. E.g. Fyfe, 2017, 123f.
16. E.g. Maur. Strat. 1.1; 1.2; 12.3; 12.5.
17. C.f. Fyfe, 2017, 133f.
18. Kelly, 2008, 27.
19. Gillett, 2003, 8.
20. The conspiracy mentioned here is dealt with in detail in Chapter 7.
21. In conversation, Evan Schultheis.
22. Scapilumancy is attested as a method used by the Huns: see e.g. Chapter 9.
23. Elishe (Eghishe): Egise, O. *Vardane i voine armyanskoe*, trans. (into Russian) by I.A. Orbeli (Erevan, 1971), p.31, 127, as referenced by Golden, 1992, 90.
24. See the quote from Priscus above.
25. Maenchen–Helfen, 1973, 269.
26. Prisc. frg. 11.1: c.f. Kim, 2015, 82–3.
27. Prisc. frg. 13: c.f. Kim, 2015, 83.
28. Prisc. frg. 49: Kim, 2015, 84.
29. The most obvious example is the stationing of the Spartans to the right of the battle line in Ancient Greece: c.f. Kim, 2015, 83.
30. C.f *Zacharias of Mitylene*: Kim, 2015, 85.
31. Lindner, 1981, 4ff.
32. Horses and sieges, Lindner, 1981, 9–10: on Aquileia, see Chapter 9.
33. C.f. Lindner, 1981, 10.
34. Lindner, 1981, 10–11.
35. Lindner, 1981, 4. Although talking about the Middle Ages in this extract, the comparison stands for the vast majority of the settled population of both of the empires named.

Chapter 3

1. Maenchen–Helfen, 1973, 59.
2. Pritsak, 1982, 437.
3. Kim, 2016, 77.
4. Marc. *com. s.a.* 427.
5. Zos. 4.57.2; 58.2: Joh. Ant. frg. 187.
6. Soz. 8.4.5, 18–20: Soc. 6.6.1: Theod. 5.32.1: Zos. 5.19.6 – 21.4: Joh. Ant. frg. 190: Eunap. frg. 82.
7. Zos. 5.21.9–22.3: Soz. 8.4.20: Marc. *com. s.a.* 400, 402: Joh. Ant. frg. 190: Soc. 6.6.1f: Philost. 11.8.

8. Zos. 5.27.1–3.
9. Soz. 8.25.1: Niceph. Call. 8.35; 13.35: dating, Maenchen-Helfen, 1973, 62–3: c.f. PLRE 2, *Uldin*, 1180.
10. Oros. 7.37.2: Marc. *com. s.a.* 406: Jord. *Rom.* 321.
11. On the lack of opposition to the invasion, c.f. *Cod. Th.* 7.8.15 (24 March, 406): c.f. Gračanin, 2006, 43.
12. Gračanin, 2006, 41.
13. Soz. 9.25.1.7: C.f. *CTh.* 5.6.
14. C.f. Jerome, Ep. 123.17: Gračanin, 2006, 44.
15. Soz.11.4.1.
16. C.f. Soc. 6.1: *CTh* 5.6.3 (12 April 409).
17. For translation and full references, Maenchen-Helfen, 1973, 64.
18. *Cod. Th.* 5.6.2.
19. Heather, 1995, 15.
20. Independent, e.g. Maenchen-Helfen, 1973, 59f: subordinate, e.g. Kim, 2016, 77f.
21. C.f. Maenchen-Helfen, 1973, 71.
22. Zos. 5.34.1.
23. Zos. 5.50.1; c.f. 5.46.6.
24. Maenchen-Helfen, 1973, 69.
25. Zos. 5.37.1: c.f. Maenchen-Helfen, 1973, 69–70.
26. Heather, 1995, 26.
27. Heather, 1995, 26, n. 4.
28. Zos. 5.46.2: 5.37.1: Maenchen-Helfen, 1973, 70–1.
29. Soz. 7.37.3.
30. For a more detailed analysis of the following events, see Hughes, 2012, 14f.
31. Greg. Tur. 2.8: Merob. *Pan.* 2.1–4. Sadly, neither source gives the date or duration of the hostage agreement.
32. Heather, 1995, 14–17.
33. C.f. Olymp. frg. 19.
34. Danubian fleets: *CTh.* 7. 17. 1 (cf. 7.16.2): Walls: C. Mango, *Le développement urbain de Constantinople (IVe-VIIe siècles)* (Paris, 1990) pp.46 ff. References, Heather, 1995, 18, and n.2.
35. East, e.g. Kelly, 2008, 53: West, e.g. Maenchen-Helfen, 1973, 73–4.
36. C.f. PLRE 2, Donatus 2, 376.
37. In conversation with Evan Schultheis.
38. C.f. Heather, 1995, 11: c.f. Akatziri, Prisc. frg. 11.2.
39. Heather, 1995, 11.
40. For more on this, see 'Rua and Octar' below.
41. Marc. *com. s.a.* 422.
42. *Chron. Pasch.* s.a. 421.
43. Croke, 1977, 347–8.
44. Theoph. A.M. 5931.
45. For a more detailed analysis of the controversy, see Croke, 1977, 358f.

46. *Cod. Th.* 7.10.10.
47. Theod. 5.37. 4–10: c.f. Croke, 1977, 349.
48. Croke, 1977, 349; 351–2, n.14.
49. Croke, 1977, 351–2, n.14.
50. PLRE 2, *Rua*, 951; *Octar*, 789–80.
51. PLRE 2, *Mundiuch*, 767.
52. Priscus, as preserved in Jordanes, quote and reference Golden, 1992, 90, n.22.
53. Prosp. a. 423 and 425: Greg. Tur. 2.8: Philost. 12.14: Soc. 7.43.3: c.f. Joh. Nik. 84.81.85.
54. *Pseudo. Aug. Ep.* 4: c.f. Maenchen-Helfen, 1973, 76–7.
55. Soc. 7.43.3: Joh. Nik. 84, 81, 85.
56. Hughes, 2102, 22.
57. C.f. Soc. 7.43.3: Joh. Nik. 84.81.85: Greg. Tur. 2.8.
58. E.g. Prosp. a. 425: details, Philost. 22.14.
59. E.g. Gordon, 1960, 59.
60. Marc. *com. s.a.* 427, possibly an exaggeration, based on Marcellinus' source, the lost *Historia Romana* of Symmachus; Maenchen-Helfen, 1973, 77: c.f. Jord. Get. 166.
61. Croke, 1977, 354.
62. C.f. Gračanin, 2006, 47, but see note 55.
63. On some of these, Gračanin, 2006, 47–9.
64. C.f. Maas, 2015, 8.
65. Kim, 2016, 80.
66. *Chron. Gall.* 452 No. 112 (s.a. 433).
67. 'Per Pannonias', Prosp. a. 432: C.f. *Chron. Gall.* 452 112(a. 433): Croke, 1977, 354: Heather, 1995, 17.
68. Croke, 1977, 354.
69. It has been suggested that Aetius returned solely with the *threat* of Hunnic assistance. This is deemed unlikely as the word of a 'renegade' may not have carried the weight of a large army.
70. Prisc. frg. 11.2, 627–631: *Chron. Gall.* 452 116 (s.a. 434).
71. Gračanin, 2006, 49–50.
72. Cass. *Var.* 1.4.10–12.
73. Gračanin, 2006, 51.
74. For a more detailed overview of the debate, Gračanin, 2006, 53.
75. Prisc. frg. 11.1.
76. Prisc. frg. 11.2.
77. Gračanin, 2006, 52.
78. Gračanin, 2006, 53.
79. C.f. Kelly, 2008, 71.
80. Soc. 7.43: Theod. 5.3.64: C.f. Kim, 2015, 80.
81. Soc. 7.43.

Chapter 4

1. Jord. *Get.* 35 (182).
2. Jord. *Get.* 180, 257: Prisc. frgg. 8, 12: Theoph. AM 5942.
3. Prosp. s.a. 444: Marc. *com. s.a.* 442: Prisc. frg. 1: *Cass. Chron.* s.a. 444: Theoph. AM 5942: Suid Z 29.
4. Heather, 2009, 208.
5. Gordon, 1960, 61, 200 n.12.
6. Prisc. frg. 21.1: c.f. Malal. 19.5–12: *Lakatos Quellenbuch*, 55: Kim, 2015, 87: conversation with Evan Schultheis.
7. Prisc. frgg. 11.2 and 13.3.
8. C.f. Kelly, 2008, 70.
9. Ellac, Prisc. frg. 8; Jord. *Get.* 262: Dengizich and Ernach, Prisc. frg. 36; Marc. *com. s.a.* 469; Jord. *Get.* 272; *Chron. Pasch.* s.a. 468.
10. C.f. Hughes, 2012, 105.
11. Tombs, Prisc. frg. 6.1: Gračanin, 2006, 17.
12. Envoys, Priscus frg. 2: Plinta, *Fl. Plinta*, PLRE 2, 892–3: Epigenes, *Epigenes*, PLRE 2, 396 (where the treaty is dated to 438).
13. Lindner, 1981, 9.
14. Kelly, 2015, 199: dated by Kelly, 2008, to 439.
15. PLRE 2, *Attila*, 182–3.
16. Thompson, 1950, 63.
17. C.f. Kelly, 2008, 111–12.
18. Prisc. frg. 2.
19. Prisc. frg. 11.1.
20. Prisc. frg. 1.
21. C.f. Gordon, 1960, 62.
22. Sarris, 2015, 55–6.
23. Kelly, 2008, 73–5.
24. Heather, 2015, 221.
25. Heather, 2015, 222: c.f. Jord. *Get.* 50.264.

Chapter 5

1. Prisc. frg. 1.
2. C.f. Gordon, 1960, 61–2; PLRE 2, *Valips.* 1147: c.f. Given, 2014, 11–12.
3. Kelly, 2008, 89.
4. Sid. Ap. *Carm.* 7.234.
5. Soc. 7.30: see Chapter 3.
6. *Gall. Chron.* a 452. s.a. 435.
7. Gračanin, 2006, 63: c.f. Hughes, 2012, 97–8.
8. Prosp. 1322: *Gall. Chron.* a 452, 118: Hyd. 102.
9. Kelly, 2015, 198.
10. Hyd. s.a. 438: Merob. Pan. I, frg. IIB: c.f. Prosp. s.s. 438. See Hughes, 2012, 99 for a more detailed description.

11. Jord. *Get.* 37 (196).
12. Jord. *Get.* 37 (196): c.f. Kelly, 2015, 198–9.
13. Hyd. 101, 108: Prosp. 1324, 1335.
14. Hughes, 2012, 102–3 for more coverage of events.
15. C.f. Kelly, 2008, 72–3.
16. Prisc. frg. 8.
17. C.f. Sarris, 2015, 57.
18. Kelly, 2008, 94.
19. *Nov. Val.* 23.1, 27 March 347: c.f. Maenchen-Helfen, 1973, 110.
20. Thompson, 1950, 63.
21. C.f. Kelly, 2015, 199.
22. Kelly, 2015, 199.
23. Marc. *com. s.a.* 441.
24. Lee, 2006, 122.
25. Marc. *com. s.a.* 442.
26. C.f. e.g. Croke, 2001, 58.
27. Lenski, 2015, 233.
28. Marc. *com. s.a.* 441: Prisc. frg. 6.18, 9.1, 11.2: c.f. Theoph. AM 5942.
29. Prisc. frg. 3: Marc. *com. s.a.* 441, 442: *Chron. Pasch.* s.a. 442.
30. Prisc. frg. 6.1: c.f. Kelly, 2008, 95–6.
31. 'Annexation' of Pannonia II. Gračanin, 2006, 68.
32. Balkans, Marc. *com.* 441.1.
33. Marc. *com. s.a.* 411: PLRE 2, *Fl. Ardabur Aspar*, 164–9: c.f. Croke, 2001, 57. Croke (*ibid.*) also suggests that at this point the Huns had sacked the cities between Sirmium and Naissus, but as already stated this would mean the Huns traversing the same roads at least twice.
34. Prisc. frg. 9.4.
35. Prisc. frg. 9.4.
36. Priscus acknowledges (fragment 11.1) that the city is five days' march from the Danube. Therefore this is either the ancient name of the River Nischava or the text is corrupt: Blockley, 1983, 380, n.11.
37. Blockley, 1983, 381, n.15.
38. Prisc. frg. 11.2.51–3.
39. Kelly, 2008, 96.
40. Prisc. frg. 9.3.39–41.
41. On the problematic dating of the Asemus affair: dated 443 Conant, 2015, 161: dated 433 Thompson (p.239): dated 447 Greatrex, 2015, 39, all based on Prisc 9.3. C.f. Maenchen-Helfen, 1973, 111–2 for a more detailed analysis of the dating problems.
42. C.f. Huntzinger, 2012, 213.
43. Prisc. frg. 9.3.34–81.
44. Prisc. frg. 11.2.
45. Kelly, 2008, 97: c.f. Kelly, 2015, 200.

46. *Cod. Just.* 2.7.9.
47. Prisc. frg. 5: PLRE s, Anatolius 10, 85.
48. Prisc. frg. 9.3.1–10. On the date, Jones, 1986, 193.
49. Prisc. frg. 9.3.21–38, esp. 28–33.
50. Olymp. 41.2: Elton, 2014, 246.
51. C.f. Kelly, 2015, 205.
52. Conversation with Evan Schultheis.
53. Maenchen-Helfen, 1973, 114 referencing Nov. Theod. 26.1, 29 November 444.
54. It should be noted that the dating of the events described here is extremely insecure. It is possible for this treaty to be dated to any year prior to 446, when it is mentioned by Merobaudes (*Pan.* 2.1–4). This date has been chosen as it allows other events the time to happen and so fits in best with the proposed chronology.
55. Cass. *Var.* 1.4.11: expecting an attack, Merob. *Pan.* 2. 55: c.f. Heather, 2005, 338.
56. Conversation with Evan Schultheis.
57. *Nov. Val.* 6.2.3.1: See also earlier in the Chapter, '444'.
58. Cass. *Var.* 1.4.11–12: Prisc. frg. 11.2.194–5, 11.3.
59. Maenchen-Helfen,. 1973, 89–90; Priscus 21–3. This would explain the passage in Priscus (frg. 11.1) which notes that Orestes, Attila's *notarius* (secretary), was by origin a Roman who 'lived in Pannonia close to the river Save which became subject to the barbarian [Attila] by the treaty made with Aetius'.

Chapter 6

1. Kim, 2015, 83.
2. Heather, 1995, 28.
3. Golden, 1992, 91.
4. Prosp. s.a. 444, 451: Marc. *com. s.a.* 445: Jord. *Get.* 181: *Chron. Gall.* a 452 no. 131 (s.a. 446): *Cass. Chron.* s.a. 444: Theoph. AM 5942.
5. Prisc. frg. 13.2.
6. C.f. Prisc. frg. 13.3.
7. Marc. com. 444–5.1.
8. Cass. *Var.* 1.4.11.
9. *Nov. Th.* 24, 12 September 443.
10. Dinchev, 2007, 518–9: conversation with Evan Schultheis.
11. C.f Kelly, 2008, 100–101.
12. Theoph. AM 5942: Prisc. frg. 9.1.
13. Prisc. frg. 9.2.
14. On the problems of the dating and context of Senator's embassy, see Maenchen-Helfen, 1973, 118–9.
15. Marc. com. 447.1: Malal. 14.22: *Chron. Pasch.* 4.50.
16. Prisc. frg. 9.2: Marc. *com. s.a.* 447: Theoph. AM 5942: Illyricum, Thrace, both Dacias, Moesia and Scythica, Jord. *Rom.* 331.

17. Marc. *com. s.a.* 447: Theoph. AM 5942.
18. Kelly, 2008, 103: c.f. *Chron. Pasch.* p.589: Theoph. AM 5942: Prisc. frg. 11.2.
19. Priscus, frg. 9.4.
20. Kelly, 2015, 200.
21. Marc. com. 447.3.
22. Kelly, 2015, 200–1.
23. Marc. com. 441.3, 447.5: c.f. Theoph. AM 5942.
24. Golden, 1992, 91.
25. 70 cities, *Gall. Chron.* a 452, s.a. 447: Callinicus, *Vita Hypatii*, 23–9.
26. Sarris, 2015, 63: c.f. Aug. *Cit. God.* 3.16.
27. Van Dam, 2015, 82.
28. Dinchev, 2007, 482–3.
29. Iron-working sites, Dinchev, 2007, 508–9.
30. Dinchev, 2007, 4.
31. Lenski, 2015, 235–6.
32. Lenski, 2015, 231.
33. *Chronicon Miscellaneum ad annum* 724, 3.136–7 = 4.106–7.
34. Proc. *Anec.* 18.17.21: *Wars*, 2.4.4–11; c.f. 7.11.13–16.
35. Lenski, 2015, 234, who suggests that, rather than these numbers applying to a single year, they may apply to the whole decade of the 440s.
36. Leo, Ep. 159, 156.
37. Lenski, 2015, 240.
38. Prisc. frg. 11.2.
39. Secretary, Prisc. frg. 14; Anon. Val. 2.38: Architect, Prisc. frg. 11.2.
40. Kelly, 2008, 111.
41. Anatolius, PLRE 2, *Anatolius 10*, 84–6: Theodulus, PLRE 2, *Theodulus 2*, 1105–1106: c.f. Croke, 2015, 120–1.
42. Prisc. frg. 9.3: PLRE 2, *Scottas*, 983.
43. Gračanin, 2003, 53.
44. Western, e.g. *PLRE 2, Attila*, 182–3: embassy Prisc. frg. 11.2.630–5.
45. Gračanin, 2006, 51–2.
46. Prisc. frg. 11.1: c.f. Kelly, 2008, 113.
47. Prisc. frg. 11.1.
48. PLRE2, Eudoxius 2, 412: *Chron. Gall.* 452 s.a. 448.
49. C.f. Kim, 2015, 97–8.

Chapter 7
1. Prisc. frg. 8. 77–81, 137–143: c.f. Lenski, 2015, 230–1: Gračanin, 2006, 65.
2. Croke, 2015, 121.
3. Promotus, PLRE 2, *Promotus 1*, 926: Romanus, PLRE 2, *Romanus 2*, 946–7.
4. Tatulus, PLRE 2, *Tatulus*, 1055: Romulus, PLRE 2, *Romulus 2*, 949.
5. Prisc. frg. 11.1.
6. Constantius, PLRE 2, *Constantius 7*, 319.

7. Gračanin, 2003, 72.
8. Prisc. frg. 8.
9. Prisc. frg. 11.1; c.f. frg. 10.
10. PLRE 2, *Edeco*, 385–6: PLRE 2, *Eslas*, 402.
11. Kim, 2016, 85–6.
12. Prisc. frg. 11.1.6–18: see Chapter 6.
13. Prisc. frg. 11.1.25–58.
14. PLRE 2, *Maximinus 11*, 743.
15. Prisc. frg. 11.1. 230f.
16. Prisc. frg. 15.1.
17. Prisc. frg. 15.2.
18. Prisc. frg. 15.4: date, Gračanin, 2003, 67.
19. Although the distances are not much greater than during the invasion of Gaul, the invasion of Persia would need far more troops, plus Attila may not have been able to demand that his 'Germanic' allies travel so far away from their homes.
20. Gračanin, 2003, 65.
21. Croke, 1995, 80–1, n.434.
22. Gračanin, 2003, 66, n.64.
23. C.f. Marc. *com. s.a.* 434: Jord. *Get.* 224.
24. Gračanin, 2003, 71–2.
25. Common knowledge by 450: Gračanin, 2003, 65: c.f. Croke, 1995, 80–1, n.434.
26. Contra, Gračanin, 2003, 66, 71–2, who claims that Hyacinthus was sent to Attila in spring 449 and that the embassy sent concerning the plates had as a secret mission to negotiate concerning Honoria.
27. On the doubts, see Maenchen-Helfen, 1973, 130.
28. Heather, 2005, 335.
29. C.f. Gračanin, 2003, 67.
30. Prisc. frg. 17.16f.
31. Gračanin, 2003, 67.
32. Gračanin, 2003, 67.
33. Prisc. frg. 16, c.f. Greg. Tur. 2.7.
34. The chronology is based on the description given by Priscus, frg. 20.3, where Attila's support of the elder son followed the death of the king. But c.f PLRE 2, *Aetius 7*, 27, where the assumption is that the king of the Franks died during the Battle of the Catalaunian Plain.
35. Conversation with Evan Schultheis.
36. Prosp. s.a. 448.
37. Jord. *Get.* 184–5.
38. Prisc. frg. 15.
39. On the strained relations between Gaiseric and Valentinian in 450, Clover, 1973, 108.
40. *Chron. Pasch.* s.a. 450.

41. The accident happened near the River Lycus not far from the city: *Chron. Pasch.* s.a. 450: Joh. Mal. 14.10 (358), 14. 27 (367); *Cass. Chron.* s.a. 450. Vict. Tonn. s.a. 450.1.
42. Kelly, 2008, 186.
43. Kelly, 2008, 186.
44. Prisc. frg. 20.1: c.f. PLRE 2, *Apollonius 3*, 121: Croke, 2015, 121.
45. Prisc. frg. 20.1.4–6.
46. Prisc. frg. 20.1.
47. Prisc. frg. 20.2.7–8.
48. Prisc. frg. 20.2.12–15.
49. Heather, 2005, 366.
50. Prisc, frg. 11. 2. 585f.
51. C.f. Kelly, 2015. 201.
52. PLRE 2, *Attila*, 182: 'East Roman interlocutors' mistakenly praised, Heather, 2005, 334.
53. Kelly, 2008, 187.
54. Prisc. frg. 20.3.
55. Jord. *Get.* 36 (185).
56. Kim, 2015, 96.
57. Joh. Ant. frg. 199.2.

Chapter 8

1. Hyd. s.a. 451.
2. Conversation with Perry Gray. The date of Carpilio's return from being a hostage – or even if he was ever sent home – are unrecorded.
3. Jord. *Get.* 194 (37). The reality of this claim is insecure, as will be discussed in the next chapter.
4. Jord. *Get.* 186 (36).
5. The fact that the Romans sent more than one messenger is a possible conclusion from the passage in Jordanes' *Getica* (188–189: 36) where 'several arguments' were needed by the ambassadors to convince Theoderic to fight, possibly from more than one embassy.
6. The list is based on Jordanes, *Get.* 36 (191). It may be confused due to the fact that Jordanes was writing approximately 100 years after the events being described, and so has confused the peoples fighting alongside Aetius. Additional information and some of the analysis, Hodgkin, 1892, 109f.
7. Prisc. frg. 16; c.f. Greg. Tur. 2.7.
8. Jord. *Get.* 37 (194).
9. The list is derived from Jordanes, *Get.* 36 (191).
10. Hodgkin, 1892, 109.
11. Jord, *Get.* 36 (191).
12. Hodgkin, 1892, 109.
13. Hodgkin is followed by Bury, 1923, 292, n.55: Boulogne and Bessin, Rouche, in Fossier, 1989, 55.

14. c.f Prisc. frg. 17.
15. Maenchen-Helfen, 1973, 131; esp. ns. 614–616.
16. *Chron. Gall.* 452, s.a. 451.
17. Sid. Ap. *Carm.* 7.319–325. Sidonius (and Jordanes) may have embellished their lists to reflect that the two armies were formed from many peoples.
18. Locations, Hodgkin, 1892, 106f.
19. Jord. *Get.* 38 (199–200).
20. Hodgkin, 1892, 117–118.
21. The relevant lives in the *Acta* are summarized by Hodgkin, 1892, 114f.
22. Maenchen-Helfen, 1973, 129, n. 604.
23. Kelly, 2015, 194.
24. Greg. Tur. 2.6.
25. Sid. Ap. *Ep.* 2.5; Greg. Tur. 2.6: Hyd. s.a. 451.
26. Greg. Tur. 2.7.
27. This hypothesis is supported by Gordon, 1960, 107.
28. Hodgkin, 1892, 115f.
29. Maenchen-Helfen, 1973, 131, and n.618.
30. Conversation with Perry Gray.
31. Hodgkin, 1892, 116f.
32. See Chapter 10.
33. Sid. Ap. *Carm. 7*, 329–330.
34. Maenchen-Helfen, 1973, 129, referencing letters of Pope Leo I: see esp. n. 605 and 606: Leo, *Ep.* 41.
35. Sid. Ap. *Carm. 7*, 329–330.
36. As implied by *Nov. Val.*, 29 (24 April 450) and Nov. Val. 33 (31 January 451): Clover, 1973, 116, and see Thompson, 1996, 161.
37. Sid. Ap. *Carm.* 7.215–317; see Chapter 7.
38. Sid. Ap. *Carm.* 7.339f. The agreement was reached when the Huns were already in Gaul; Aetius persuaded Theoderic via Avitus to join with him against Attila, 'who had attacked many Roman cities', Joh. Mal. 14.10 (358). C.f. Sidonius, who claims that Theoderic waited until the last minute, Sid. Ap. *Carm.* 7. 328–331. See also Bury, 1923, 292.
39. Thorismund, Greg Tur. 2.7: Theoderic, Jord. *Get.* 190.
40. Greg Tur 2.7.
41. Greg Tur. 2.7.
42. Sid. Ap. *Carm.* 7.12.3.
43. Conversation with Perry Gray.
44. Theoph. AM 5943.
45. Greg Tur. 2.7. Modern sources, for example Bury (1923, 292, n.58) suggest that there was no siege, but that Aetius and Theoderic arrived at the city first. The versions given by Gregory of Tours and in the *Acta Sanctorum*, supported by the testimony of Sidonius (*Ep.* 8.15. 1) have been preferred.
46. Hodgkin, 1982, 121, n.1: 'The Life of Saint Anianus', from the *Acta Sanctorum*.

47. For the date, *Vita Aniani*, Chap. 7, p.113: *octavodecimo kal. Iulias*, Bury, 1923, 292, n.59.
48. Greg. Tur. 2.7.
49. C.f. Sid. Ap. *Ep.* 8.15.1, where the city was 'invaded but never plundered'.
50. Hodgkin, 1892, 122.
51. Greg Tur. 2.7.

Chapter 9
1. Jord. *Get.* 41 (217).
2. Date following Bury, 1923, 292–293, n. 59.
3. Jord. *Get.* 36 (191–192) and 38 (196–197): Hyd. s.a. 451: *Chron. Caes.* s.a. 450.
4. *Chron. Gall. 511*, s.a. 451, '*Tricassis pugnat loco Mauriacos*'; *Consul. Ital. (Prosp. Havn.)*, '*quinto miliario de Trecas loco nuncupato Maurica in eo Campania*'; Greg. Tur. 2.7, '*Mauriacum campum*'; *Lex Burg.* 17.1, '*pugna Mauriacensis*'.
5. Theoph. AM 5943.
6. Joh. Mal. 14.10 (358).
7. For further analysis, Bury, 1923, 293, esp. n.60: MacDowall, 2015, *passim*.
8. Jord. *Get.* 37 (196).
9. Jord. *Get.* 37 (195–6).
10. Jord. *Get.* 38 (197f).
11. Kim, 2015, 101.
12. This is the story given by Gibbon, who notes that: 'This spacious plain was distinguished, however, by some inequalities of ground; and the importance of an height which commanded the camp of Attila was understood and disputed by the two generals': Gibbon, 1861, Vol. 2, 370–371.
13. Jord. *Get.* 38 (197–8).
14. Jord. *Get.* 24 [123–6] = Prisc. frg. 10.
15. My thanks to Evan Schultheis for drawing my attention to Jordanes' earlier description and the apparent change of tone.
16. E.g. Hodgkin, Vol. 2, 1842, 126.
17. Jord. *Get.* 37 (197).
18. Again, the detail given here is obtained from Jordanes, *Getica*, 38–40 (197–212). It is probable that he derived his material from Priscus: Mitchell, 2007, 28–29.
19. Jord. *Get.* 38 (197).
20. The use of pre-battle speeches is an old tradition and is usually included in histories even if the words are pure fiction. The authors followed a format. Jordanes was writing well after the period so much of his account may be based on oral history rather than written accounts and he wanted to please his Gothic audience: conversation with Perry Gray.
21. Joh. Mal. 358. *Chron. Pasch.* s.a. 450.
22. Jord. *Get.* 41 (215–217): Greg Tur. 2.7; see also *Addit. Ad Prosp. Haun.* s.a 451.
23. Jord. *Get.* 41 (218).
24. For the viewpoint that the Huns were victorious, e.g. Kim 2015, 101–2: contra, e.g. Pritsak, 1982, 428.

25. Prosp. s.a. 451; Hyd. s.a. 451; *Chron. Pasch.* s.a. 451 (who confuses Theoderic with the earlier Gothic 'king' Alaric); Greg. Tur. 2.7; *Cass. Chron.* s.a. 451. c.f. *Cass. Variae* 3.3.
26. Sid. Ap. *Carm.* 7, esp. 330f.
27. Maenchen–Helfen, 1973, 126.
28. Possibly following Creasey, 1851, Chapter 7.
29. Bury, 1923, 294.

Chapter 10
1. Clover, 1973, 109, esp. n.20.
2. *Chron. Gall. 511*, s.a. 452.
3. Prisc. frg. 22.1 = Jord. *Get.* 42. 219–24.
4. Maenchen–Helfen, 1973, 132.
5. 'Hot springs', probably Aquae Calidae Superiores or Budafelhéviz, near Óbuda (Budapest): Budavár [Buduuar], probably Óbuda or Etzelburg: 'Circular Wall' probably the old Roman amphitheatre: Etzelburg probably Ecilburgu: Rayd, 7, n.30 and 31.
6. Travelling through Pannonia, Prosp. s.a. 452: Date, Maenchen–Helfen, 1973, 132–135: probably before Aetius issued *Nov. Val.* 36 (29 June 452), as this talks of warfare, possibly in Italy.
7. Prosp. s.a. 452.
8. Disputed, Maenchen–Helfen, 1973, 134.
9. Prosp. s.a. 452, who notes that the invasion was unexpected and so Aetius had accordingly taken no actions to defend the passes across the Julian Alps.
10. See Paul. Diac. 2.9: Maenchen–Helfen, 1973, 135.
11. For example, Theodosius defeating Magnus Maximus at the Battles of Siscia and Poetovio.
12. Hughes, 2010, 138.
13. Prisc. frg. 22: Marcell. *com. s.a.* 452: *Cass. Chron.* s.a. 452: Greg. Tur. 2.7. Siege engines, Jord. *Get.* 42 (221).
14. See Chapter 9.
15. Prisc. frg. 22.
16. Paul Diac. 14.9. Paul gives 'three years', but this is obviously an error: cf. Maenchen–Helfen, 1973, 133, n. 628.
17. Hyd. 146.
18. Prisc. frg. 22; Paul Diac. 14.9.
19. Jord. *Get.* 219–221: Proc. BV 3.4.30–5.
20. Burning of Aquileia Theoph. AM 5945; Jord. *Get.* 42 (221): analysis, Maenchen–Helfen, 1973, 136–137.
21. *Nov. Val.* 36 (29 June 452).
22. Prosp. s.a. 452.
23. This is proved by later events: see below.
24. Prisc. frg. 22.1 = Jord. *Get.* 42. 219–24.: 'Taken some cities by storm' Hyd. s.a. 452–3.

25. Paul Diac. 14.11.
26. *Suid. Lex*: Suda Online = http://www.stoa.org/sol/,entry 2123. Possible the original source was Priscus, frg. 22.3: Maas, 2015, 3.
27. Conversation with Perry Gray.
28. Hyd. s.a. 452–3.
29. Compare this to the invasion by the Franks during the Wars of Belisarius, when the Franks lost a third of their army to disease: Hughes, 2009, 172.
30. Heather, 2005, 340.
31. Prisc. frg. 22.1 = Jord. *Get*. 42. 219–24. Alaric had died shortly after the sack of Rome.
32. Hyd. s.a. 452–3.
33. Discussed Burgess. 1988, pp.360–1. Burgess also suggests that the entry does not justify a campaign by the East at the same time, but rather a different campaign.
34. Freeman (1887) claims that 'we first hear of Aetius in his own peninsula as prefect of Constantinople in the consulship of Maximus and Plintha' (p.428). He also notes that 'Aetius' was made consul in 454 and that therefore 'Aetius was killed during his fourth consulship' (p.418). In this he is combining the careers of the two Aetiuses. Muhlberger also denies that there was a second Aetius (2006, 231. n. 86).
35. PLRE 2, *Aetius 1*, 19–20.
36. PLRE 2, *Aetius 1*, 19–20.
37. PLRE 2, *Aetius 8*, 29–30.
38. Although earlier attested as a civilian administrator, Hydatius calls Aetius *Aetio duce*, implying that he commanded the army: Hyd. s.a. 452: PLRE 2, *Aetius 8*, 29.
39. Burgess, 1988, *passim*.
40. Prisc. frg. 22.1 = Jord. *Get*. 42. 219–24.
41. Prosp. s.a. 452: Vict. Tonn. s.a. 449: *Cass. Chron.* s.a 452: Prisc. frg. 22.1.
42. Trygetius, PLRE2, *Trygetius*, 1129: Gennadius Avicanus, PLRE 2, *Gennadius Avicanus 4*, 193–4.
43. Paul Diac. 14.12: Maenchen-Helfen, 1973, 140–141.
44. Maenchen-Helfen, 1973, 141: Patrologiae Latina 52, 59–60.
45. Prisc. frg. 22.1 = Jord. *Get*. 42. 219–24.
46. Prisc. frg. 23.1, 2: Jord. *Get*. 225.
47. Prisc. frg. 23.3.
48. Maenchen-Helfen, 1973, 143: Jord. *Get*. 255.
49. See also Prisc. frg. 24.2; Marcell. *com. s.a.* 454; *Cass. Chron.* s.a. 453; Vict. Tonn. s.a. 453.2; Theoph. AM 5946.
50. Jord. *Get*. 254: Theoph AM 5946 (accident): Marc. com. 454.1 (Ildico or accident).
51. Joh. Mal. 14.10 (359).

Chapter 11

1. Theoph. AM 5946: Prisc. frg. 25 = Jord. *Get.* 50 (259–263).
2. Prisc. frg. 25 = Jord. *Get.* 50 (259–63).
3. Date, Hyd. s.a. 453. PLRE 2, *Pulcheria*, 930; *Chron. Pasch.* s.a. 453; Theoph. AM 5945.
4. Prosp. s.a. 453.
5. Jord. *Get.* 38 (199–200): Prisc. frg. 30. 1. = Joh. Ant. frg. 201.
6. Kim, 2015, 111–12.
7. The information on this battle is drawn from Priscus (frg. 30. 1. = Joh. Ant. frg. 201.) unless otherwise stated.
8. Prisc. frg. 30. 1. = Joh. Ant. frg. 201.
9. C.f. Pritsak, 1982, 429.
10. Lindner, 1981, 9 and n. 25: Kelly, 2015, 205.
11. Kelly, 2015, 195.
12. Golden, 1992, 91.
13. Political and military weakness, c.f. Kelly, 2015, 204.

Bibliography

Primary Sources

Ambrose, *Epistulae*, http://www.tertullian.org/fathers/ambrose_letters_00_intro. htm.

Ambrose, *Expositio Evangelii secundum Lucam*, https://archive.org/details/ expositioevange00schegoog.

Chronicon Paschale, Whitby, M. and Whitby, M. (1989), *Chronicon Paschale 284–628 AD*, Liverpool.

Claudian, http://penelope.uchicago.edu/Thayer/E/Roman/Texts/Claudian/home. html.

Code of Justianian, http://www.uwyo.edu/lawlib/blume-justinian.

Gesta Hungarorum ('The Anonymous Notary of King Béla') trans. M. Rady, *discovery.ucl.ac.uk/18975/1/18975.pdf*.

Ghazar P'arpets'I, *History of the Armenians*, http://www.attalus.org/armenian/ gpintro.htm.

Herodotus, *History*, http://www.gutenberg.org/ebooks/2707.

Jerome, *Commentary on Isaiah*, https://www.ccel.org/ccel/schaff/npnf206.vii. iv.viii.html; https://www.ccel.org/ccel/schaff/npnf206.pdf.

John of Ephesus, *Ecclesiastical History*, http://www.tertullian.org/fathers/index. htm#John_of_Ephesus.

John of Nikiu, *Chronicle*, http://www.tertullian.org/fathers/nikiu2_chronicle. htm.

Marcellinus *comes*, http://www.documentacatholicaomnia.eu/02m/0474 0534,_ Marcellinus_Comes_Chronicum,_MLT.pdf; Croke, B. (1995), *The Chronicle of Marcellinus: a Translation and Commentary*, Sydney.

Merobaudes, *Flavius Merobaudes: A Translation and Historical Commentary*, Clover, F.M. (1971) Philadelphia.

Philostorgius, *Church History*, Amidon, P.R. (2007) http://www.hourofthetime.com/ 1-LF/November2012/Hour_Of_The_Time_11042012-The_Ecclesiastical_ History_Of_Sozomen_And_Philostorgius-1855.pdf.

Quintus Aurelius Symmachus, *Relationes*, https://archive.org/details/qaureliisy mnach00meyegoog.

Socrates Scholasticus, *Ecclesiastical History*, http://www.newadvent.org/fathers/ 2601.htm.

Sozomen, *Ecclesiastical History*, http://www.hourofthetime.com/1-LF/November 2012/Hour_Of_The_Time_11042012The_Ecclesiastical_History_Of_ Sozomen_And_Philostorgius-1855.pdf.

Vita Aniani, http://www.dmgh.de/de/fs1/object/display/bsb00000750_00112. html?sortIndex=010:020:0003:010:00:00.

Secondary Sources

Amidon, P.R., *Philostorgius: Church History* (Society of Biblical Literature, 2007).

Atwood, C.P., 'Huns and Xiōngnu: New Thoughts on an Old Problem', in Boeck, B.J., Martin, R.E. and Rowland, D. (eds), *Dubitando: Studies in History and Culture in Honor of Donald Ostrowski* (Bloomington, 2012), pp.27–52.

Bayless, W.N., 'The Treaty with the Huns of 443', *The American Journal of Philology* (1976), 97(2), 176–179.

Blockley, R.C., *The Fragmentary Classicising Historians of the Later Roman Empire: Eunapius, Olympiodorus, Priscus and Malchus: Vol. 2* (Liverpool, 1983).

Burgess, R.W., 'A New Reading for Hydatius "Chronicle" 177 and the Defeat of the Huns in Italy', *Phoenix*, Vol. 42, No. 4 (Winter, 1988), pp.357–363.

Bury, J.B., *History of the Later Roman Empire* (London, 1923) http://penelope. uchicago.edu/Thayer/E/Roman/Texts/secondary/BURLAT/home.html.

Cameron, A. and Garnsey, P., *Cambridge Ancient History, Volume XIII* (Cambridge, 1998).

Clover, F.M., 'Geiseric and Attila', *Historia: Zeitschrift für Alte Geschichte*, Vol. 22, No. 1 (1st Qtr, 1973), 104–117.

Clover, F.M., *Flavius Merobaudes: A Translation and Historical Commentary* (Philadelphia, 1971).

Collins, R., *Visigothic Spain 409–711* (Oxford, 2006).

Conant, J.P., 'Romanness in the Age of Attila', in Maas, M. (ed.), (2015), pp.156–172.

Creasy, E., *The Fifteen Decisive Battles of the World* (1851) http://www.gutenberg. org/dirs/etext03/tfdbt10.txt.

Croke, B., 'Dynasty and Aristocracy in the Fifth Century', in Maas, M. (ed.), (2015), pp.98–124.

Croke, B., *Count Marcellinus and His Chronicle* (Oxford, 2001).

Croke, B., *The Chronicle of Marcellinus: a Translation and Commentary* (Sydney, 1995).

Croke, B., 'Evidence for the Hun Invasion of Thrace in AD 422', *Greek, Roman, and Byzantine Studies 18* (1977), pp.347–367.

Dinchev, V., 'The Fortresses of Early Thrace', *Proceedings of the British Academy 141* (2007) 479–546.

Drinkwater, J. and Elton, H., *Fifth Century Gaul: a Crisis of Identity?* (Cambridge, 2002).

Elton, H., *Warfare in Roman Europe AD 350–425* (Oxford, 1996).

Elton, H., 'Defence in fifth-century Gaul', in Drinkwater, J. and Elton, H., *Fifth Century Gaul: a Crisis of Identity?* (2002) 167–76.

Fossier, R. (ed.), *The Cambridge Illustrated History of the Middle Ages 350–950* (Cambridge, 1989).

Freeman, E.A., 'Aetius and Boniface', *The English Historical Review*, Vol. 2, No. 7 (July 1887), pp.417–465.

Fyfe, L.E., 'Hunnic Warfare in the Fourth and Fifth Centuries C.E: Archery and the Collapse of the Western Roman Empire' (thesis, Trent University, Ontario, 2017).

Gibbon, E., *The History of the Decline and Fall of the Roman Empire* (Liverpool, 1861).

Gillett, A., *Envoys and Political Communication in the Late Antique West, 411–533* (Cambridge University Press, 2003).

Gillett, A., 'Embassies and Political Communication in the Post-Imperial West' in Gillett, A., *Envoys and Political Communication in the Late Antique West, 411–533* (Cambridge University Press, 2003).

Given, J., *The Fragmentary History of Priscus: Attila, the Huns and the Roman Empire, AD 430–476* (Huntingdon, 2014).

Golden, P.B., *An Introduction to the History of the Turkic Peoples: Ethnogenesis and State Formation in Medieval and Early Modern Eurasia and the Middle East* (Wiesbaden, 1992).

Golden, P.B., 'The Peoples of the South Russian Steppes' in *The Cambridge History of Early Inner Asia*, ed. Denis Sinor (Cambridge University Press, 1990, download *Academia*) pp.256–284.

Gordon, C.D., *The Age of Attila: Fifth-Century Byzantium and the Barbarians* (University of Michigan Press, 1960).

Gračanin, H., 'The Huns and South Pannonia', *Byzantinoslavica LXIV*, 2006, pp.29–76.

Gračanin, H., 'The Western Roman Embassy to the Court of Attila in AD 449', *Byzantinoslavica*, Vol. 61 (2003), pp.53–74.

Greatrex, G., 'Government and Mechanisms of Control, East and West' in Maas, M. (ed.), (2015), pp.26–43.

Greatrex, G. and Greatrex, M., 'The Hunnic Invasion of the East of 395 and the Fortress of Ziatha', *Byzantion, Tome LXIX* (1999), pp.65–75 https://www.academia.edu/2470426/The_Hunnic_Invasion_of_the_East_of_395_and_the_fortress_of_Ziatha.

Halsall, G., *Barbarian Migrations and the Roman West* (Cambridge, 2007).

Heather, P., 'The Huns and Barbarian Europe' in Maas, M. (ed.), (2015), pp.209–229.

Heather, P., *Empires and Barbarians: The Fall of Rome and the Birth of Europe* (Oxford University Press, 2009).

Heather, P., *The Fall of the Roman Empire: A New History* (London, 2005).

Heather, P., *The Goths: The Peoples of Europe* (London, 1998).

Heather, P., *The Goths* (Oxford, 1996).

Heather, P., 'The Huns and the End of the Roman Empire in Western Europe', *The English Historical Review*, Vol. 110, No. 435 (February 1995), pp.4–41.

Heather, P., *Goths and Romans 332–489* (Oxford, 1991).

Henning, W., 'The Date of the Sogdian Ancient Letters', *Bulletin of the School of Oriental and African Studies, University of London*, 12(3/4), 601–615 (1948). Retrieved from http://www.jstor.org/stable/608717.

Hodgkin, T., *Italy and Her Invaders* (Oxford, 1892). http://www.archive.org/stream/italyandherinva04hodggoog#page/n11/mode/1up.

Holum, K.G., 'Mediterranean Cities in the Fifth Century: Elites, Christianizing, and the Barbarian Influx' in Maas, M. (ed.), (2015), pp.61–79.

Hughes, I., *Aetius: Attila's Nemesis* (Barnsley, 2012).

Hughes, I., *Stilicho: The Vandal Who Saved Rome* (Barnsley, 2010).

Hughes, I., *Belisarius: The Last Roman General* (Barnsley, 2009).

Huntzinger, H., 'L'affaire d'Anasamos (443): une négociation entre Attila, Anatolius et les habitants d'une place forte danubienne' in Becker, A. and Drocourt, N. (eds), *Aux origines d'une diplomatie méditerranée. Les ambassadeurs, moyens humains de la diplomatie* (2012) Metz, pp.211–226.

Jones, A.H.M., *The Later Roman Empire 284–602* (Baltimore, 1986).

Kelly, C., 'Neither Conquest Nor Settlement: Attila's Empire and its Impact' in Maas, M. (2015), pp.193–208.

Kelly, C., *Attila The Hun: Barbarian Terror and the Fall of the Roman Empire* (Bodley Head, 2008).

Khazanov, A.M., *Nomads and the Outside World* (University of Wisconsin Press, 1994).

Kim, H.J., *The Xiongnu* (2017) http://asianhistory.oxfordre.com/view/10.1093/acrefore/9780190277727.001.0001/acrefore-9780190277727-e-50?rskey=73POhU&result=1.

Kim, H.J., *The Huns* (Routledge, 2016).

Kulikowski, M., *Rome's Gothic Wars* (Cambridge, 2007).

Kulikowski, M., 'Nation versus Army: a Necessary Contrast?' in Gillett, A., *On Barbarian Identity: Critical Approaches to Ethnicity in the Early Middle Ages* (Turnhout, 2003), 69–84.

Lee, A.D., *Information and Frontiers: Roman Foreign Relations in Late Antiquity* (Cambridge, 2006).

Lenski, N., 'Captivity Among the Barbarians and its Impact on the Fate of the Roman Empire' in Maas, M. (2015), pp.230–246.

Lindner, R.P., 'Nomadism, Horses and Huns', *Past and Present No. 92* (August 1981), pp.3–19.

Maas, M. (ed.), *The Cambridge Companion to the Age of Attila* (Cambridge, 2015).

MacDowall, S., *Catalaunian Fields AD 451: Rome's Last Great Battle* (Osprey, 2015).

Maenchen-Helfen, O.J., *The World of the Huns: Studies in Their History and Culture* (University of California Press, 1973).

Mangaltepe, I., 'Attila: The ruler of the Huns (434–453)', *International Journal of Multidisciplinary Thought* (2011), pp.7–15.

Masek, Z., 'Hun Period Cauldrons in Hungary: Current Research in the Light of a New Find', *Hungarian Archaeology Journal* (Summer 2015).

Mathisen, R.W., 'Peregrini, Barbari, and Cives Romani: Concepts of Citizenship and the Legal Identity of Barbarians in the Later Roman Empire', *The American Historical Review*, Vol. 111, No. 4 (October 2006), pp.1011–1040.

Muhlberger, S., *The Fifth-Century Chroniclers: Prosper, Hydatius and the Gallic Chronicle of 452* (Francis Cairns, 2006).

Oost, S I., 'Aetius and Majorian', *Classical Philology*, Vol. 59, No. 1 (January 1964), 23–29.

Payne, R., 'The Reinvention of Iran: The Sasanian Empire and the Huns' in Maas, M. (2015), pp.282–299.

Pritsak, O., 'The Hunnic Language of the Attila Clan', in *Harvard Ukrainian Studies* Vol. 6, No. 4. (December 1982) 428–477; http://projects.iq.harvard.edu/files/huri/files/vvi_n4_dec1982.pdf.

Pulleyblank, E.G., 'The Consonantal System of Old Chinese', *Asia Major 9* (1962).

— Part 1: www2.ihp.sinica.edu.tw/file/1110cxVuiEg.PDF.

— Part 2: www2.ihp.sinica.edu.tw/file/1114AUnNESH.pdf.

— Part 3: http://s155239215.onlinehome.us/turkic/29Huns/Pulleyblank1963 Appendix_HsiungNuLanguageEn.htm.

Sarris, P., 'Rural and Urban Economies in the Age of Attila', in Maas, M. (ed.) (2015), pp.44–61.

Thompson, E.A., *The Huns* (Oxford, 1996).

Thompson, E.A., 'The Foreign Policies of Theodosius II and Marcian', *Hermathena*, No. 76 (November 1950), pp.58–75.

de la Vaissière, E., 'The Steppe World and the Rise of the Huns' in Maas, M. (ed.) (2015), pp.175–192.

Van Dam, R., 'Big Cities and the Dynamics of the Mediterranean During the Fifth Century' in Maas, M. (ed.) (2015), pp.80–97.

Vovin, A., 'Did the Xiong-nu Speak a Yeniseian Language?', *Central Asiatic Journal*, Giovanni Stary (ed.), 44 (2000) 1, CAJ 44/1 (2000), Harrassowitz Verlag; http://s155239215.onlinehome.us/turkic/29Huns/AVovin_XiongnuLanguageEn.htm.

Walden, C. and Mason, C., *Encyclopedia of European Peoples* (2 volumes), (New York, 2006).

Whitby, M. and Whitby, M., *Chronicon Paschale 284–628 AD* (Liverpool, 1989).

Index